D0231409

United States Interest Rates
and the
Interest Rate Dilemma
for the Developing World

Recent Titles from QUORUM BOOKS

United States Interest Rates and the Interest Rate Dilemma for the Developing World

J. PIERRE V. BENOIT

QUORUM BOOKS

WESTPORT, CONNECTICUT • LONDON, ENGLAND

Library of Congress Cataloging-in-Publication Data

Benoît, J. Pierre V.
  United States interest rates and the interest
rate dilemma for the developing world.

  Bibliography: p.
  Includes index.
  1. Interest rates—United States. 2. Loans,
American—Developing countries. I. Title.
HG1623.U5B46 1986   332.8′2′0973   85–12348
ISBN 0–89930–131–2 (lib. bdg. : alk. paper)

Library of Congress Catalog Card Number: 85–12348
ISBN: 0–89930–131–2

First published in 1986 by Quorum Books

Greenwood Press
A division of Congressional Information Service, Inc.
88 Post Road West
Westport, Connecticut 06881

Printed in the United States of America

The paper used in this book complies with the
Permanent Paper Standard issued by the National
Information Standards Organization (Z39.48–1984).

10 9 8 7 6 5 4 3 2 1

To those who forty years ago
founded the United Nations, which remains
the best instrument for promoting understanding
and cooperation among states

If help is given to us let us accept it,
but let us not sit down and say nothing can be done
until the rest of the world out of its goodness of
heart is willing to grant us charity.

Sir Arthur Lewis

Contents

Abbreviations and Acronyms

ATS	automatic-transfer service
BIS	Bank for International Settlements
CATS	Certificates of Accrual on Treasury Securities
CPI	consumer price index
DM	Deutsche mark
DMI	Dar Al Maal Al-Islami
ESF	Exchange Stabilization Fund
FDIC	Federal Deposit Insurance Corporation
GATT	General Agreement on Tariffs and Trade
GDP	gross domestic product
GNP	gross national product
GSP	Generalized System of Preferences
IBI	Islamic Bank International
IBSI	Islamic Banking System International
IDA	International Development Agency
IDB	Islamic Development Bank
IET	interest equalization tax
IMF	International Monetary Fund
IRA	individual retirement account
IRS	Internal Revenue Service
KFH	Kuwait Finance House
LDC	less-developed country
LIBOR	London Interbank Offered Rate
MLR	minimum lending rate
MMDA	money-market deposit account
NOW	negotiable order of withdrawal
OCD	other checkable deposits
ODA	Official Development Assistance
OECD	Organisation for Economic Co-operation and Development
OPEC	Organization of Petroleum Exporting Countries
RP	repurchase agreement

SDR   special drawing rights
SELA   Latin American Economic System
SIBOR   Singapore Interbank Offered Rate
TIGRS   Treasury Investment Growth Receipts
TRs   Treasury Receipts
UNCTAD   United Nations Conference on Trade and Development

List of Tables

Acknowledgments

I am grateful to the following friends with whom I have had the pleasure of discussing for the past fifteen years the issues involved in the mobilization of personal savings in developing countries: Jean-Marie Pesant, General Manager, International Savings Banks Institute; José Manuel Pittaluga, General Manager, Banco Inmobiliario Dominicano, Dominican Republic; Uno Tenfalt, Senior Vice-President, Swedish Savings Banks Association; Ashok M. Thadani, Deputy General Manager, International Savings Banks Institute; and David Wirmark, former member of the Swedish Parliament, Ambassador of Sweden to Mexico, Advisor to the Swedish Savings Banks Association and Chairman of the Development Co-operation Committee of the International Savings Banks Institute.

I am also grateful to Mayer Gabay, a friend and former colleague in the Fiscal and Financial Branch of the United Nations Secretariat, now Director General of the Israeli Ministry of Justice, who helped me greatly with the section in this book on the practice of charging or taking interest in Judaism.

Finally, I want to thank my colleagues in the Fiscal and Financial Branch of the United Nations Secretariat, Jean Causse, Andrew Ezenkwele and Juergen Holst, for their constructive comments on various chapters.

I assume full responsibility for any shortcomings in the book and for the views expressed therein, which are strictly personal and should not be construed as reflecting the position of the United Nations Secretariat.

Introduction

Although Keynesianism was included in university curricula after the publication of *The General Theory of Employment, Interest and Money* in 1936, it did not become the cornerstone of fiscal policy until after the Second World War. A similar fate was to await monetarism, which did not leave the confines of academia until the 1970s, when, as a result of unusually persistent and pervasive inflation, it penetrated the realm of politics. Numerous public officials and politicians then became converts to the monetarist thesis, propounded in the 1950s by a group of monetary economists in Chicago led by Milton Friedman and already accepted by numerous other economists, that inflation is always and everywhere a monetary phenomenon and can be slowed by slowing the growth of the money supply. In that context the United States Congress adopted the Full Employment and Balanced Growth Act of 1978, which led the United States Federal Reserve to decide, in October 1979, to begin formally targeting the growth of the money supply with a view to controlling such growth and to cease seeking to maintain the federal funds rate and other interest rates within a given range. Since that decision, interest rates in the United States have risen to unprecedentedly high levels.

Interest rate liberalization in the United States has generated a long overdue continuing trend toward more realistic interest rate levels, not only in industrialized countries but also in an increasing number of developing countries. This trend has, however, exacerbated the interest rate dilemma for the developing world, the origin and nature of which are discussed in Chapter 1 against the background of a general analysis of United States interest rates and their world-wide impact on international flows of capital.

The question of interest rate levels is, of course, linked to the basic principle of charging or taking interest, a principle that has been a source of controversy throughout the ages. This controversy has been reanimated since the 1970s by the spread of interest-free banking as an offshoot of the Islamic revival. To place the question of interest rate levels in the proper perspective, Chapter 2 contains a review of attitudes toward the practice of charging or taking interest not only in Islam but also in Judaism and Christianity, a discussion of the principles and practices of Islamic banking and a comparative analysis of the latter and Western banking.

One major effect of the increase in United States interest rates was an aggravation of the 1982–1984 international debt crisis. Resolving the interest rate dilemma would help developing countries mobilize more domestic financial resources; this in turn would, directly or indirectly, help ease their debt-servicing difficulties and make them progressively less dependent on foreign borrowing. It would help provide a lasting solution to the current international debt imbroglio, the sequel to the debt crisis. Chapter 3 describes the scope and causes of the crisis and the strategies of the parties involved (creditor banks, debtor countries and countries of the creditor banks). It emphasizes that declining United States interest rates, although desirable, would in no way constitute a panacea for developing countries' financial ills, the only lasting cure for which is greater self-reliance on their part.

If developing countries are eventually to find their way back to solvency, reestablish creditworthiness over the long term and at the same time create structural conditions for sustained economic growth, they will have to enhance the probity of their public administration, make a greater tax effort and take stronger action to mobilize personal savings. A priority aim of that action will be to find a solution to the interest rate dilemma. The dilemma has arisen primarily because developing countries have in most cases been setting interest rates, by administrative decision, at levels so low as to prompt households to hold their savings in the form of physical assets or to devise ever more ingenious ways of escaping foreign exchange controls and transferring their funds abroad. The options available to governments as regards the determination of interest rates are analyzed in Chapter 4, which describes three alternative systems for determining interest rates—the administered interest rate system, the modified administered interest rate system and the market rate system—and reviews the arguments in favor of administered interest rates and market rates.

The choice of an interest rate determination system depends on conditions in each country. Whatever the system chosen, the aim should be to ensure that interest rates reach levels that can be considered just for both savers and borrowers. Chapter 5 introduces and discusses the concept of a just interest rate and emphasizes that the interest rate dilemma facing the developing world can be resolved only by establishing a just interest rate structure.

United States Interest Rates
and the
Interest Rate Dilemma
for the Developing World

1 United States Interest Rates and Their World-Wide Impact

THE 6 OCTOBER 1979 FEDERAL RESERVE DECISION: BACKGROUND AND EFFECTS

In any economy, over a given period, some economic agents spend more than their income while others hold spending within their income level. The agents that spend more than they receive have a deficit that they can finance in one or more ways: by depleting their existing cash reserves; by converting other liquid financial assets into cash; by realizing securities; by realizing physical assets (real assets, jewelry, stocks of merchandise and so on); and by borrowing. The agents who do not spend all of their income have a surplus that they can use in one or more ways: to constitute or increase their cash reserves; to accumulate other liquid financial assets; to purchase securities; to acquire physical assets; and to repay debts.

At both the national and international levels, the financial operations of the surplus agents and the deficit agents are complementary; the ones with a surplus finance the requirements of the ones with a deficit. They do this either directly, through direct loans to the deficit agents or direct purchases of securities or physical assets from the deficit agents; or indirectly, through intermediaries such as financial institutions (which collect surpluses in the form of deposits, investments in various financial assets and insurance premiums) and brokerage firms, individual stockbrokers and other intermediaries (such as *notaires* in France) who bring together the surplus agents and the deficit agents.

Whereas the major surplus agents (net savers) are households, the major deficit agents (net borrowers) are central governments, local authorities, enterprises, and households wishing to borrow for capital formation or current consumption. The price that deficit agents pay to surplus agents (either directly or through intermediaries) for the use of their funds is *interest*. Like other prices in a free market, the rate of interest should normally be determined by the interplay between supply (the supply of money belonging to the surplus agents and available for lending) and demand (the demand for credit on the part of the deficit agents). However, interest is not like other prices, because money is a good created by the monetary authorities, which through monetary policy, constantly regulate or influence the quantity in circulation.

Before the First World War it was considered a sufficient objective for monetary policy to maintain the convertibility of a country's currency at a fixed gold value or to maintain a more or less constant exchange value for that currency *vis à vis* other currencies on the gold standard. In the period immediately following the First World War, monetary policy was viewed primarily as a means of preserving stability in the value of money as measured in terms of a standard index number of prices. Later, monetary policy was assigned broader objectives, and it was widely believed that progress in the application of monetary-policy techniques had put an end to wide fluctuations of the business cycle. But this optimism was shattered by the Great Depression, which caused the efficacy of monetary policy to be called in question. Informed opinion on the role that should be assigned to monetary policy in the management of the business cycle swang to the other extreme. For about two decades thereafter, under the influence of Keynesian economics, monetary policy was given, at best, a small role compared to fiscal policy. The latter is concerned with the effects of changes in the level of public revenue and spending and the effects of changes in the budget surplus or deficit on the economy; fiscal policy was believed to exert an important effect on national income and employment through the multiplier process. In the words of Milton Friedman, the "only role" of monetary policy in Keynesian economics was the "minor role of keeping interest rates low, in order to hold down interest payments in the government budget, contribute to the 'euthanasia of the rentier' and maybe, stimulate investment a bit to assist government spending in maintaining a high level of aggregate demand."[1]

The role of monetary policy remained minor compared to that of fiscal policy, even when it was assigned the additional function of preserving the value of government bonds in order to enable governments to obtain money at low cost. In 1945 the Director of the Research Division of the Federal Reserve Board, after defining the primary objective of monetary policy as being to "maintain the value of government bonds," observed that the United States would "have to adjust to a 2 1/2 percent interest rate as the return on safe, long-time money, because the time has come when returns on pioneering capital can no longer be unlimited as they were in the past." In a 1945 book entitled *Financing American Prosperity*, John H. Williams, a professor at Harvard University and an adviser to the New York Federal Reserve Bank, declared, "I can see no prospect of revival of a general monetary control in the postwar period."[2] A similarly skeptical view concerning the power of monetary policy to influence the economy was expressed by another professor, Arthur Smithies, who, writing in *A Survey of Contemporary Economics*, published in 1948, stated, "In the field of compensatory action, I believe fiscal policy must shoulder most of the load. Its chief rival, monetary policy, seems to be disqualified on institutional grounds. This country appears to be committed to something like the present low level of interest rates on a long-term basis."[3]

However, in the late 1950s and early 1960s, the policies inspired by Keynesianism began to be reevaluated in the context of continually increasing prosperity in industrialized countries and waning faith in the ability of government to plan and operate the economy. As a result, increasing attention was directed to the potential importance of monetary policy in economic management, and between the mid-1960s and the mid-1970s, progressively less reliance was placed on interest rates as a policy guide. At the same time, greater attention was paid to the macroeconomic role of money, the control of the money supply, the setting of growth ranges for money and credit aggregates, and the behavior of such aggregates as an intermediate guide in formulating policy. The change of emphasis from interest rates to monetary aggregates can be at least partly attributed to the influence of the monetarists. They had become so numerous that United States economists (except those who believed that any anti-inflationary policy other than government price controls is bound to fail) were divided into two main camps: the monetarists and those whom the monetarists called the "Keynesians" or the "neo-Keynesians" (although it is not certain that Keynes himself would have endorsed the eponymous label for all of those so designated).

Although the early Keynesians believed that "money does not matter," the neo-Keynesians acknowledged that "money matters" to a certain extent, in that changes in the money supply can exert some influence on output and the general level of prices. But they regarded that influence as so minimal that it rendered monetary policy relatively ineffective in bringing about macroeconomic stabilization. The monetarists, on the other hand, thought that fiscal policy is an ineffective tool, since it cannot influence real output, unemployment or inflation; that inflation is always and everywhere a monetary phenomenon; and that it is the money supply that matters, because monetary policy is the only key to macroeconomic stabilization. According to the monetarists, *monetary policy* means, essentially, regulation of the money supply, and *velocity*—the speed with which money circulates in the economy—behaves in a regular and predictable way. In their view, it is enough to monitor the money-supply figures and to use the monetary-policy instruments to make the money supply increase or decrease as appropriate, and it is essential to refrain as much as possible from using monetary-policy instruments to influence other parameters, especially interest rates, which they believe should be determined by market forces. The monetarists believe that inflation is caused by the continuing growth of the money supply, resulting from the fact that in the postwar period most countries relied more and more on central bank financing, either to achieve full employment or to fund public expenditures.

The basic monetarist tenets may be considered to have been officially sanctioned in the United States by the Full Employment and Balanced Growth Act of 1978. That act amended the Employment Act of 1946, which stated that the objectives of governmental policy were, among other things, "to promote maximum employment, production and purchasing power." The 1978 act stipulated that "Congress further declares that inflation is a major national problem requiring improved government policies relating to food, energy, improved and co-ordinated fiscal and monetary management." The act also amended the Federal Reserve Act to require the Federal Reserve to send to Congress twice a year "the objectives and plans of the Board of Governors and the Federal Open Market Committee with respect to ranges of growth or diminution of the monetary and credit aggregates." The act likewise stipulated that nothing therein "shall be interpreted to require that the objectives and plans with respect to the ranges of growth or diminution of the monetary and credit aggregates disclosed in the reports submitted under this section be achieved if the Board of Governors and the Federal Open Market Committee determine they cannot or should not be achieved because of changing conditions."

Pursuant to that act, the Federal Open Market Committee, the policy-making organ of the Federal Reserve Board, decided on 6 October 1979 to adopt a new approach to the conduct of open-market operations. This approach emphasized supplying a volume of bank reserves estimated to be consistent with the desired rates of growth in monetary aggregates while permitting much greater fluctuations in interest rates than before. Previously, open-market operations had been oriented essentially toward maintaining the *federal funds rate*—the fee that banks in the United States charge on overnight loans to one another—and other short-term interest rates at levels that appeared to conform to the committee's objectives for growth in the money supply measuring gauges.

The strategy applied by the Federal Reserve from October 1979 to late 1982 allowed interest rates to respond semiautomatically to deviations from the desired course of growth of the money supply. However, the strategy applied since then has ruled out purely mechanistic responses and has enabled the Federal Reserve to exercise judgment to a much greater extent. The Federal Reserve, having succeeded in reducing inflation, has been willing to accommodate M1 deviations provided they fit in with its underlying monetary strategy and has been placing more emphasis on the broader money supply figures M2 and M3 and paying more attention to general economic trends and to the rest of the world.[4]

Significant variations in the United States money supply figures may trigger speculation about the likelihood of the Federal Reserve tightening or loosening its grip on the amount of currency in circulation sufficiently to push up or bring down the federal funds rate. A higher federal funds rate places upward pressure on the rate of three-month Treasury bills (a rate set on the basis of bids from investors), on the *prime rate* (the rate posted by large banks as a reference for loans to corporations in line with their own cost of funds and the demand for credit), on the *discount rate* (the interest rate charged by Federal Reserve banks on loans to depository institutions), and on other United States interest rates, both short term and long term.[5]

Since the October 1979 decision of the Federal Reserve, United States interest rates have risen to historically high levels. From the beginning of 1953 to the end of the third quarter of 1979, the average nominal short-term interest rate had been 5.27 percent while the average real short-term rate had been 1.39 percent. From the fourth quarter of 1979 to the end of the second quarter of 1984, the average nominal rate on three-month Treasury bills was 11.10 percent and the average real rate on such bills was 4.35 percent, rates which were as much as two and three times higher than in the preceding quarter of a century. The average nominal rate from the fourth quarter of 1979 to mid-1984 exceeded by more than two thirds the average nominal rate between 1976 and the end of the third quarter of 1979, while the real rate barely exceeded zero during that period.

The measured *real prime rate*—the quarterly nominal prime rate minus the rate of inflation as measured by the percentage change at an annual rate in the gross national product deflator—climbed from an average of 1.5 percent in 1970–1974 and 1.8 percent in 1975–1979 to 5.5 percent in 1980, 10.2 percent in 1981, and 10.7 percent in 1982. It declined to 7.1 percent in 1983 but rose to 8.3 percent in 1984.[6] Between 1972 and 1981, the nominal interest rate on prime commercial paper of four- to six-months' maturity more than tripled, and the rate on ten-year government bonds and Moody's AAA corporate bonds more than doubled (see Table 1).

In late 1984, with unemployment persistently exceeding 7 percent—a level usually reached only in recessions—the Federal Reserve began trying to edge interest rates downwards in order to stimulate the economy. The Federal Reserve allowed the federal funds rate to decline and then confirmed the relaxation of its previously restrictive stance by lowering the discount rate it charges on loans to banks. By May 1985, despite the fact that the money supply had grown by roughly 10 percent during the previous eight months, a rate that far exceeded the rate of growth of the United States economy and might well be interpreted as a sign that faster inflation might be in the offing, the Federal Reserve's discount rate had fallen to 7.5 percent (its lowest level since October 1978, when it was 8.5 percent) and the banks' prime lending rate had slipped to 9.5 percent (its lowest level since October 1978). Heavy federal borrowing notwithstanding, short-term interest rates—whose behavior reflects more closely than that of long-term rates the degree of tightness or relaxation of current monetary pol-

Table 1
United States Interest Rates and Bond Yields
(In Percentages)

Year	Three-Month Treasury Bills	Ten-Year Government Bonds	Corporate Bonds (Moody's AAA)	Prime Commercial Paper of Four-to Six-Months' Maturity
1972	4.071	5.63	7.21	4.69
1973	7.041	6.30	7.44	8.15
1974	7.886	6.99	8.57	9.87
1977	5.265	7.42	8.02	5.61
1978	7.221	8.41	8.73	7.99
1979	10.041	9.44	9.63	10.91
1980	11.506	11.46	11.94	12.29
1981	14.077	13.91	14.17	14.76

Source: U.S. Council of Economic Advisers, Economic Reports of the President.

icy—plummeted, with the ninety-day Treasury bill rate dropping from more than 11 percent in the early fall of 1984 to 7.3 percent in May 1985. Even so, since the annual inflation rate was then 3.7 percent as compared with 8.9 percent in October 1978, real interest rates remained very high. In fact, real interest rates are likely to remain higher than they were during the 1950s, 1960s and 1970s.

REASONS FOR THE RISE IN UNITED STATES INTEREST RATES SINCE THE 1979 FEDERAL RESERVE DECISION

The unprecedentedly high levels, relative to current inflation, to which United States interest rates have risen since the Federal Reserve's decision of 6 October 1979 are widely regarded as being essentially the result of the staggering overall United States public and private credit-market debt. Even disregarding a number of items for which no aggregate figures are available (such as currency swaps, lines of credit between companies and credit guarantees by banks and insurance companies), the overall credit-market debt increased sevenfold over two decades, rising from about $1.0 trillion in the mid-1960s to about $2.5 trillion in the mid-1970s and an estimated $7.2 trillion in 1984.

In particular, the high dollar interest rates are widely viewed as being caused primarily by United States government borrowing to finance the budget deficit, which has become partly structural in that spending exceeds revenues even when the economy is not experiencing a cyclical slowdown.

The deficit reached $57.9 billion in the fiscal year 1981, climbed to $110.7 billion in 1982 and $195.4 billion in 1983, and amounted to $175.3 billion in 1984. On 1 August 1985, the United States Congress approved a 1986 budget plan that was projected to shrink the federal budget deficit from an estimated $209.8 billion in 1985 to $171.9 billion in 1986, $154.75 billion in 1987 and $112.9 billion in 1988. A 1988 deficit of between $150 billion and $160 billion was nevertheless considered more realistic, because the projection for 1988 was based on an earlier forecast of economic growth that was acknowledged to be outdated. Federal borrowing pushed the national debt from $709 billion in 1977 to $1,430 billion in 1983, and in 1984 the United States paid more than 5.0 times as much for debt service as it had in 1974 and 13.5 times as much as in 1964.

However, both the federal budget deficit and federal borrowing are more manageable than they appear to be. The budget deficit gives less cause for concern when it is viewed as a percentage of the gross national product (GNP): in 1983, for example, the United States budget deficit represented 5.8 percent of GNP, compared with 6.2 percent for Canada and 16.5 percent for Italy (the budget deficit represented 5.5 percent of GNP in Japan, 4.9 percent in the United Kingdom, 3.3 percent in France, and 2.0 percent in the Federal Republic of Germany). Adjusted for inflation, the United States budget deficit represented 4.4 percent of GNP in 1983, com-pared with 4.5 percent for Canada and 6.5 percent for Italy (the inflation-adjusted budget deficit represented 5.3 percent of GNP in Japan, 3.0 per-cent in the United Kingdom, 1.4 percent in France and also 1.4 percent in the Federal Republic of Germany). Similarly, the United States national debt seems much less alarming when it is considered that the portion owed to foreigners, like the portion owed to residents, is denominated in dollars; therefore, the United States could, if necessary, meet its debt obligations toward foreigners by printing more of its own currency. This option is not open to countries whose foreign debt is denominated in foreign currencies since they must service that debt out of export surpluses or new borrowing.

Despite the growing budget deficit, government borrowing has not crowded out private borrowing: government borrowing declined from 38 percent of aggregate borrowing in 1982 to 28 percent in 1984. Borrowing by the United States private sector has been sustained by the tax privileges provided under a tax system that is unusually favorable to borrowers, which by reducing the effective interest rates paid by borrowers have increased the tolerance of United States corporations and households for higher borrowing costs. Taxpayers, whether individuals or businesses, are gen-erally allowed to deduct all interest paid or accrued on indebtedness during the taxable year. The tax system's treatment of interest payments encour-ages corporations to obtain money for new investment and acquisitions by borrowing rather than by raising capital through offerings of common stock. Similarly, the United States tax system, more than the tax systems of most other industrialized countries, encourages borrowing and buying on credit by households. In most industrialized countries, an individual borrowing to purchase a principal residence receives mortgage interest relief and pays no tax on the imputed income (the income saved in the form of rent that he would have paid to a landlord had he been renting his home), and he pays no capital gains on the increasing value of his home (or enjoys privileged treatment in this regard). In the United States, on the other hand, households have been allowed unlimited tax deductions not only for mortgage interest on their principal residences but also for all interest payments, including mortgage interest payments on their second homes. However, under the package of tax revisions proposed by President Reagan on 28 May 1985, interest payments on mortgages on second homes and other interest payments would be deductible up to $5,000 in excess of the taxpayer's net investment income; moreover, homeowners would no longer be allowed to deduct their property taxes, a major factor in an individual's decision whether to rent a home or to borrow in order to buy one. Gains on the sale of property would no longer be eligible for preferential capital gains treatment; they would be taxed at regular rates, although gains on the sale of property would be adjusted for inflation. Deductions for depreciation of real estate would be increased with inflation, but the depreciation schedule would be stretched out from eighteen to twenty-eight years.

The extent of consumer borrowing is reflected in the proliferation of credit cards, which have become a status symbol. According to the Federal Reserve, 70 percent of families hold at least one credit card; 35 percent have gasoline cards; 51 percent have bank cards; 14 percent have travel and entertainment cards; and 63 percent have retail store cards. It has been estimated that there are about six hundred million valid credit cards in the United States and that such cards are used in some 30 percent of retail sales. Indeed, in the past quarter of a century it has become trendy to be a borrower.

The propensity of households to borrow for consumption was perhaps sustained by the 1981 Economic Recovery Tax Act which was, ironically, designed to encourage saving. The cuts it made in marginal tax rates for all taxpayers and the reduction in the top marginal tax rate on nonearned income from 70 percent to 50 percent, which were intended to encourage households to save more by leaving them with more disposable after-tax income, may instead have prompted them to borrow more by increasing their repayment capacity. By the end of the third quarter of 1985, United States households were saving less of their disposable income than at any time since the 1950s: the personal savings rate dropped from an average of 5 to 7 percent in eight of the previous nine years to barely 4 percent for the first three quarters of 1985 and to only 1.9 percent in September of that year.

The propensity of United States corporations and households to borrow has been stimulated not only by the tax system but also by the policy of keeping interest rates artificially low, which prevailed for half a century in the United States and elsewhere following the Great Depression. At one time interest rates were so low that in the United States the rediscount rate of the Federal Reserve Bank of New York, which had been 7 percent in 1920, fell gradually to reach a low of 1 percent in 1940 and remained at that level through 1945, rising slightly to 1.60 percent in 1950 and 1.92 percent in 1955.

Artificially low interest rates have encouraged households to live beyond their means by making it easy for them to live "ahead of their means" through borrowing, that is, by spending money they have not yet received. The tendency of households to borrow has also been encouraged by inflation, which has taught people to appreciate the difference between "a dollar borrowed today" and "a dollar repaid tomorrow."

The contemporary attitude toward borrowing and saving in the United States, and to a certain extent in other countries, contrasts sharply with the beliefs and behavior that predominated in the nineteenth and early twentieth centuries, when saving was considered virtuous. In those times, entrepreneurs usually financed their businesses with their own funds and funds provided by relatives or friends (as is still the custom in many developing countries). Individuals usually tried to avoid buying on credit, and financed their purchases from accumulated savings or current income. Although credit was considered necessary in commercial transactions, it was generally frowned upon in the case of personal transactions, and individuals who borrowed for personal purposes (other than in serious emergencies) were regarded as feckless. Keynes questioned that attitude toward saving, and under his influence saving came to be regarded not as an intrinsically virtuous act of self-denial that was always constructive but as a form of egocentric conduct that could reduce demand and increase unemployment. Thus Keynes wrote:

An act of individual saving means—so to speak—a decision not to have dinner to-day. But it does not necessitate a decision to have dinner or to buy a pair of boots a week hence or a year hence or to consume any specified thing at any specified date. Thus it depresses the business of preparing to-day's dinner without stimulating the business of making ready for some future act of consumption. It is not a substitution of future consumption-demand for present consumption-demand, it is a net diminution of such demand. . . .

If saving consisted not merely in abstaining from present consumption but in placing simultaneously a specific order for future consumption, the effect might indeed be different. . . . In any case, however, an individual decision to save does not, in actual fact, involve the placing of any specific forward order for consumption, but merely the cancellation of a present order. Thus, since the expectation of consumption is the only *raison d'être* of employment, there should be nothing paradoxical in the conclusion that a diminished propensity to consume has *cet. par.* a depressing effect on employment.[7]

Those views were not new, for similar ideas had been expressed much earlier. Pierre Samuel Dupont de Nemours, in his commentary on Turgot's *Reflexions sur la formation et la distribution des richesses*, had condemned saving that did not lead to productive spending and had observed that in a society based on the division of labor, saving viewed as a simple setting aside of money was bound to have deleterious effects by reducing demand. Thomas Malthus had praised luxurious consumption for its beneficial economic effects, and John Atkinson Hobson and some of his contemporaries at the end of the nineteenth century had considered that saving, taken to the extreme, was a major cause of poverty among workers. However, the ideas of Keynes seemed all the more convincing in a world shaken by the First World War and the Great Depression.

In the 1940s and 1950s the public was particularly receptive to the Keynesian emphasis on spending and even on borrowing in order to spend. This emphasis, characteristic of the consumer society of the past half a century, represented a break with the traditional view that the enjoyment that comes from spending must be preceded by a period of effort and self-denial while one accumulates the necessary funds for future spending. Memories of past deprivation and suffering, possibly combined with apprehension about the Cold War, reinforced the natural desire for instant gratification epitomized in two popular songs of the period, one American, the other French. The American song, addressed to people who "never take a minute off, too busy making dough" and "only think of dollar bills tied neatly in a stack" gave them the following advice: "Enjoy yourself, it's later than you think."[8] The French song, associated with the singer Juliette Greco, echoed a sonnet by the sixteenth-century poet Ronsard, urging people to *"cueillir dès aujourd'hui les roses de la vie"* (gather the roses of life today).

This attitude toward present enjoyment was fully consistent with the ideas of Keynes, who believed that "we have been trained too long to strive and not to enjoy." The emphasis on enjoying life now rather than postponing pleasure until later was not new: even in Augustan Rome, Horace had advised *"Carpe diem, quam minimum credula postero"* (Snatch the sleeve of today and trust as little as you may to tomorrow), and in the seventeenth century, Robert Herrick, in "To Virgins, to Make Much of Time," added his version of the same theme when he wrote:

> Gather ye rosebuds while ye may,
> Old Time is still a-flying:
> And the same flower that smiles today
> Tomorrow will be dying.

The conflict between the urge to save and the urge to spend is inherent in the human psyche. Freud related the urge to save to the anal personality and the urge to spend to the oral personality. However, the individual's basic oral impulse to seek instant gratification is inhibited or encouraged by social conditions. In the postwar period the propensity to consume and to spend was stimulated not only by psychological factors but by the introduction of new social security benefits and the expansion of existing social security schemes. During the twentieth century, and particularly since the Second World War, most countries have come to accept the principle that the community as a whole, through the government, must bear the responsibility of ensuring a minimum of social protection to all of its members.[9] In the United States and a number of other countries, social security benefits represent the major source of postretirement consumer spending, and in general such contractual benefits, by allaying to some extent the fears of financial need resulting from old age, unemployment or illness, have made it less necessary to set aside money for a "rainy day" and have encouraged people to "make hay while the sun shines."

UNITED STATES INTEREST RATES AND INTERNATIONAL CAPITAL FLOWS

Because the United States not only is at the center of the international monetary system but accounts for a very large part of world trade and economic output, increases in United States interest rates have placed upward pressure on interest rates in other financial centers and other countries.[10] Specifically, they have pushed up the London Interbank Offered Rate (LIBOR, usually the average of the rates quoted at five of the major London banks and used as a base rate in international lending) and other Eurodollar interest rates, which tend to fluctuate in tandem with short-term interest rates in the United States. Similarly, they have pushed up the Singapore Interbank Offered Rate (SIBOR) and other Asian dollar rates, which generally follow the United States prime rate and LIBOR.

High United States interest rates aggravate the debt-servicing problem of developing countries and impose on them an additional adjustment burden. This in turn erodes much of any increase in export earnings they may achieve. Every time the prime rate in the United States—to which many loans to foreign countries by United States banks are tied—and the international lending rates jump, so do the interest costs of the developing countries' external debt, a substantial portion of which bears variable interest rates: a 1.0 percent rise in international rates adds some $3 billion to $4 billion a year to the developing countries' interest payment burden. However, the impact of such increases on the developing countries' outstanding debts was softened somewhat by the fact that they have had access to external finance on concessional terms. Consequently, *average interest costs* (interest payments as a ratio of the stock of debt outstanding at the beginning of each year) were on the whole much lower for developing countries than for industrialized countries. Although in the period 1974–1981 the average interest cost increased for Sweden by 7.4 percent (from 7.5 to 14.9 percent) and for Belgium by 4.9 percent (from 7.6 to 12.5 percent), it increased for Pakistan by only 1.4 percent (from 3.0 to 4.4 percent), for the Philippines by only 1.3 percent (from 4.5 to 5.8 percent) and for Tunisia by only 0.2 percent (from 3.9 to 4.1 percent). Developing countries with the highest increases in average interest costs during the same period include the Republic of Korea and Venezuela (each with an increase of 6.6 percent) and Morocco (5.3 percent).

High United States interest rates—combined with the United States tax exemption of interest on funds deposited by nonresident aliens with qualifying depository institutions and the perception of the United States as a safe haven for foreign funds and of the dollar as a store of value—have likewise aggravated the developing countries' financial difficulties. These factors have been a powerfully attractive force, drawing funds into the United States from developing countries as well as funds from industrialized countries that, to a certain extent, might otherwise have been invested in, or lent to, developing countries. On the other hand, the inflow of foreign funds has maintained United States interest rates at levels below those they would otherwise have attained.

Aggregate foreign investment in the United States has doubled since 1979, and it amounted to more than $800 billion by mid-1984. Recorded foreign inflows into United States assets reached a peak of $113 billion in 1982 and remained high at $93 billion in 1983 and $83 billion at an annual rate in the first nine months of 1984. In the third quarter of 1983, United States investment and lending abroad declined dramatically, and United States banks became net borrowers from the rest of the world. Those banks, which have drastically curtailed their lending to developing countries and their Eurodollar activities, have now become net borrowers from the Eurodollar market. Thus increased foreign investment in the United States and reduced United States investment abroad have brought about a reversal in the situation that prevailed in previous decades, transforming the United States position in global accounts from that of a net creditor to that of a net debtor.

The inflow of foreign investment, on which the growth of United States economic activity has become heavily dependent, is likely to be sustained or even stimulated further by the 1984 Tax Reform Act, which eliminated the 30 percent withholding tax on new government and corporate bonds and notes issued in the United States and sold to foreign investors. The elimination of that tax increased the effective yield received by foreign holders of United States domestic bonds. But the additional yield was less than 30 percent in the case of foreign investors who previously claimed the benefits available under bilateral agreements for the avoidance of double taxation between their own countries and the United States in respect of their interest income from United States domestic bonds. The stepped-up flow of foreign funds into the United States as a result of the strength of the dollar has compelled Western European countries to raise their interest rates to prevent increased capital outflows and further declines in the exchange values of their currencies. Such increases could hinder their economic recovery, increase unemployment and reduce their imports from developing countries, thus aggravating the latter's financial difficulties.

Before the adoption of the 1984 act, the United Kingdom was virtually the only major financial center where the yield on certain bonds (War Loan bonds and some gilt-edged stocks issued in the late 1970s when sterling was weak) was free of tax to foreign investors, although the general rule of the British Inland Revenue is that foreign bondholders, like domestic bondholders, receive their interest net of tax. However, the attraction of the tax-free British bonds was limited by the fact that foreign investors had to register with the Inland Revenue before being allowed to buy them and by the relatively low yield of the War Loan bonds compared with the yield of other British Government bonds.

Concern about the power of attraction for foreign investors of the more generous tax treatment accorded foreign bondholders in the United States led France to eliminate the 25 percent *prélèvement libératoire* (final withholding) in the case of bonds issued on or after 1 October 1984, when the actual beneficiary of the interest income is domiciled outside France, Monaco and the countries of the franc area. A similar concern led the Parliament of the Federal Republic of Germany to repeal in December 1984 the 25 percent coupon withholding tax on interest paid to foreign holders of new and old domestic bond issues, the aim being to bolster the Deutsche mark *vis à vis* the United States dollar by encouraging foreigners to purchase securities denominated in Deutsche marks (DM). The 25 percent withholding tax was originally imposed in 1965 to deter foreigners from investing heavily in DM-denominated securities, for fear that the Deutsche mark might become a reserve currency like the dollar, thereby reducing the Bundesbank's control of the money supply and stepping up inflationary pressures in the Federal Republic.

Although there had been increasing lobbying in the United States Congress in favor of the repeal of the 30 percent withholding tax for a number of years, one of the major aims of the repeal was to make it easier for the United States Treasury to tap foreign investors for funds and thus not only to help finance the federal budget deficit but to do so at lower cost. The potential for selling more of the United States debt to foreign investors is evident from the fact that in mid-1984 foreign investors held only 10 percent of the $1.56 trillion in outstanding United States Treasury borrowings, and that official institutions accounted for about three-quarters of that 10 percent.

Another important feature of the 1984 Tax Reform Act was that it empowered the Treasury to determine whether issues should be made in registered or bearer form. Bankers and financiers in the United States had contended that eliminating the 30 percent withholding tax was only one step in the international competition to attract capital, that bonds in bearer form, on virtually an equal footing with Eurobonds, were necessary to boost demand for United States bonds, and that it was in the interest of the United States to tailor a bond specifically to the requirements of foreign investors. The availability of bonds issued in the United States that were not only free of United States tax to foreign buyers but marketable to such buyers in bearer form was expected to make such bonds particularly attractive to foreign investors, not so much institutional investors as secretive individual investors. These investors are persons who for various reasons (tax minimization, a desire for privacy or even a desire to invest the proceeds of criminal activity) like to buy bonds on which the names and addresses of the owners are not recorded and on which the interest is paid to whoever presents the bond coupons to the paying agent.

In a 16 August 1984 announcement the Treasury said it would issue specially registered government securities targeted at foreign investors but it was ruling out, at least for the time being, the issue of government securities in bearer form with ownership not registered. The decision to create a new class of United States Government bonds for sale only to foreign investors was a compromise between those who favor issuing bearer bonds and those who think such bonds are a new way for United States taxpayers to use Treasury bonds to evade taxes.

On 20 August 1984 the Internal Revenue Service (IRS) released its temporary regulations implementing the Treasury's decisions. But the regulations were ambiguous and caused confusion in the international capital markets. In particular, many interpreted them as meaning that under the IRS rules aimed at combating tax evasion by United States citizens, foreign buyers of United States domestic bearer bonds would have to prove that they were not United States citizens or United States residents or be liable to a 20 percent "backup" withholding tax. This process would force them to reveal their identity and cancel out the advantages they were seeking by investing in bearer bonds. The confusion prompted the IRS to issue on 28 August a "clarification" in question-and-answer form. It confirmed that foreign banks and brokerage firms acting as paying agents for United States corporate bearer bonds were not subject to the information-reporting requirements and "backup" withholding tax rules that applied to United States financial institutions. Thus non-United States financial institutions holding United States corporate bearer bonds could receive the interest payments without having to report that the beneficial owners of the bonds were not United States citizens or residents.

Following the clarification, United States borrowers began making their issues direct from their United States companies instead of taking the off-shore route. The IRS clarification had not, however, allayed the fear that a future change in the United States tax regime might resubject foreign investors to withholding tax or identification requirements. Consequently, on 6 September 1984 the top syndicate managers devised a form of wording, which was expected to be accepted by both borrowers and investors, whereby the borrowers would undertake to redeem their bonds from the investors at par (with accrued interest) within one year should the United States reintroduce the requirement that the identity of purchasers of United States bearer bonds must be revealed. According to the wording, such bonds must be marketed under arrangements "reasonably designed to ensure that the obligation (debt) is sold to a person who is not a United States person." In particular, the bonds must be offered for sale outside the United States as well as delivered outside the United States. When a bearer bond is sold to a United States citizen or resident, it must be converted into a registered bond and cannot subsequently be reconverted to bearer form. This September 6 development, which completely dissipated investors' fears concerning possible future changes in the United States tax regime, removed the last potential impediment to the launching of more Eurocurrency issues directly from the United States.

Apparently surprised by the early criticism of its efforts to broaden its funding base, the United States Treasury announced on 7 September 1984 that it had decided to ban the issue of government-backed securities in bearer form that might facilitate tax evasion by United States citizens and residents. On that occasion, the Treasury observed that it was "basic to our tax law that a transaction be treated according to its substance and not its form" and that the same registration requirements should consequently be applied to government securities and repackaged government securities. The Treasury noted that a repackaged government issue in bearer form would be competing against normal government issues, but if the repackaged government issue were to obtain a better yield, the latter would "not accrue to the benefit of the United States Government or our taxpayers but will go instead to the private intermediary." The Treasury's decision put an end to the lingering uncertainty about whether, after the Salomon Brothers initiative of 9 August 1984, it would ban further issues of repackaged government bonds in bearer form. The initiative had involved the purchase of a large portion of a United States Treasury bond auction and the repackaging of the bonds after "stripping" them of their interest with a view to marketing them in bearer form.

On 11 September 1984 the United States Treasury announced that the registered United States government securities targeted at foreign investors—its major new instrument for tapping foreign markets, which had been announced on 16 August 1984—would be introduced in mid-October 1984. The targeted securities making up the first issue and subsequent issues were to form part of regular domestic bond auctions but would be marketed in a special registered form. Financial institutions bidding for the targeted obligations would be required to certify that the ultimate beneficial owners are not United States citizens or residents. Furthermore, the institutions paying the interest on behalf of the Treasury would be required to certify each year when the interest is paid that the recipient is not a United States citizen or resident, although it was to be left to each individual institution to determine what proof it requires of those receiving interest. A Treasury spokesman is reported to have said: "We will accept the certification they give us at face value." The Treasury announcement concerning the first issue of the targeted registered bonds prompted the French newspaper *Le Monde* to observe in its 12 September 1984 issue: "*Le trésor américain organise l'afflux des capitaux étrangers*" (The United States Treasury is organizing the flight of foreign capital [to the United States]).

On 24 October 1984 the first offering of government foreign-targeted securities consisting of $500 million to $1 billion in new three-year, eleven-month notes attracted almost $4 billion in bids, largely by securities firms in Europe and Asia. The 11.41 percent average yield on the notes, which pay interest only once a year, was equivalent to a yield of about 11.1 percent for regular Treasury notes paying interest twice a year. The yield on the foreign-targeted notes was nearly three-tenths of a percentage point lower than the equivalent yield on the regular Treasury four-year notes, which were offered for sale on 24 October at an average yield of 11.42 percent. The lower yield on the foreign-targeted notes resulted in significant interest cost savings to the Treasury. The success of the issue, which was four times oversubscribed, led *The Economist* on 27 October 1984 to accuse "spendthrift America" of "raiding the rest of the world's piggy bank."

The flows of foreign capital into dollar-denominated assets have helped to strengthen the dollar, which by mid-1985 was estimated to have risen some 35 to 40 percent against the other major currencies since 1980. The surge in the international purchasing power of the dollar has reduced the competitiveness of United States industry in both domestic and foreign markets. The value of the dollar, combined with the developing countries' debt problems, the continuing United States dependence on foreign oil and the narrowing United States technological edge, has aggravated the United States trade deficit. The latter, which rose from $28 billion in 1981 to $36 billion in 1982, $69 billion in 1983 and $123 billion in 1984, and was likely to soar above $140 billion in 1985, has added considerably to the rest of the world's net claims on the United States. This forms a great contrast with the uninterrupted trade surpluses that the United States enjoyed for more than three quarters of a century before the 1970s. Although the strong dollar has increased the price of United States goods abroad and in March 1985 was estimated by the United States Secretary of Commerce to be "25 percent too high for the full range of American industries to be able to compete," it has also helped to reduce inflation in the United States by making foreign goods relatively inexpensive in that country.

In 1984, after three years of a strong dollar, inflation in the United States stood, as noted earlier, at 3.7 percent, its lowest level since 1967. The task of the Federal Reserve was then to accommodate low inflation with a strong recovery: the real gross national product increased by 6.8 percent in 1984 (its fastest rate of growth since 1951) compared with an average growth rate of 2.3 percent for the four largest European economies and a growth rate of 5.5 percent for the economy of Japan. However, the annual GNP growth rate, after averaging 7.1 percent during the first six quarters of the economic recovery which began in November 1982, started to decline and fell so low as to average only 2.2 percent in the last two quarters of 1984 and the first quarter of 1985. In an appeal to the Senate and House Conference Committees published in *The New York Times* on 23 June 1985, five former Secretaries of the Treasury and one former Secretary of Commerce and other "Founding Members of the Bipartisan Budget Appeal" made the following comments on the economic slowdown:

This abrupt deceleration is neither accidental nor a consequence of faulty monetary fine tuning by the Federal Reserve. Instead, it reflects the continuing hemorrhage in the U.S. trade sector, the 10-month stagnation of industrial production, budding inventory excesses, and rapidly diminishing prospects for strong capital spending. These fundamentally unhealthy trends result from the nation's drastic fiscal imbalance that clashes with the anti-inflationary policies of the Federal Reserve. If these trends worsen, they may paralyze our capacity to take needed corrective actions.

As a result of the "continuing hemorrhage in the U.S. trade sector," the concern over inflation—quiescent at an annual rate of about 4 percent—of the Federal Open Market Committee, which meets about eight times a year to set monetary policy, was replaced by concern over the exchange rate of the dollar (which is now essentially a market price determined by the interplay of supply and demand with only occasional intervention by the monetary authorities) and its impact on United States tradeable goods. In the 24 June 1985 issue of its *Financial Digest*, the Manufacturers Hanover Trust Company observed: "Imports are not simply increasing in pace with U.S. economic growth, but are displacing U.S. production at an accelerating rate." At the end of July 1985, the Federal Reserve's real aim seemed to be to allow or even arrange a gradual decline in the exchange value of the dollar that would reduce the United States trade deficit. Many academic economists and some central bank officials believed that solving the problems of the overvalued dollar and the growing United States trade deficit would require cooperative action by the leading Western industrialized countries aimed at expanding their economies and their imports of United States goods.

Measured against the Morgan Guaranty Bank's index (100 = the average value of the dollar during the period 1980–1982), the dollar soared from 88.1 on 18 July 1980 to 140.9 on 25 February 1985 but had fallen to 125.4 by 12 July 1985. However, that decline was not sufficient to have much effect on the trade deficit. The National Association of Manufacturers had estimated in May 1985 that the dollar would have to decline by 20 percent over the next two years to make United States products competitive in world markets.

Although a weaker dollar would help the United States manufacturing sector become more competitive, a "crash landing" of the dollar might lead to increasingly large outflows of foreign capital. As the chairman of the Federal Reserve Board observed when addressing the Congress early in 1985, United States "capital markets and interest rates have become hostage to a continuing flow of foreign capital." Consequently, large outflows of such capital combined with a significant decline in inflows could, in the absence of substantial reductions in the budget deficit, lead United States interest rates to soar several percentage points above the level they would otherwise have reached. That situation would bring about a recession, increased unemployment and rising inflation, with adverse effects on other industrialized countries and the developing world.

During his July 1985 appearance before the Congress, the chairman of the Federal Reserve Board complained "we are piling up debts abroad in amounts unparalleled in our history." He commented: "When we are living on this much borrowed money, we are also living on borrowed time." Nevertheless, he seemed also to imply that, if confronted with the possibility that foreign investors might reduce their dollar holdings much more quickly than the United States could reduce its need for inflows of foreign funds to compensate for its low domestic savings rate, the Federal Reserve would act to stop the decline in the exchange value of the dollar and the outflow of capital, even if that meant tightening monetary policy and thus pushing up interest rates. On the other hand, if the United States were to reduce its need for foreign funds by gradually reducing the federal budget deficit, the Federal Reserve would be freer to pursue an accommodating monetary policy more likely to cause interest rates to return to and remain at normal levels.

THE INTEREST RATE DILEMMA FOR THE DEVELOPING WORLD

Even though interest rates admittedly have reached historically high levels in the United States, the widespread complaints about those rates and about international interest rates which have followed in their wake have been all the more indignant because such levels reflect a departure from the view, which has prevailed since the 1930s, that borrowing should be cheap. For half a century, until recently in certain countries, interest rates were among the few prices that moved slowly up the inflationary ladder, and although money is the good most affected by inflation (in that inflation deprives it of some of its real value), its price usually has failed to increase as rapidly as other prices. It is only in the past six years that in the United States the financial system has been more or less able to equilibrate the supply of, and demand for, savings at market prices for the first time since the years of the Great Depression: before 1979 the system of federal financial regulations and state usury laws severely restricted the levels of interest rates on most financial instruments and thereby impeded effective market competitiveness.

Like the United States government between 1933 and 1978, governments in all parts of the world have been or are imposing, within the context of policies inspired by Keynesianism, limits on nominal interest rates payable on deposits and/or on nominal interest rates chargeable on loans in general or on loans to special categories of borrowers or to particular economic sectors. Alternatively, they have achieved the same objective by indirect means, such as subsidized loan rates for such borrowers or sectors, preferential rediscount rates, credit floors, general or sector credit ceilings and the creation of specialized financial institutions endowed with public funds. With the acceleration of inflation in the 1970s, *real rates of interest* (nominal interest rates minus inflation rates), net of taxes, became negative in both industrialized and developing countries. That situation was aggravated for savers in countries where the tax system was not adjusted to take into account the distortion of the tax base caused by inflation. For example, in the United States, real interest rates on thirty-year government bonds (which are indicative of the cost of long-term financing) ranged from 0.8 percent to 3.0 percent in the 1960s (averaging 1.8 percent) and from −2.3 percent (negative rate) to 1.5 percent in the 1970s (averaging 0.3 percent). The *real prime rate* (the nominal prime rate minus the rate of inflation, which is indicative of the cost of short-term borrowing) averaged 2.65 percent in the 1960s and dropped to an average of 2.05 percent in the 1970s, when it was highly volatile (during the same period, *real income*, that is, nominal income adjusted for inflation, increased markedly: by 30 percent in the 1960s and 28 percent in the 1970s).

During the 1970s, financial savings were substantially eroded in many developing countries when interest rates in those countries turned sharply negative. As can be seen from Table 2, the greatest erosion occurred in Latin America, particularly in Chile, Argentina, Uruguay, Peru and Brazil. In Africa, the countries where financial savings were most severely eroded were Ghana, Nigeria, Burkina Faso (then the Upper Volta) and Benin, and in Asia the countries most seriously affected were Indonesia, the Philippines, Bangladesh, Pakistan and India.

Interest rates were also often negative during the 1970s in industrialized

Table 2
Real Interest Rates in Selected Developing Countries, 1971–1980
(In Percent per Annum)

Country	1971	1975	1976	1977	1978	1979	1980
AFRICA							
Benin	-4.23	-8.43	-10.72	-20.63	-5.93	--	--
Botswana	--	--	-3.64	-3.93	11.23	-21.49	-12.83
Cameroon	-5.01	-5.96	-27.95	-8.23	--	--	--
Congo	--	--	--	-6.26	-3.26	-2.16	-9.13
*Gabon	1.11	-23.32	-14.97	-8.65	-5.56	-3.15	-7.54
Ghana	--	-21.95	-20.49	-59.75	-61.32	-27.64	-32.46
*Ivory Coast	1.53	-5.93	-6.57	-21.89	-7.51	-11.10	-7.16
Kenya	-4.55	-11.46	-10.56	-11.83	1.95	-1.35	-0.69
Liberia	--	-34.80	6.85	-6.45	2.31	-0.31	1.02
Malawi	-4.64	-3.75	-1.26	-6.51	5.95	3.62	-2.67
*Mauritania	-1.76	-5.91	-8.38	-4.31	-1.20	-2.98	-2.26
*Mauritius	6.04	-8.56	-6.74	-1.18	-1.00	-6.01	-31.95
Morocco	-3.96	2.41	1.28	-7.44	0.47	-0.60	-0.20
*Niger	-4.18	-3.64	-18.04	-17.77	-4.56	-1.78	-2.80
Nigeria	-0.64	-17.27	-6.87	-0.11	-24.65	-7.72	-1.89
Senegal	-3.07	-5.82	0.75	1.01	-12.41	-1.04	--
Sierra Leone	1.23	-10.86	-3.49	-12.56	-6.87	-4.68	0.99
*Somalia	5.57	-12.86	-7.61	-4.06	-3.45	-17.77	-50.34
Tanzania	1.80	-7.96	-11.00	6.25	-10.93	-2.40	-2.61
*The Gambia	3.03	-19.90	-11.07	-5.41	-1.81	2.89	5.30
Togo	-4.74	6.67	-1.24	-11.82	1.31	--	--
Tunisia	-5.15	1.39	-0.67	-5.09	-2.53	-6.32	-8.80
*Upper Volta (now Burkina Faso)	-2.10	-13.28	13.90	-24.51	-2.76	-9.41	-4.78
Zambia	6.96	19.25	-6.16	-2.27	-2.60	-20.96	-3.13
Zimbabwe	1.70	-3.51	-4.45	-4.73	0.84	-12.40	-7.31
ASIA							
Bangladesh	--	-64.09	30.87	11.48	-6.70	1.77	-0.91
*Burma	-0.30	21.82	-13.15	7.85	12.10	5.20	9.20
*Fiji	-6.55	-6.72	-4.65	0.75	0.48	-0.77	-7.50
India	1.25	9.51	-0.22	4.55	3.90	-8.49	-4.99
Indonesia	14.22	-0.48	-2.46	-1.00	-1.95	-23.49	-20.14
Korea	9.41	-9.47	-1.63	-2.09	-2.22	-0.42	-2.95
Malaysia	6.47	11.56	-4.22	-0.35	-3.34	-1.91	-0.86
*Nepal	--	4.58	15.82	2.23	4.82	9.20	-1.92
Pakistan	39.49	-16.65	-3.85	0.23	1.73	0.23	-0.23
Philippines	-6.01	0.07	-1.48	-1.18	-0.98	-4.81	-0.98
Singapore	1.55	3.36	3.89	3.77	3.53	3.75	4.30
Sri Lanka	2.11	4.20	2.18	-5.10	1.89	-4.75	-9.14
Thailand	5.45	5.21	4.06	-0.58	-0.62	-2.60	-4.42

Table 2—*continued*

Country	1971	1975	1976	1977	1978	1979	1980
EUROPE							
*Portugal	-6.64	-11.02	-9.31	-12.17	-3.54	-4.75	2.35
*Turkey	-15.69	-13.21	-11.34	-21.08	-39.30	-44.68	-69.08
*Yugoslavia	-15.53	-13.42	-1.22	-4.54	-3.60	-11.82	-13.38
LATIN AMERICA							
Antigua	--	--	--	2.71	-10.27	-4.34	-1.57
Argentina	-33.00	-163.00	-334.51	-64.30	-41.81	-40.16	-24.08
Barbados	7.03	-2.13	-4.21	-1.19	-2.03	--	--
Bolivia	5.64	3.45	1.86	-0.86	-3.45	-3.21	-21.92
Brazil	8.19	-10.61	-17.21	-3.66	-0.21	-31.87	-40.70
Chile	--	-227.78	-78.25	-10.56	12.12	-1.88	6.80
Colombia	2.56	3.20	0.33	-4.31	4.92	-1.08	8.28
Costa Rica	4.50	-10.50	0.60	0.00	10.00	v.vv	0.vv
Dominica	--	-14.21	-25.01	-6.45	-7.95	-13.46	-1.62
Dominican Republic	2.81	-9.23	4.64	-3.09	6.59	-3.58	-6.27
Ecuador	1.35	-1.01	-3.93	-8.50	1.10	-6.61	-11.51
El Salvador	4.64	-1.56	-16.07	-11.91	11.64	-1.35	-0.93
Grenada	--	--	-6.41	-5.43	-15.14	-9.84	-9.41
Guatemala	8.26	-4.09	-2.48	-7.46	3.51	0.40	-1.29
Haiti	1.62	-11.19	-10.93	-2.88	9.46	11.82	-9.25
Honduras	5.22	-0.28	0.55	-4.47	4.08	3.52	0.36
Jamaica	0.27	-8.99	3.43	0.28	-14.14	-6.58	-6.71
Mexico	5.10	-3.78	-8.57	-16.38	-1.74	-5.02	-6.71
Panama	2.10	-4.39	0.47	0.84	-2.42	-3.73	-4.88
Paraguay	1.94	1.40	2.95	-1.18	-2.44	-12.48	-5.84
Peru	4.58	-11.07	-20.94	-25.23	-34.91	-43.25	-20.94
St. Vincent	--	--	-0.80	-5.38	-10.23	-4.37	-2.00
Trinidad and Tobago	-0.31	-16.98	-0.95	-7.70	4.86	-13.29	-24.96
Uruguay	-1.34	-23.86	13.67	9.28	1.89	-23.77	-2.73
Venezuela	0.45	7.76	1.46	-0.84	0.80	-10.66	-11.56
MIDDLE EAST							
Jordan	--	1.36	-5.38	-8.51	-0.96	-7.95	-4.71
Yemen Arab Republic	3.45	-12.05	-8.69	-16.08	-9.02	-8.15	2.56
*Yemen People's							
Democratic Rep.	-0.33	-5.50	2.25	0.84	6.05	-13.80	-10.04

Source: International Monetary Fund, International Financial Statistics.

*The real interest rate is calculated by correcting the nominal interest rate
for a percentage change in the gross domestic product (GDP) deflator:
$r = \frac{1+i}{1+P} = 1$, where i is the nominal interest rate and P is the GDP deflator.
For the countries with an asterisk, the consumer price index (CPI) is used
instead of the GDP deflator, in view of its nonavailability.

Table 3
Real Interest Rates in Industrialized Countries[a]
(In Percentages)

Country	1975	1976	1980	1981	1982	1983[b]
Canada						
Short term	-3.1	-0.5	1.0	6.4	3.5	2.7
Long term	-1.6	-0.3	1.3	4.2	3.7	4.9
France						
Short term	-4.8	-1.4	-0.3	3.6	1.8	3.3
Long term	-2.6	0.5	1.4	4.5	2.8	4.8
Germany, Federal Republic of						
Short term	1.7	0.4	4.4	6.7	3.7	1.8
Long term	3.9	4.3	3.8	5.7	3.8	4.4
Italy						
Short term	-6.5	-2.0	-3.1	1.9	1.9	4.5
Long term	-5.2	-4.0	-7.2	-2.9	-0.4	4.8
Japan						
Short term	2.2	0.3	7.9	4.7	4.8	5.2
Long term	1.2	0.7	6.0	6.2	6.1	6.6
United Kingdom						
Short term	-13.7	-3.2	-3.2	-1.3	2.1	2.5
Long term	-10.5	-0.9	-4.5	1.5	4.4	5.2
United States						
Short term	-3.2	-0.2	3.7	6.3	5.9	4.4
Long term	-1.0	2.5	1.9	4.1	6.4	6.6
Memorandum item, nominal rate of interest:						
United States						
Short term	5.8	5.0	13.3	16.3	12.2	9.0
Long term	8.2	7.8	11.4	13.9	12.7	11.3

a. Both short- and long-term rates are period averages net of the change in the GNP deflator. The short-term rate is the bank rate in Canada and the United Kingdom; the call money rate in France, the Federal Republic of Germany, Italy and Japan; and the federal funds rate in the United States. The long-term rate for the Federal Republic of Germany is the yield on Public Authorities Bonds and for others the yield on long-term government bonds.

b. Preliminary estimates based on data up to and including November 1983, except for Italy, whose data extend to the end of October 1983.

Source: United Nations, World Economic Survey, 1984, p. 82.

countries, notable exceptions being the Federal Republic of Germany and Japan (see Table 3). More recently, interest rates in the industrialized countries have increased substantially and turned sharply positive as a result of tight monetary policies followed with a view to containing inflationary pressures and expectations. However, interest rates in many developing countries are still being kept artificially low, and such rates may therefore be negative by an appreciable margin owing to prevailing high rates of inflation.

The policy of keeping interest rates artificially low means that in many developing countries savers are not rewarded appropriately for sacrificing present consumption to future consumption. At the same time, privileged borrowers and favored areas of activity benefit from loans granted at rates of interest that are below the level that would equilibrate the supply of, and demand for, funds. Many projects financed with this cheap credit are only artificially profitable. Borrowers who could afford to pay equilibrium rates of interest benefit from low interest rates that are in effect subsidized by savers, while poor borrowers are compelled to resort to the money lenders who charge exorbitant interest rates. This phenomenon has been characterized as "financial repression" by the United States economist R. I. McKinnon:

Organized banking has a sorry record in penetrating the economic hinterland of less developed countries, in serving rural areas in general, and in serving small borrowers in particular. Bank credit remains a financial appendage of certain enclaves: exclusively licensed import activities, specialized large-scale mineral exports, highly protected manufacturing, large international corporations, and various government agencies, such as coffee marketing boards or publicly controlled utilities. Even ordinary government deficits on current accounts frequently preempt the limited lending resources of the deposit bank. Financing of the rest of the economy must be met from the meager resources of moneylenders, pawnbrokers and co-operatives.[11]

According to McKinnon, a major consequence of financial repression is heavy dependence on foreign capital:

Financial repression restrains domestic saving within LDCs [less-developed countries] and generates pressures for reliance on foreign capital to supplement domestic saving and to provide intermediation services capable of identifying high-return investment opportunities that would otherwise languish. Similarly, the repression of foreign trade inhibits the development of exports and creates an apparent shortage of foreign exchange that ostensibly can also be relieved by inflows of foreign capital. In the repressed economies, therefore, foreign loans or grants play the important dual role of relaxing the saving constraint on the one hand and the foreign exchange constraint on the other. (One could go further and identify a third constraint, a fiscal one, that requires soliciting budgetary support from abroad because the government cannot raise revenue domestically). . . . Governments become accustomed to foreign aid for their own fiscal support on current and capital account and feel less need for "organized" financial processes for allocating capital on a decentralized basis at much higher rates of interest.[12]

To end financial repression and reduce reliance on foreign capital, interest rates must be increased to encourage domestic saving. The positive real interest rates on savings recorded in a number of developing countries in recent years indicate a trend toward a more realistic perception of the role of interest rates; they indicate a willingness to encourage saving, not in the form of precious metals, commodities and other physical assets but in financial assets that promote investment; they indicate a willingness to turn away from policies that have constrained the capital allocation process (through setting ceilings on interest rates and through granting bank loans to privileged borrowers and sectors at rates well below the opportunity cost of capital, which is in very short supply); and they indicate a movement toward policies that encourage saving in the form of domestic financial assets and the functioning of an allocative mechanism that will direct savings to those ventures most likely to result in higher employment and growth rates.

However, a developing country which has decided to renounce a policy of negative interest rates that discourages voluntary financial savings and makes it necessary to mobilize involuntary savings by means such as inflation (through borrowing from the central bank or simply by printing notes), overvaluation of exchange rates or distortion of terms of trade through pricing policies must develop a rational and clearly defined alternative. The crucial problem facing the developing world is how to resolve what may be called the interest rate dilemma. This means steering a safe course between, on the one hand, a policy of artificially low interest rates that stimulates investment in unsound projects and the choice of capital-intensive technologies and depresses financial intermediation and saving in the form of domestic bank deposits and other income-yielding domestic financial assets and on the other, a policy of allowing interest rates to be determined essentially by market forces that, even if the conditions for the untrammeled interplay of supply and demand were met, might result—given the scarcity of capital and the high demand for credit—in interest rates rising so high that they would constrain productive investment.

If, as a result of their being set by administrative decisions, domestic interest rates deviate too much from interest rates in world financial centers, any benefits expected from keeping them abnormally low are sooner or later offset by the outflow of savings abroad to sources of higher returns. Experience has shown that erecting barriers to international capital flows does not usually reduce the outflow of savings significantly but merely drives it underground. On the other hand, if interest rates are completely deregulated, entrepreneurship, particularly small entrepreneurship, may be discouraged. This may happen because interest rates rise to unaffordably high levels as a result either of the interplay of supply and demand or of the covert manipulation of interest rates by financial institutions, which in developing countries are often so few that they constitute de facto interest-rate cartels.

One possible way of resolving the dilemma, by setting interest rates at levels considered appropriate or just for both savers and borrowers, is discussed in Chapter 5.

NOTES

1. Milton Friedman, Presidential address delivered at the Eightieth Annual Meeting of the American Economic Association, Washington D.C., 29 December 1967.

2. Paul Homan and Fritz Machlup, eds., *Financing American Prosperity*, New York: The Twentieth Century Fund, 1945, p. 383.

3. Arthur Smithies, "Federal Budgeting and Fiscal Policy," *A Survey of Contemporary Economics*, Philadelphia: The Blakiston Company, 1949, p. 155, see also pp. 174–209.

4. M1 consists of currency outside the Treasury, Federal Reserve Banks, and the vaults of commercial banks; traveler's checks of nonbank issuers; demand deposits at all commercial banks other than those due to domestic banks, the United States Government, and foreign banks and official institutions, less cash items in the process of collection and Federal Reserve float, and other checkable deposits (OCD) consisting of negotiable order of withdrawal (NOW) and automatic transfer service (ATS) accounts at depository institutions, credit union-share draft accounts, and demand deposits at thrift institutions. The currency and demand-deposit components exclude the estimated amount of vault cash and demand deposits respectively held by thrift institutions to service their OCD liabilities.

M2 consists of M1 plus overnight (and continuing contract) repurchase agreements (RPs) issued by all commercial banks and overnight Eurodollars issued to United States residents by foreign branches of United States banks world-wide, money-market deposit accounts, savings and small-denomination time deposits (time deposits—including retail RPs—in amounts of less than $100,000), and balances in both taxable and tax-exempt general purpose and broker-dealer money market mutual funds. It excludes individual retirement account (IRA) and Keogh balances at depository institutions and money market funds. It also excludes all balances held by United States commercial banks, money market funds (general purpose and broker-dealer), foreign governments and commercial banks and the United States government. Also subtracted is a consolidation adjustment that represents the estimated amount of demand deposits and vault cash held by thrift institutions to service their time and savings deposits.

M3 consists of M2 plus large-denomination time deposits and term RP liabilities (in amounts of $100,000 or more) issued by commercial banks and thrift institutions, term Eurodollars held by United States residents at foreign branches of United States banks world-wide and at all banking offices in the United Kingdom and Canada, and balances in both taxable and tax-exempt institution-only money market mutual funds. It excludes amounts held by depository institutions, the United States government, money market funds, and foreign banks and official institutions. Also subtracted is a consolidated adjustment that represents the estimated amount of overnight RPs and Eurodollars held by institution-only money market mutual funds.

The United States also uses another money stock measure, namely L, which consists of M3 plus the nonbank public holdings of United States savings bonds, short-term Treasury securities, commercial paper and banker's acceptances, net of money market mutual fund holdings of these assets.

5. The prime rate is in fact no longer the "base" rate that the banks offer to their largest corporate customers. The latter have long been benefiting from rates well below the prime rate, because the banks have feared that in the absence of such concessional rates their customers would turn to alternative sources of credit, such as the commercial paper market or overseas credit markets. However, the prime rate is used by banks as a base for rates on loans to many small and medium-sized corporations and is watched closely because its movements usually affect interest charges throughout the United States economy and elsewhere. Indeed, an increase in the prime rate (usually decided in order to protect banks' profit margins over the cost of borrowed funds) may trigger a wave of dollar buying, which will push up the exchange value of the dollar and cause a decline in stock and gold prices. Lending by United States banks to developing countries is typically 1.5 points above the prime rate.

6. Federal Reserve Bank of Kansas City, "The U.S. Economy and Monetary Policy in 1984" by J. A. Cacy and Glenn H. Miller, Jr., *Economic Review*, December 1984, 12.

7. John Maynard Keynes, *The General Theory of Employment, Interest and Money*, New York: Harcourt, Brace and Company, 1936, pp. 210–211.

8. "Enjoy Yourself (It's Later Than You Think)" by Herb Magidson and Carl Sigman. © 1948, 1949 Edwin H. Morris and Company, a Division of MPL Communications. © Renewed 1976, 1977 Edwin H. Morris and Company, a Division of MPL Communications. International Copyright Secured. All rights reserved. Used by permission.

9. The idea that the state should be responsible for the social welfare of all of its citizens, and particularly the underprivileged, was first given practical political expression in Germany in the imperial proclamation by Kaiser Wilhelm I, read to the Reichstag, the lower chamber of the federal Parliament, on 17 November 1881 by Chancellor Otto von Bismarck. The proclamation, drafted by Bismarck, declared that the state "should not be confined to defensive action designed to protect existing rights, but should also seek to promote actively, by means of appropriate institutions and by using the available resources of the community, the well-being of all its members and in particular of the weak and needy."

10. From 1944, when the Bretton Woods Agreement on a new international monetary system was concluded, until the early 1970s, when the system of pegged exchange rates under the Agreement came to an end with the suspension of the gold convertibility of the dollar, the international monetary system operated on a dollar standard. During that period the United States business cycle tended to be followed by that of the rest of the world. By the end of 1983, however, the international financial system could be considered to have returned, for the time being at least, to a dollar standard but this time within the context of world-wide floating exchange rates. In effect, the dollar holdings of the central banks of the industrialized countries, which had fallen in the second half of the 1970s and early 1980s, had risen strongly again. In the Eurodollar market, dollars as a percentage of total liabilities, which had likewise declined rapidly in the second half of the 1970s and early 1980s, had rebounded. Thus the dollar has not only held its own as the world's main trading currency but has regained its position as the world's main international

reserve currency. The dollar represents 75 to 80 percent of the world currency market.

11. R. I. McKinnon, *Money and Capital in Economic Development*, Washington, DC: The Brookings Institution, 1973, pp. 68–69.

12. Ibid., pp. 170–171.

2   Charging or Taking Interest:
A Source of Controversy
throughout the Ages

The interest rate dilemma theoretically could be sidestepped through full Islamization of a country's banking system. However, experience has not dispelled the doubts about the extent to which a modern banking system can in practice become fully or even predominantly Islamic. Islamic banking is based on the premise that the Koran prohibits the practice of charging or taking interest, irrespective of the rate. But that strict interpretation of the Koran is not accepted by all Muslims, and the principle of charging interest is today a subject of renewed debate in the Muslim world. In fact, that principle has often been a source of controversy throughout the centuries, and to place Islamic banking and the current concern about interest rates and indebtedness in their proper perspective, this chapter reviews historical attitudes toward charging or taking interest, with particular emphasis on Judaism, Christianity and Islam, before taking up the question of Islamic banking.

CHARGING OR TAKING INTEREST IN ANTIQUITY

Lending at interest was not only practiced but was accepted in many very ancient civilizations, although it was generally subject to regulation, especially in the form of legal maximum interest rates. Limits on interest rates were set in ancient China and also in India, where the Laws of Manu, probably compiled between 200 B.C. and A.D. 200 from ancient sources, recognized a customary annual interest rate of 24 percent. However, ancient Indian texts vilify usury. Papyrus records indicate that interest was charged on loans in Egypt at least from the ninth century B.C.; some of the annual interest rates recorded are very high (75 percent and 100 percent, for example), but since the economy of ancient Egypt was essentially authoritarian and the state owned most of the nation's resources, the use of credit was inevitably limited.

Historical records show that lending at interest was common as early as 3000 B.C. in ancient Sumer, and many Sumerian lending practices were subsequently codified under King Amraphel, sixth king of the Semitic dynasty of Babylonia, usually known as King Hammurabi and a contemporary of Abraham. The Code of Hammurabi (circa 1800 B.C.) covered, among other things, commercial and financial transactions, including the granting of credit. In Sumer the usual annual interest rate charged for a loan of silver was 20 percent, and the rate charged for a loan of barley (the medium of exchange for most commercial transactions) was 33.3 percent. Those rates became the prescribed maximum rates in the Code of Hammurabi and remained in force until about 600 B.C., when the maximum rate for loans of grain was lowered and made equal to the maximum rate for loans of silver.

To ensure that both debtor and creditor fulfilled their obligations, the Code of Hammurabi provided that the terms and conditions of all loans had to be set out in a contract drawn up before an official and duly witnessed. Failure to follow such a procedure meant that the creditor forfeited his right to repayment. A creditor found guilty of having resorted to stratagems to obtain a rate of interest higher than the prescribed maximum was penalized by having the debt cancelled. On the other hand, the creditor could protect his interests by demanding pledges. The borrower could pledge not only his land, house, utensils or doors (the latter being a valuable possession because timber was scarce in Mesopotamia) but also his own person or that of his wife, concubine, child or slave. However, the creditor could not detain the wife, concubine or child for more than three years, and if they died as a result of mistreatment he had to pay full compensation to the debtor. The Code of Hammurabi protected women's property rights, for a husband could not pledge joint property without his wife's consent; nor could his creditors seize her property for payment of his antenuptial debts. The code regulated joint borrowing by partners in a venture, and a partner could contribute credit instead of risk capital; partnerships had, in fact, existed in ancient Sumer before partnership practices were embodied in the code. The Babylonian temples owned substantial wealth and used it to engage in lending operations, granting loans of silver and grain, sometimes free of charge (when the borrower was poor) and often at rates below the legal maximum. The Babylonian Temple of Marduk even made loans to slaves so that they could purchase their freedom.

Lending practices similar to those in Babylonia existed in Assyria, where customary rates of interest were recognized, but apparently, no formal maximum rate was set. Interest–free loans with heavy penalties for failure to comply with the terms of a loan appear to have been more frequent in Assyria than in Babylonia.

For many centuries, the nations of Mesopotamia had the most highly developed credit practices in the world, but by the sixth century B.C. the focus of economic activity had moved to the Mediterranean and especially to Greece. Probably the earliest reference to lending in the Greek world is found in the *Works and Days* of Hesiod (eighth century B.C.), which mentions interest-free loans of seed repayable in kind. During the seventh century B.C., the Greeks developed a complex commercial and financial system in which credit played an important role. Early in the sixth century B.C. an economic crisis in Attica was sparked by the financial difficulties of smallholders, who owned much of the land but were often deeply in debt and liable to be enslaved, together with their families, if they defaulted. The unrest led to legal reforms initiated by Solon, who was elected Chief Archon of Athens in 594 B.C. Solon cancelled all mortgages and debts, limited the amount of land that could be added to anyone's holdings, prohibited all borrowing in which the borrower's freedom was pledged, and prohibited the selling of men into slavery for failing to pay interest on a loan. Unlike the Code of Hammurabi, the laws of Solon removed restrictions on interest rates.

In succeeding centuries, throughout the Greek world, all social strata engaged in borrowing and lending for a wide range of purposes. The temples of the various gods, using donated and deposited funds, made loans to city-states and individuals, and private banking assumed an increasingly important role as a collector of deposits and provider of finance. The average rate of interest on ordinary loans varied from a probable range of 16 to 18 percent in Solon's time to a range of 10 to 12 percent in the fifth and fourth centuries B.C.; in the third and second centuries it dropped again to a range of between 6 and 10 percent and rose slightly to a range of between 6 and 12 percent in the first century B.C. The rates charged by individual moneylenders were often very high and in some instances reached astronomical levels, such as a daily rate of 25 percent.

Although lending at interest was widely accepted in Greek society as an essential feature of economic activity, many Greek philosophers disapproved of it. Plato, in *The Republic*, denounced "the men of business, stooping as they walk, and pretending not even to see those whom they have already ruined" who "insert their sting—that is, their money—into someone else who is not on his guard against them, and recover the parent sum many times over multiplied into a family of children." Such men "make drone and pauper to abound in the State" and render some of these victims "eager for revolution." According to Aristotle, interest "makes a gain out of money itself, and not from the natural use of it." He considered that "money was intended to be used in exchange but not to increase at interest." In his opinion, the term *interest* (tokos), "which means the birth of money from money, is applied to the breeding of money, because the offspring resembles the parent. Wherefore of all modes of making money, this is the most unnatural." Aristotle was nevertheless not opposed to the idea of profit and wealth *per se*, as is demonstrated by his approving reference in *The Politics* to the philosopher Thales, who became rich by foreseeing a plentiful olive crop well in advance and securing a virtual monopoly of the olive presses in the Greek islands of Chios and Miletus. Aristotle apparently did not disapprove of Thales' skillful business dealings, because getting rich was not Thales' "object in life."

In ancient Rome, the Twelve Tables, a codification of Roman law traditionally believed to date from 450 B.C., set a legal maximum interest rate of 8 1/3 percent, and any creditor who exacted a higher rate had to pay damages to the debtor. If the debtor defaulted, he could be seized and fettered by the creditor. The legal maximum rate of 8 1/3 percent was probably exceeded in time, because in 357 B.C. that legal maximum was reconfirmed. The legal maximum was reduced to 4 1/6 percent in 347 B.C., and the charging of all interest was prohibited in 342 B.C., but a legal maximum of 8 1/3 percent was subsequently restored. In 326 B.C. it became illegal to imprison Romans for failure to repay their debts. In 192 B.C., a number of moneylenders who had lent at rates above the legal maximum were fined, and loans by foreigners were brought within the ambit of the law on interest; however, no interest ceiling was set for maritime loans. In 88 B.C., under Sulla, the maximum interest rate was raised to 12 percent, a step that probably merely sanctioned the practice of charging rates exceeding the 8 1/3 percent legal ceiling. Within the framework of Lucullus' reform of the finances of Rome's provinces in Asia Minor, the 12 percent maximum was extended in 67 B.C. to cover loans made to borrowers in those provinces. At the same time, Lucullus decreed that the aggregate interest paid on a loan could not exceed the principal and that a lender must not demand from a borrower payments exceeding one-quarter of his income. The 12 percent legal ceiling remained in force throughout the existence of the Western Empire and was still in force (or was reconfirmed) under Constantine early in the fourth century A.D.; later in that century, it was raised to 12 1/2 percent. Lower legal ceilings were set in the Byzantine Empire (the Eastern Roman Empire) in the sixth century A.D. Under the code of Roman law (*Corpus Juris Civilis*) prepared during the reign of Emperor Justinian, the legal ceiling on interest varied according to the type of creditor: 8 percent for bankers, 6 percent for ordinary citizens and 4 percent for "distinguished" lenders such as senators. A limit of 12 percent per voyage was set in the case of maritime loans, which had not been regulated in the past. A ceiling of 12 percent was likewise imposed in the case of loans of commodities repayable in kind.

The Code of Justinian thus reflected the traditional Roman attitude toward lending at interest, which was permitted but regulated so that interest rates did not exceed what was regarded as a reasonable ceiling. However, a number of Roman philosophers and moralists, including the two Catos, Cicero and Seneca, echoed the Greek philosophers' disapproval of lending at interest. Cato the Elder, for example, thought that moneylending was dishonorable. The Roman Empire's attitude toward charging interest became more ambivalent as Christian doctrine began to exert greater influence. The Christian opposition to charging interest, in fact, came directly from the Judaic condemnation contained in the Old Testament. The basic assumption underlying the condemnation of the practice of charging interest by Judaism, Christianity and Islam was that the lender, by definition, possesses a store of capital that exceeds his requirements, while the borrower does not have enough resources to satisfy his immediate needs. It was therefore believed, consciously or unconsciously, that it would be unfair and even immoral for a "needy" borrower both to repay the capital and to increase the lender's wealth still further by paying him interest. Hence it was the duty of the prosperous to assist the needy, if not by gifts, then through interest–free loans. In the case of some other religions, no explicit condemnation of interest was necessary, since the exacting of a charge for lending goods or services was alien to the mores of the community concerned. In African societies, for example, assistance was provided—as it still is today—within the framework of the extended family or within the framework of mutual help associations.[1]

CHARGING OR TAKING INTEREST IN JUDAISM

Charging or taking interest is prohibited in both the Tanach (also referred to as the Jewish Bible) and the Talmud.[2] The Tanach draws no distinction between *interest* and *usury*, both terms being the translation of the Hebrew terms *neshech* (literally, a "bite") and *tarbit* and *marbit* (literally, "increase"). Maimonides, the twelfth-century Jewish philosopher, physician and rabbinic scholar, commenting in his Mishneh Torah on the term *neshech*, said that it was used because the person who charges interest "bites his fellow, causes pain to him and eats his flesh."[3] Maimonides also pointed out that the two virtually synonymous terms *neshech* and *marbit* had been used deliberately "so that he who would take [interest] should be chargeable with transgressing two negative commandments."[4]

The Book of Exodus prohibits the practice of charging or taking interest. It also forbids the pledging of clothes as security. It may be recalled that *pawnbroking* (the business of making loans on the basis of pledges of goods or chattels) is one of the oldest occupations of humankind, having been practiced in ancient Greece and Rome and also some three thousand years ago in China. Its main purpose was usually to satisfy the need of the poor for consumption loans, but it could easily degenerate into exploitation when would-be borrowers were prepared to pledge even their clothing. That was the rationale for prohibiting such pledges, as well as interest, in the Book of Exodus:

If thou lend money to any of My people, even to the poor with thee, thou shalt not be to him as a creditor; neither shall ye lay upon him interest.

If thou at all take thy neighbour's garment to pledge, thou shalt restore it unto him by that the sun goeth down; For that is his only covering, it is his garment for his skin; wherein shall he sleep? and it shall come to pass, when he crieth unto Me, that I will hear; for I am gracious. (Exodus 22:24–26)

The prohibition of interest is repeated in the Book of Leviticus but is extended to cover charging interest on loans to the *ger tzedek* (stranger)— interpreted in the rabbinic tradition as a non–Israelite who had become a proselyte—and to the *ger toshav* (settler)—interpreted in the rabbinic tradition as a resident alien, that is, a non–Jew who had abandoned idolatry but had not taken upon himself the life and religious practices of an Israelite:

And if thy brother be waxen poor, and his means fail with thee; then thou shalt uphold him: as a stranger and a settler shall he live with thee.

Take thou no interest of him or increase; but fear thy God; that thy brother may live with thee. (Leviticus 25:35–36)

The ban on taking clothing as a pledge is likewise extended to cover other necessities of life:

Thou shalt not give him thy money upon interest, nor give him thy victuals for increase. (Leviticus 25:37)

In the Book of Deuteronomy, the prohibition of lending at interest to Jews is repeated, and the ban on taking necessities of life as pledges from Jewish borrowers is broadened to cover the pledging of any good:

Thou shall not lend upon interest to thy brother: interest of money, interest of victuals, interest of any thing that is lent upon interest. (Deuteronomy 23:20)

However, the Book of Deuteronomy permits Jewish lenders to charge interest on loans to the *nochri* (foreigner)—interpreted in the rabbinic tradition as a person who is only temporarily among Jews and is usually a merchant visiting them for purposes of trade:

Unto a foreigner thou mayest lend upon interest; but unto thy brother thou shalt not lend upon interest. (Deuteronomy 23:21)

Furthermore, the Book of Deuteronomy calls upon those who have lent money to their "neighbors" and "brothers" to cancel their debts at the end of every seventh year, known as the sabbatical year, when in accordance with God's command to Moses the land was left fallow and allowed to rest, as men were allowed to rest on the seventh day:[5]

At the end of every seven years thou shalt make a release. And this is the manner of the release: every creditor shall release that which he hath lent unto his neighbour; he shall not exact it of his neighbour and his brother, because the Lord's release hath been proclaimed. (Deuteronomy 15:1–2)

The rationale for cancelling all debts at the end of the sabbatical year (also known as the *Shemitah*, or year of release) was that in an agricultural community, where most men were farmers and supposedly self–sufficient, they would seek a loan only if they were exceptionally hard pressed. Thus if a borrower were unable to pay his debt in the years when he could till the soil, he undoubtedly would be incapable of doing so in a year when his land must be left fallow.

The Book of Deuteronomy nevertheless excludes foreigners from the sabbatical cancellation of debts:

Of a foreigner thou mayest exact it; but whatsoever of thine is with thy brother thy hand shall release. (Deuteronomy 15:3)

The differentiation between Jews and foreigners (with the exception of resident aliens) was based on the assumption that a foreigner was probably a transient merchant, not a farmer following the Jewish practice of leaving his land fallow every seventh year. There was thus no reason to release him from his debts during the sabbatical year or to expect him to release his Jewish debtors or to lend to them without charging interest.

The prohibition of charging or taking interest contained in the three Books of the Tanach quoted above—whose violation constituted a moral transgression entailing no penal sanction—does not seem to have been widely complied with, judging from the following passages in later Books of the Tanach:

And every one that was in distress, and every one that was in debt, and every one that was discontented, gathered themselves unto him; and he became captain over them and there were with him about four hundred men. (1 Samuel 22:2)

Now there cried a certain woman of the wives of the sons of the prophets unto Elisha, saying "Thy servant my husband is dead; and thou knowest that thy servant did fear the Lord; and the creditor is come to take unto him my two children to be bondsmen."(2 Kings 4:1)

The continued failure of "the nobles and officials" to refrain from charging or taking interest prompted the prophet Nehemiah to admonish them and exhort them to abide by the scriptural injunction:

Then I consulted with myself, and contended with the nobles and the rulers, and said unto them: "Ye lend upon pledge, every one to his brother! And I held a great assembly against them." (Nehemiah 5:7)

Then said they: "We will restore them, and will require nothing of them; so will we do, even as thou sayest." Then I called the priests, and took an oath of them, that they should do according to this promise. Also I shook out my lap and said: "So God shake out every man from his house, and from his labour, that performeth not this promise; even thus be he shaken out, and emptied!" And all the congregation said "Amen," and praised the Lord. And the people did according to his promise. (Nehemiah 5:12–13)

In Psalm 15, King David stated that those who refrain from lending at interest will be rewarded by God:

Lord who shall sojourn in thy tabernacle? . . .
He that putteth not out his money on interest,
Nor taketh a bribe against the innocent.
He that doeth these things shall never be moved. (Psalms 15:5)

The prophet Ezekiel, alarmed by the disregard of the scriptural injunction, denounced the practice of charging or taking interest as a serious offense calling for appropriate punishment, and he mentioned it in the same context as "abominations" such as larceny, adultery and homicide, all punishable by death. Referring to the man who "hath given forth upon interest and hath taken increase" the prophet exclaimed, "Shall he then live?" and answered, "He shall not live—he hath done all these abominations; he shall surely be put to death, his blood shall be upon him" (Ezekiel 18:13).

The difficulty of achieving full compliance with the scriptural prohibition of interest led Talmudic jurists to clarify that prohibition and to extend its scope. They did this first by enlarging the concept of interest, second by increasing the number of people affected by the prohibition, and third by limiting the circumstances in which Jews could lend at interest to non-Jews.

The Talmud enlarged the concept of interest to cover any tangible or intangible benefit that might be deliberately or involuntarily conferred on a lender by a potential or actual borrower. Thus in the case of tangible benefits, the prohibition against lending a given quantum of wheat for a greater quantum of wheat was extended to lending a given quantum of wheat for the same quantum of wheat, because the value of the wheat might increase between the date of the loan and the date of its repayment, the increase being viewed as tantamount to interest. Because of the problems involved in such fluctuations in value, specific rules were set forth in the Mishnah, including the following:

A man may lend his tenants grain for [an equal quantity of] grain [to be returned] for sowing purposes but not for food. For Rabban Gamaliel used to lend his farmer-tenants grain for sowing; and if it was dear and became cheap, or cheap and became dear, he would accept [a return] only at the lower price; not because the halachah is so, but because Rabban Gamaliel desired to submit himself to greater stringency.

A man may not say to his neighbour, "Lend me a kor of wheat and I will repay you at harvest time"; but he may say, "lend me until my son comes, or until I find the key." Hillel, however, forbade [even this] and thus Hillel used to say: a woman must not lend a loaf to her neighbour without first valuing it, lest wheat advances and thus they [the lender and borrower] come to [transgress the prohibition of usury].[6]

Generally, the market price of wheat or any other agricultural product had to be set before the product was sold, since the purchaser could, by paying in advance a price below the eventual market value of the product, obtain a profit on his money that was analogous to interest. On the other hand, once the price of a good had been set, the owner could, if he wished, sell it below the market price; according to the Talmudic jurists, such a sale would not be a disguised interest-bearing transaction but a *bona fide* if not commercially sound operation.[7] The Talmudic jurists prohibited the payment of interest not only within the context of exchanges of goods but within the context of exchanges of labor, which they regulated as follows:

A man may say to his neighbour: "Help me to weed, and I will help you; assist me to hoe, and I will assist you." But he may not suggest: "Do you weed with me, and I will hoe with you; Do you hoe with me and I will weed with you." All the days of the dry season are equal, and likewise of the rainy season, [but] one may not say, "plough with me in the dry season, and I will plough with you in the rainy season."[8]

The Talmud extended the prohibition of interest to cover any arrangement whereby a party to a transaction receives compensation when he leaves money in the possession of the other party when it should have already been paid according to law or custom.[9] The Talmud further prohibited contracts of partnership under which one partner provides financing for a venture and the other manages it, the losses being borne by the manager alone while the profits are shared between both partners. Such contracts were valid under the Talmud only if the partner providing the funds shared the burden of an eventual loss or if the manager of the venture received a salary instead of or in addition to his right to a share of the profits.[10]

The Talmud also prohibited borrowers or would-be borrowers from allowing actual or potential lenders to live free of rent in buildings or apartments they owned; even if the lender had not been paying rent before granting the loan, the borrower had to begin charging rent once the loan was contracted.[11] Furthermore, the borrower might not send the lender gifts before or after he granted the loan:

Rabban Gamaliel said: There is [a form of prepaid interest, and one of postpaid interest], e.g. if one made up his mind to borrow from his neighbor and sent him [a gift] saying: "it is in order that you should lend me"—that is interest in advance. If he borrowed from him, repaid his money, and then sent him [a gift] saying: "it is on account of your money which [as far as you were concerned] lay idle with me," that is postpaid interest."[12]

The lender may not ask the borrower to entertain his friends or acquaintances:

He who has lent something to his fellow must not say to him "Ascertain whether such a one has arrived hither from such a place," that is to say "Pay him respect, dine and wine him fittingly and the like."[13]

With regard to intangible benefits, the Talmud prohibited acts such as the transmittal of information to potential lenders: "A man may not say to his creditor, 'Know thou that such a man has come from such a place,' thus giving information of value in consideration of receiving a loan;"[14] or purely social acts of courtesy: "He who borrowed something from his fellow must not be quick to greet him first if he was not accustomed to do so before the loan was made and, needless to say, must not flatter him with words of praise and pay him visits frequently at his house . . . . Similarly, the borrower is forbidden, while the loan remains unpaid, to teach the lender Scripture or Gemara if he was not accustomed to do so before the loan was made."[15]

Numerous persons were affected by the prohibition; the obligation not to lend at interest applied not only to lenders who charged interest but to borrowers who committed themselves to paying interest, to guarantors who guaranteed the repayment of loans, to the witnesses to loan contracts or arrangements and even to scribes who prepared the written texts of loan contracts.[16] It is significant that this is one of the few instances in which accessories to an offense incurred responsibility to the same extent as the principals.

Lending at interest to foreigners (excluding resident aliens) was considered allowable in Deuteronomy 23:20. However, it was generally frowned upon by Talmudic scholars, some of whom asserted that it should be tolerated only when no other means of earning a living was available.[17] Although the Talmud interpreted the psalmist's admiration for the man who would not lend at interest (Psalms 15:5) as applying to the man who would not lend at interest to foreigners, it nevertheless advised Jews who were prepared to provide interest-free loans to give priority to their neighbors:[18]

If a poor man and a rich man stand before you to borrow, the poor man should be given preference. If it be your own poor relative and the poor of your city, your own poor should be given preference over the poor of your city. If it be the poor of your city and the poor of another city, the poor of your city should be given preference.[19]

According to the Talmud, loans are the best form of charity, because they do not humiliate the receiver.

Greater is he who lends than he who gives, and greater still is he who lends, and with the loan, helps the poor man to help himself. Lending money to the poor man is a more meritorious deed than giving charity to him who begs for it, for the one has already been driven to begging, while the other has not yet reached that stage. Severe, indeed, is the censure of the Law against him who withholds a loan from the poor. For it is written, "Beware that there be not a base thought in thy heart and thine eyes be evil against thy needy brother, and, thou give him nought."[20]

Throughout the ages, attitudes toward charging interest have been molded not only by religious principles and injunctions but by the realities of everyday life, social conditions and the logic of economics. As early as the Amoraic period in Babylonia, the Judaic ban on charging interest proved to be incompatible with the economic needs of the community, owing to a change in economic conditions. The first century A.D. (the first century of the Common Era according to Judaism) witnessed the emergence in Palestine of a class of wealthy merchants and bankers who found it difficult to operate their businesses without evading the scriptural injunctions against charging interest, and that situation led to the adaptation of Jewish law to the new commercial requirements.

Although Talmudic jurists had extended the scope of the biblical prohibition of interest to encompass activities that had only a tenuous connection with the concept of interest, they devised particularly ingenious techniques for legitimizing transactions that, on the basis of any reasonable criterion, involved charging interest. The need to find ways to circumvent the injunctions prohibiting interest, rather than simply disregarding them or declaring them inoperative, can probably be explained by the fact that those injunctions formed part of a complex structure of religious principles and practices based on the Tanach; to ignore or cancel any part of that structure might have been taken as calling in question the validity of other parts or even the whole. On the other hand, certain precepts, such as the ones relating to interest, although appropriate and constructive in a simple pastoral or agricultural society, became inappropriate and constrictive in a more sophisticated urban, commercial society—hence the need to devise legal but often casuistic stratagems to circumvent rather than disregard the injunctions.

One method devised by Talmudic scholars was to grant a loan disguised as the sale of goods. The lender arranged to sell goods to the borrower on credit at a price of, say, one hundred units payable at a given time in the future. Under a companion arrangement, the borrower immediately resold the goods to the lender at a price of, say, ninety units payable cash down. The borrower thus received ninety units of cash and was to repay one hundred units at a future date. The difference of ten units in fact constituted interest on the ninety units, but since the arrangements ostensibly involved merely two contracts of sale (although in fact the goods never left the possession of the lender), they were deemed to be technically in conformity with the law.

Another stratagem made it possible for a farmer who wanted a loan to convey all or part of his land to the lender while remaining on the land as the lender's tenant; the crops obtained from the land or the proceeds from their sale would be transferred to the lender as income from his property and not as payment of interest. One Talmudic jurist even argued that money, like chattels, could be let out on hire in exchange for the payment of rent, a process that in his view was essentially different from making a loan and collecting interest on it.

To circumvent the rule concerning the cancellation of debts in the sabbatical year and thus encourage loans to the needy, one Talmudic scholar devised the prosbul, whereby the creditor deposited with a court a note stating that a debt owed to him by a given debtor might be collected whenever the creditor chose. Any loan not covered by a prosbul was subject to the Pentatcucal rule concerning the year of release and was therefore forfeited if not repaid before that year.

The Talmudic rule that partnership contracts under which one partner provides the funds and the other manages the venture are valid only if the latter partner receives a salary instead of or in addition to his share of the profits was circumvented by permitting the salary to be nominal. Furthermore, the rabbinic authorities decided that such partnerships could be made valid under Talmudic law by specifying that half of the funds contributed by the financing partner constituted a loan and the other half a deposit; the managing partner would be responsible for the repayment of the loan but not for any eventual loss of the deposit. This meant that the financing partner would share in any losses, thus removing the rationale for the Talmudic prohibition of such partnerships. Partnership arrangements were accepted as valid even when the financing partner received his share of the profits in advance through a down payment, provided that there was a reasonable expectation that the business would be profitable.

The concept of partnership as a means of legalizing the payment of interest was developed further in post-Talmudic law, leading to what is known as *hetter iskah*, "permission to form a partnership." This practice is described in *The Principles of Jewish Law*:

A deed, known as *shetar iskah*, was drawn up and attested by two witnesses, stipulating that the lender would supply a certain sum of money to the borrower for a joint venture; the borrower alone would manage the business and he would guarantee the lender's investment against all loss; he would also guarantee to the lender a fixed amount of minimum profit. The deed would also contain a stipulation that the borrower would be paid a nominal sum as a salary, as well as an agreement on the part of the lender to share the losses. In order to render this loss–sharing agreement nugatory, provision would normally be made for such losses to be proved by particular, mostly unobtainable evidence . . . .The amount of the capital loan plus the guaranteed minimum profit would be recoverable on the deed at the stipulated time it matured. In the course of the centuries this form of legalizing interest has become so well established that nowadays all interest transactions are freely carried out, even in compliance with Jewish law, by simply adding to the note or contract concerned the words *al–pi hetter iskah*. The prohibition on interest has lost all practical significance in business transactions and is now relegated to the realm of friendly and charitable loans where, indeed, it had originated.[21]

Although lending at interest to non-Jews tended to be disapproved of from an ethical angle, it was not illegal under Judaic law, since it was assumed that a foreigner would be a transient, usually a merchant who needed money for commercial purposes, and not an unfortunate individual needing money to cope with a personal emergency. The lawfulness of lending at interest by Jews to non-Jews provided a way for Jews to evade the scriptural prohibition of interest. A Jew could lend money at interest to a non-Jew, who would then relend it to the intended Jewish borrower: both loan transactions would be valid under Judaic law.

The fact that Judaic law allowed Jews to lend at interest to non–Jews assumed great importance in Europe after 1179, when the Church decreed that charging or taking interest was contrary to Scripture and the laws of nature and that all Christians lending at interest would be subject to ex-communication. In twelfth–century Europe the Jews, unlike their ancestors in Palestine and Mesopotamia, were not tillers of the soil, since they were not integrated in the feudal system. They therefore tended to concentrate on commerce to such an extent that in Carolingian capitularies the terms *Jew* and *merchant* are almost interchangeable. However, with the emerg-ence of an indigenous non-Jewish merchant class in the various countries of Europe, the Jews were excluded from trade. As early as A.D. 945 Venice had prohibited Venetian ships from transporting Jewish merchants and their goods to the Eastern Mediterranean to prevent them from competing with Venetian merchants. In time the Jews were to be excluded from other occupations as well in the greater part of Europe, although they were to continue as farmers and artisans in Sicily and Spain. The fact that the canonical prohibition could not be enforced against the Jews tended to give them a virtual monopoly of moneylending, which was practically the only occupation left to them, as is indicated in the following passage from the Talmud:

If we nowadays allow interest to be taken from non-Jews, it is because there is no end to the yoke and the burden King and ministers impose on us, and everything we take is the minimum for our subsistence, and anyhow we are condemned to live in the midst of the nations and cannot earn our living in any other manner except by money dealings with them; therefore the taking of interest is not to be prohibited.[22]

The steady increase in economic activity between the twelfth and fourteenth centuries was accompanied by a corresponding increase in the demand for credit, created not only by the poor but also by the affluent, who were ready to pay very high interest rates. That period therefore witnessed a considerable increase in moneylending, particularly in the form of pawnbroking, which was carried out not only by Jews but by other categories of people (the Lombards in England and the Low Countries, now Belgium and the Netherlands, and the Cahorsins in France).

Since moneylending by definition was assumed to be very lucrative, the Jewish community was subjected to heavier taxation than the community at large. However, the association of moneylending with wealth was not sufficient to account for the fact that in the twelfth century the Jews, who represented only 0.25 percent of the population of England, contributed more than 8 percent of the yearly royal revenue and contributed a similarly disproportionate share of tax revenue in other European countries in the Middle Ages. Clearly, that situation also was attributable to the fact that the Jews constituted a visibly different religious and ethnic group.

The role of moneylender virtually thrust upon the Jews made them the focus of the ambivalent attitude that lenders of money tend to inspire. Although moneylenders are sought after for the services they can provide, they are envied and even hated for being in a financial position that gives them power over their debtors. The negative emotions aroused by financial considerations in the case of all moneylenders were intensified in the case of the Jews, who not only formed a separate ethnic and religious group but were held by the Christians to have been implicated in the death of Jesus. All of those factors gave the Jews the reputation of being grasping, and they were periodically victims of riots and mob violence directed allegedly against usury. The injustice of that situation was emphasized by Martin Luther, who observed: "If we prohibit the Jews from following trades and other civil occupations, we compel them to become usurers." A similar view was expressed some two centuries later, on the eve of the French Revolution, by Abbé Grégoire, who was opposed not only to aristocratic privileges but to racial prejudice, and who had cooperated with the Societé des Amis des Noirs with a view to achieving the abolition of Negro slavery. He declared in an address to the National Assembly, which was hesitant to accord full rights to the Jews because they were accused of practicing usury: "O nations, if you record the past faults of the Jews, let it be to deplore your own work."

The distorted stereotype image of the Jews provided the basis for literary creations such as Marlowe's Barabas in *The Jew of Malta* and Shakespeare's Shylock in *The Merchant of Venice*. Marlowe portrayed Barabas as a rich merchant of the Renaissance who earlier in his life had been "a usurer" who:

> With extorting, cozening, forfeiting,
> And tricks belonging unto broking
> . . . filled the jails with bankrupts in a year,
> And with young orphans planted hospitals
> And every moon made some or other mad,
> And now and then one hang himself for grief,
> Pinning upon his breast a long great scroll
> How [he] with interest tormented him.

However cruel this melodramatic "monster" may appear, Marlowe provided him with extenuating circumstances: because he is a Jew he is hated by the Christians, who confiscate his entire fortune to pay Malta's tribute to the Turks.

Shakespeare, writing at a time when a Portuguese Jewish doctor had been executed for allegedly participating in a plot against Queen Elizabeth I and the current of anti-Semitism was running high, portrayed Shylock as a vindictive usurer who hates Antonio, the merchant of Venice, because:

> he lends out money gratis, and brings down
> The rate of usance here with us in Venice.

However, Shakespeare, who believed in making money and "saw nothing wrong with high interest so long as he himself was not paying it," showed Shylock to have been a loving husband and father, gave him a certain dignity, and motivated his vengeful behavior by having him describe his humiliation at the hands of the Christians:[23]

> You call me misbeliever, cut-throat dog,
> And spit upon my Jewish gabardine,
> And all for use of that which is mine own.

The stereotype image of the Jew as a moneylender persisted in literature well into the eighteenth century. In Voltaire's *Candide*, Cunégonde is taken prisoner by a Bulgarian captain who runs out of money and sells her to Don Issachar, "a Jew with business connexions in Holland and Portugal" who is "the Court banker." Jews were thus to continue for over a century to be portrayed in literature as the typical moneylenders.

CHARGING OR TAKING INTEREST IN CHRISTIANITY

In Christian dogma, the attitude toward charging or taking interest was based not only on the Old Testament but the New Testament. In the Gospel according to Saint Luke, Jesus warns Christians against the dangers of wealth and exhorts them to lend freely:

And if ye lend to them of whom ye hope to receive, what thanks have ye? for sinners also lend to sinners, to receive as much again, But love ye your enemies, and do good and lend, hoping for nothing again; and your reward shall be great, and ye shall be the children of the Highest. (Luke 6:34–35)

However, the New Testament does not specifically prohibit the practice of charging interest; indeed, the parable of the talents seems to reflect a certain tolerance of it.

Originally, the Fathers of the Church, like the Talmudic scholars, interpreted the biblical writings as banning the practice of taking any interest, not merely excessive interest. In Christian dogma, as in Judaic dogma, the underlying assumption was that any would-be borrower was indigent, and it would be contrary to charity and mercy or even immoral to try to profit from his misfortune; the fortunate should aid the indigent through gifts or, failing that, through interest-free loans.

Several ecumenical councils, including the first Council of Arles (A.D. 314) and the first General Council of Nicaea (A.D. 325), voiced general disapproval of the practice of charging interest but expressly prohibited it only to the clergy. The Council of Carthage (A.D. 345) declared it reprehensible for laymen. Saint Jerome (circa A.D. 347–420) asserted that the prohibition of lending at interest among "brothers" had been extended by the pronouncements of the prophets and the New Testament, so that the permission granted in the Book of Deuteronomy to lend at interest to foreigners had been invalidated. Saint Ambrose (circa A.D. 340–97) considered that usury was permissible only when it involved lending to the enemies of God's people. Saint Leo the Great (circa A.D. 400–61), who was Pope from A.D. 440 to 461, enjoined the clergy not to exact interest and stated that laymen who did so were guilty of "shameful gain." In the reign of Charlemagne, the state as well as the Church prohibited usury; the capitularies (a body of legislative and administrative decrees and written commands) made it illegal for laymen to practice usury, which was said to exist "where more is asked than is given."

In succeeding centuries, both the Church and the state continued to view lending at interest as reprehensible, an attitude that led in A.D. 850 to the excommunication of Christian lay usurers by the Synod of Pavia. However, it was not until the Middle Ages that the Church strictly forbade the practice of charging interest to combat "the insatiable rapacity of usurers"; charging

interest was viewed as a failure to obey the seventh commandment. In
A.D. 1139, at the Second Council of Lateran, the prohibition of interest
was reaffirmed. Pope Eugene III (A.D. 1145–53) proclaimed as reprehensible "mortgages in which the lender enjoyed the fruits of a pledge without
deducting them from the principal." Pope Alexander III (A.D. 1159–81),
who was to preside at the Third Council of Lateran (A.D. 1179), also
considered credit sales at a price higher than the cash price as reprehensible.
The Council went further and decreed that all Christians lending at interest
would be subject to excommunication.

From the twelfth century onwards, as the development of commerce
and later of industry rendered the need for credit more and more pressing
and prompted more and more people to disobey the Church's prohibition,
the arguments against charging or taking interest broadened in scope, being
based increasingly on references to the *jus humanum* (human justice), the
jus naturale (natural justice), and the teachings of ancient philosophers in
addition to the *jus divinum* (divine justice) and Jewish and Christian
revelation.

Reference to *jus naturale* and the Aristotelian argument concerning the
barrenness of money were very frequent. In keeping with the Aristotelian
view that money could not produce money, canonists argued that it was
inadmissible and unfair for the lender to receive anything more than the
sum lent, since the additional amount must be taken from the fruit of the
borrower's industry. Canonists also argued that charging interest was unjust
because the lender derived a profit from the use of goods the borrower
had acquired with the borrowed money, goods that were the borrower's,
not the lender's, property.

A third argument, based on the fact that the use of certain goods consists
in the consumption of the goods themselves, was advanced by the scholastic
philosophers, whose aim was to defend the right of reason without en-
croaching on the right of revelation, since they believed that revelation
cannot contradict reason nor reason contradict revelation. The scholastics—Alexander of Hales, St. Albertus Magnus and especially St. Thomas
Aquinas—condemned interest as contrary to *commutative justice*, justice
bearing on the relations between individuals, particularly in regard to the
equitable exchange of goods and the fulfillment of contractual obligations.
They thought that in the case of a *mutuum*, a loan of fungible or perishable
or generic goods such as bread or wine, it was inequitable to be repaid
more than the amount actually lent. They regarded money as a fungible
since the borrower could no longer use it once he had exchanged it for
goods. In their opinion, money was consumed in the act of being used and
had no use that could be distinguished from its substance; charging interest
for its use (unlike charging rent for the occupancy of a house) was charging
interest for something nonexistent and was therefore unacceptable. In the
words of St. Thomas, who considered that wealth could be morally ac-

ceptable if used for legitimate purposes, "it is in itself illicit to accept a price for the use of money loaned."

The arguments of the scholastics and other canonists remained virtually unchallenged at the theoretical level throughout the thirteenth and fourteenth centuries. Like the Third Council of Lateran, the Second Council of Lyons, in 1274, proclaimed that Christians who lent at interest would be excommunicated. In 1311 the Council of Vienna declared that secular legislation that did not prohibit interest was invalid and that anyone who asserted that lending at interest was not sinful should be declared a heretic and punished as such. Thereafter, stringent measures were taken to uncover the many disguises devised to evade the prohibition and to punish the offenders. However, punishments did not stop the continuing violation of the prohibition, openly or with the aid of ever more sophisticated stratagems.

In the fifteenth and sixteenth centuries, increasing attention was devoted to the question of the licitness of new financial institutions and practices. Churchmen saw the need to make interest-free loans available to the poor to rescue them from the clutches of private pawnbrokers and began to establish *montes pietatis*, charitable pawnshops that granted loans secured by pledges, usually of household goods and used clothing; the funds were obtained from gifts or bequests. The first *montes pietatis* was established in Perugia by Barnabas, a Franciscan friar; subsequently, others were set up in various cities, including Turin (1519), Rome (1539), Bruges (1572) and Avignon (1577). In 1515 the Fifth Lateran Council (the eighteenth ecumenical council of the Roman Catholic Church, convened by Pope Julius II) legalized the *montes pietatis* as charitable institutions, and Pope Leo X (who had succeeded Julius II) issued a bull to that effect, permitting the charging of fees to defray the necessary administrative expenses. Private pawnshops run by Jews had long been allowed to operate, sometimes on a *de facto* basis and sometimes as a result of specific legal authorization.

A steadily increasing volume of credit was granted in the form of sales of goods against future payment. Credit sales were considered legitimate and even desirable, because they fostered trade at the wholesale and retail levels. Wholesalers usually did not need cash loans, because they generally had a store of gold and silver and could pay cash; retailers and consumers did not need cash loans, because they could buy on credit, the former from the wholesaler and the latter from the retailer. Personal cash loans continued to be viewed as tending to encourage laziness and dissipation, and individuals seeking such loans to cope with genuine emergencies were still expected to be granted outright charity or could have recourse to *montes pietatis* or similar institutions. In Germany, where the pressures of practical life had led many local laws to sanction the practice of charging or taking interest, Martin Luther denounced the practice as the greatest misfortune of the German nation and blamed the Pope for having tolerated it. Loans for production purposes (for example, for the purchase of tools or raw materials) continued to be considered unjustified. It was still believed that such purchases should be financed from savings and that increases in production depended more on a worker's manual skill and industriousness than on his tools.

Although many continued to regard the practice of charging interest, or "usury" in the old sense of the term, as morally wrong, the growing credit needs of trade in the sixteenth century led to a gradual reassessment of the basic concept of usury. The need for commercial credit had intensified in particular as a result of the expansion of trade brought about by the explorations that, beginning in the fifteenth century, had placed under the sway of European powers far-away territories that became new markets for exports and sources of precious metals and raw materials. In a kind of practical compromise or accommodation between religious ideals and day–to–day reality, the canon doctrine on interest was supplanted by secular laws. These laws recognized circumstances under which a lender was entitled to charge interest on loans, and a distinction was drawn between low interest and interest above certain limits, with only the latter regarded as usury and therefore objectionable. That interpretation met with the approval of Huldrych Zwingli, the most influential personality in the Swiss Reformation, and even with that of Martin Luther, who hitherto had been a harsh critic of interest, as well as Philip Melanchthon, a German theologian who made the first systematic presentation of the principles of the Reformation and at the Diet of Augsburg wrote and presented the Augsburg Confession, which influenced every subsequent important credal statement in Protestantism. Under a 1541 statute of Henry VIII, England removed the prohibition of interest and made it legal to charge interest at a rate not exceeding 10 percent. The law was repealed soon afterwards by Edward VI, who in 1547 paid 14 percent for a loan in London, but was subsequently reenacted by Elizabeth I, who in 1561 borrowed £30,000 at 10 percent in London.

The changing attitudes toward interest were linked not only to the rise of Protestantism but also to a reassessment of the theoretical premises of the canonic prohibition of interest by theologians, in particular the Geneva reformers such as John Calvin, and also by lay lawyers such as Charles Dumoulin (who wrote in Latin as Carolus Molinaeus), a French jurist who was an expert in customary law. Calvin challenged Aristotle's dictum that money is barren by noting that when money is used to buy land, it can be correctly regarded as yielding additional money in the form of the annual return on the land. Calvin observed that although money remained barren when it was not put to use, a borrower often did not allow it to be idle, and in paying interest such a borrower was paying it from the profits he made with the money. Calvin therefore concluded that charging or taking interest should be accepted in so far as it was consistent with justice and charity. To that end he stated that interest should not be sought from people in dire need, and that in charging interest the welfare of the state should be taken into consideration and the interest ceiling established by law should be strictly complied with. On the whole, he considered interest legitimate only if the borrower obtained a return as large as, or larger than, that of the lender.

Dumoulin, in his *Tractatus Contractuum et Usurarum Redituumque Pecunia Constitutorum* (1546), analyzed the *jus divinum* and contended that the parts of the Scriptures generally interpreted as banning the practice of charging or taking interest were meant only to prohibit interest that contravened the principles of charity and brotherhood and not interest in general. Dumoulin argued that by foregoing the use of his money while it is on loan the lender sustains an injury and that it is just and economically necessary that he be compensated for that injury by the payment of interest. He therefore considered that the position taken in the Code of Justinian, which permitted the practice of charging interest but regulated its level, was entirely justified since it enabled people to borrow money that they could then use to make a profit. He refuted the scholastic argument that money was consumed in the act of being used by pointing out that the use of money could be dissociated from the actual sum borrowed, since the borrower could use and derive profit from the goods acquired with that money. Referring to Aristotle's contention that money is barren, Dumoulin pointed out that even land yields no crop without effort and expense and that money can produce "fruits" as a result of human skill and industriousness.

Toward the end of the sixteenth century, the German scholar Christopher Besold, in his dissertation *Questiones Aliquot de usuris* (1598), reasoning along the same line as Dumoulin, argued that money used in trade could not be considered barren. Anticipating the position taken by the English philosopher Jeremy Bentham roughly two centuries later, he observed that since every individual should be permitted to pursue a course that he deemed to be to his own best advantage, insofar as it was not harmful to others, there were no grounds in the *jus naturale* for prohibiting interest.

During the seventeenth century, the practice of taking interest and granting cash loans came to be more generally accepted in the major trading nations in the context of mercantilist policies and practices (known as *colbertism* in France and *cameralism* in Austria and Germany). Even so, many writers continued to express opposition to the practice. In England, for example, Sir Thomas Culpepper, in his *Tract against the High Rate of Usury* (1621), tried to show how much evil ensued from the practice of taking interest but found himself compelled to direct his arguments against high interest rates rather than interest in general. In France the economist and merchant Jacques Savary, in his book *Le Parfait Negociant* (1675), widely regarded as a milestone in the history of economics, warned merchants that they "should not borrow money unless they needed it urgently to pay bills of exchange that had fallen due because they had no cash reserves, or to make some other payment that could not be deferred" and that "they should not borrow to obtain capital for normal trading activities, for nothing is more dangerous." Savary likewise warned lenders, who were also wholesalers, that although they could charge interest, "the rate should not be high," because "charging a high rate of interest is abominable usury before God and men, which brings God's curse upon you," and "such conduct is forbidden to Christians."

In keeping with the idea that interest rates should not be high, steps continued to be taken in the seventeenth century to lower the legal interest rate ceilings, which represented socially acceptable maximum interest rates and separated legal lending operations from illegal lending operations. Thus in France in 1665, Colbert, the Minister of Finance of Louis XIV, imposed a maximum interest rate of 5 percent, arguing that higher rates would inhibit trade; he also trimmed the public debt by reducing the value of some obligations and repudiating others. In England the statutory maximum interest rate was lowered to 8 percent in 1624 and 6 percent in 1660. The general trend among theorists, as well as among statesmen and merchants, was definitely in favor of charging interest. The pragmatic spirit of the period is perhaps best exemplified by the philosopher John Locke, who in *Some Considerations of the Consequences of Lowering the Interest and Raising the Value of Money* (1691) concluded: "Borrowing money upon use is not only, by the necessity of affairs and the constitution of human society, unavoidable to some men, but to receive profit from the loan of money is as equitable and lawful as receiving rent for land, and more tolerable to the borrower, notwithstanding the opinion of some over-scrupulous men."

In the eighteenth century, attitudes toward charging interest became even more liberal. In 1745 the scholastic position that interest was licit in certain circumstances was formally endorsed by the Church in the encyclical *Vix Pervenit*, issued by Pope Benedict XIV, which was not an infallible decree. Despite these developments, an underlying current of moral and religious disapproval of the practice of charging interest persisted. Thus in England, when John Wesley drew up his first printed rules for Methodists, he originally sought to condemn the practice because it was prohibited in the Bible. He was finally persuaded that the changed condition of society made a return to the medieval ban on interest impossible, and he therefore relented sufficiently to permit the practice of charging a moderate rate of interest. In France the Physiocrats, a group of economists predominant between 1760 and 1770, advocated free trade—in opposition to the mercantilists—except in the case of trade in money, that is, lending. The Marquis de Mirabeau, the forerunner and subsequently a leader of the

Physiocrats, referred to interest as tribute extracted by "the rodent order of rentiers." Robert Joseph Pothier, a French jurist whose work paved the way for the adoption of the French Civil Code, based his opposition essentially on the old scholastic argument that money was "a fungible" that was "consumed in the using" and that it was therefore impossible to imagine it "as having a price distinct from the thing itself." He therefore argued as follows:

> If I lend you a sum of money for your use under the condition of paying me back as much again, then you receive from me simply that sum of money and nothing more. The use that you will make of this sum of money is included in the right of property that you acquire in this sum. There is nothing that you have received outside of the sum of money. I have given you this sum, and nothing but this sum. I can therefore ask you to give me back nothing more than this amount lent without being unjust; for justice would have it that only that should be claimed which was given.[24]

Pothier's great contemporary Anne Robert Jacques Turgot, who had been an abbé at the Sorbonne before opting for a career as a civil servant, was a Physiocrat but, unlike the other members of the group, advocated not only freedom of lending but also the removal of controls on interest rates.[25] In his *Réflexions sur la formation et la distribution des richesses* (1766), Turgot argued that since capital was "the indispensable basis of any enterprise" and since the possessor of capital could invest in any type of production venture (industrial or commercial as well as agricultural), he would not lend his capital unless the borrower offered him at least as much as he could obtain by investing in agricultural, industrial or commercial ventures. Unlike the other Physiocrats, Turgot did not regard industry or trade as sterile and considered that any enterprise could be productive. Turgot further buttressed the case for freedom of lending at interest with an argument based on a similarity between interest and the fee charged by moneychangers: the charging of the fee was regarded as justified because the moneychanger could not regain his capital without transferring the foreign exchange to its place of issue (distance in space); similarly charging interest was justified because the lender had to wait for the borrower to return his capital (distance in time). Interest constituted compensation for the distance in time just as the exchange fees represented compensation for the distance in space. A similar argument was advanced by Etienne Bonnot de Condillac in *Le Commerce et le Gouvernement considérés relativement l'un à l'autre* (1776).[26]

Like Turgot and others, the English philosopher Jeremy Bentham approached the question of lending money at interest from a scientific as opposed to a moral, philosophical or religious standpoint. In his *Defence of Usury*, written in Russia and cast in the form of a series of letters from that country, he asserted that since every man was the best judge of his own advantage, it would be in the public interest to allow him to seek that advantage without hindrance and that there was no reason why that doctrine should not be applied to the practice of lending money at interest.

In 1795, in the first course on political economy ever offered in France, which was given at the newly established Ecole Normale Supérieure, Alexandre Vandermonde told his audience: "It is only very recently that money has become, by some mysterious process, an asset that yields annual returns. Today, every merchant, before thinking of calculating his profit, deducts his interest payments from his earnings. In French trading circles, the interest rate is usually 6 percent."

In keeping with the theories of Adam Smith, it came to be generally recognized in the eighteenth century that cash loans could serve a very useful purpose and could be put to profitable use. In fact, credit was so widely used that the eighteenth century became known as the century of credit, just as the seventeenth century was designated the century of trade and the nineteenth was known as the century of industry and currency.

In the nineteenth century, in the context of the laissez-faire doctrine—which had developed during the second half of the eighteenth century as a reaction against almost two centuries of mercantilism and which urged reliance on natural mechanisms or laws and confinement of the State to general functions—more and more writers (including clerical writers) began to question whether the Catholic Church's position on interest should not be clarified by stating that charging a market rate of interest or an interest rate determined by bargaining between individual lenders and borrowers was acceptable. During the reigns of Pope Pius VIII (1829–1830) and Pope Gregory XVI (1831–1846), the Congregations of the Holy Office, the Penitenciary and the Propaganda took a number of decisions embodying the position that the faithful who lent money at moderate rates of interest were "not to be disturbed," provided that they obeyed any future decisions of the Holy See.

By 1867 the prevailing liberal current of opinion had caused all controls over interest rates to be removed in England and most European countries. In the United States, on the other hand, most states continued to impose statutory ceilings on interest rates. The removal of interest rate controls gave rise to much abuse and extortion, and in England, for example, the courts decided in 1880 to empower Chancery to reopen any transaction involving interest with a view to freeing a borrower from excessive interest and alleviating the terms of harsh or unconscionable transactions in various other ways. That power—which constituted a qualitative rather than a quantitative way of solving the question of the fairness of interest rates charged in particular transactions—was embodied in the Money-Lenders Act of 1900. The act, as rewritten and amended in 1937, stipulates that unless the contrary is proved, a transaction shall be deemed harsh and unconscionable if the interest exceeds 48 percent a year. That figure was merely a convenient guideline and not a statutory maximum in the legal sense.

At the same time, in the United States the general interest and usury statutes of individual states often prescribed two rates of interest: a *legal rate* that an obligation will yield in the absence of any agreement stipulating a different rate and a *maximum rate* that may be charged by contract or written agreement. In the second half of the twentieth century, legal rates were set, depending on the state, at 4, 5, 6 or 7 percent. Ten states set the maximum contract rate at the same level as the legal rate; Rhode Island set the maximum contract rate at 30 percent for loans of more than $50; a number of states permitted the practice of charging a contract rate of 1 to 6 percent above the legal rate; and the other states (Colorado, Maine, Massachusetts and New Hampshire) had no maximum contract rates. Although these other states imposed no penalty for usury, the remaining states prescribed penalties that included forfeiture of interest, forfeiture of excessive interest, forfeiture of as much as three times excessive interest, forfeiture of twice the total amount of interest, the annulation of the loan and the imposition of a fine or imprisonment or both.

CHARGING OR TAKING INTEREST IN ISLAM

In Islam, as in Judaism and Christianity, the rationale for the ban on charging interest is that a person who needs a loan is a person in distress and that it would be wrong to seek to profit from his misfortune.

The Koranic Prohibition of Interest

The Arabic word for interest is *riba* ("addition," or "increase"), which can also mean *usury* ("excess") and has been so translated in various foreign language versions of the Koran.[27]

In the following verses, the Koran denounces and prohibits *riba*:

> Those who devour usury
> Will not stand except
> As stands one whom
> The Evil One by his touch
> Hath driven to madness.
> That is because they say:
> "Trade is like usury"
> But God hath permitted trade
> And forbidden usury. (2:275)

Riba is subsequently contrasted with charity:

God will deprive
Usury of all blessing
But will give increase
For deeds of charity. (2:276)

Believers are urged to abandon the practice of *riba* if they wish to avoid the anger of God:

O ye who believe!
Fear God, and give up
What remains of your demand
For usury, if ye are
Indeed believers. (2:276)

This exhortation is repeated in a later verse:

O ye who believe!
Devour not Usury,
Doubled and multiplied;
But fear God; that
Ye may (really) prosper. (3:130)

Those who seek to profit through *riba* at the expense of others are again warned in the following verse that this is displeasing to God:

That which ye lay out
For increase through the property
Of (other) people, will have
No increase with God:
But that which ye lay out
For charity, seeking
The Countenance of God,
(Will increase): it is
These who will get
A recompense multiplied. (30:39)

Creditors are urged not only to refrain from charging *riba* but to be lenient with debtors who are finding it hard to repay and if possible to release them completely from their debts:

If the debtor is
In a difficulty
Grant him time
Till it is easy
For him to repay,
But if ye remit it

By way of charity
That is best for you
If ye only knew. (2:280)

In footnote 324, Chapter 2, verse 275, of the English translation of the Koran quoted above, the translator observes that "usury is condemned and prohibited in the strongest possible terms" and that "there can be no question about the prohibition." However, he also observes that when it comes "to the definition of usury there is room for difference of opinion." He recalls that "Hadhrat 'Umar, according to Ibn Kathir, felt some difficulty in the matter as the Apostle left this world before the details of the question were settled," and that "this was one of the three questions on which he [Hadhrat 'Umar] wished he had had more light from the Apostle, the other two being Khilafat [usually translated as 'successor'] and Kalafat [usually translated as 'descendant']".[28]

Similarly, the article on *riba* in the *Shorter Encyclopaedia of Islam* states that "the traditions give varying answers to the question what forms of business come under the Koranic prohibition of riba, none of which can be regarded as authentic."[29] In the absence of an authoritative definition, the term *riba* has been interpreted in various ways. According to the most conservative view, *riba* means not only "usury" (excessive interest) but also simply "interest" (any amount, even minimal, received by a creditor from a debtor in addition to the amount originally lent). Many of those who adhere to this interpretation also believe that Muslims should use their capital for trading rather than lending at interest, so that those who provide the capital for a given venture will share the risks involved with those who provide the labor. According to another interpretation, *riba* means only "excessive interest," or usury, in the modern sense of the English term. A third interpretation excludes bank interest as it is known today from the Koranic prohibition of *riba*, the rationale being that at the time of the Prophet there was no banking system of the type that exists today. Similarly, it has been asserted that the prohibition does not cover interest on loans made for productive purposes, which were virtually unknown at that time. With regard to the third and fourth interpretations, the scholar whose translation of the Koran is quoted above stated in footnote 324:

Our 'Ulama, ancient and modern, have worked out a great body of literature on Usury, based mainly on economic conditions as they existed at the rise of Islam. I agree with them on the main principles, but respectfully differ from them on the definition of Usury . . . . The definition I would accept would be: undue profit made not in the way of legitimate trade, out of loans of gold and silver, and necessary articles of food, such as wheat, barley, dates and salt (according to the list mentioned by the Holy Apostle himself). My definition would include profiteering of all kinds, but exclude economic credit, the creature of modern banking and finance.[30]

According to a fifth interpretation, *riba* refers only to compound interest, and simple interest is therefore permitted. A sixth interpretation is that the prohibition of interest applies only to interest paid by one physical person to another and not to interest paid by one corporate body or juridical person to another, the rationale being based on verses of the Koran that mention only physical persons when referring to the prohibition of interest. A seventh interpretation excludes from the prohibition the practice of taking interest by an individual from a corporate body such as a bank, since according to that interpretation, the prohibition of *riba* is prompted by the element of exploitation involved, and an individual cannot exploit a large organization such as a bank, which mobilizes savings in financial forms with a view to financing remunerative activities. An eighth interpretation is that the Koranic prohibition of *riba* does not extend to loans granted by government institutions, since under Islam the state is a religious institution that is called upon to protect, not exploit, its citizens.

The Development of Islamic Banking in the Context of the Contemporary Islamic Revival

Even when Islamic civilization was at its zenith, economic activity focused on trade, with emphasis on credit sales and markup. The need for production loans was minimal, and hence the question of lending at interest does not seem to have been an important issue. That situation continued to prevail in the eighteenth and nineteenth centuries, as the Muslim countries began to fall under the direct or indirect control of European countries. Today, thirteen and a half centuries after the death of the Prophet, the Islamic world is experiencing a spiritual rebirth known as the Islamic revival. In recent decades an increasing number of Muslims have been voicing apprehension about what they see as the debilitating spread of Western-style materialism, pop culture and permissiveness and have been advocating with mounting fervor a return to basic Islamic values. This attitude is epitomized by the views of the government of Pakistan expressed in the *Pakistan Economic Survey, 1982–83*:

It was the departure from moral conduct in all social affairs which led to the eclipse of over a thousand years of Muslim supremacy, and the beginning of a second Dark Age for mankind starting some two to three hundred years ago. In this modern (dark) age man has forgotten his fundamental obligations and is guided exclusively by the pursuit of pleasure, seeking ever higher levels of consumption, enjoying full social approval for accumulating wealth by depriving his fellow men, and neglecting his duties to Allah. It is the duty of Muslims today, just as it was fourteen hundred years ago, not to be intimidated by the technologically advanced super-powers which existed then and exist today, to invite humanity to the transcendent values of Islam which are the only solution to the potential ills of modern civilization.

Against the background of a renewed assertion of Islamic identity on the part of governments and renewed dedication to Islamic principles on the part of individuals, various steps have been taken in Muslim countries to bring personal conduct and various aspects of community life, including law, politics and economics, more into line with the tenets of the Islamic *shariah*.[31] In the economic sphere, the desire to comply with the Koranic prohibition of interest and the need to mobilize, in the form of financial assets, the funds hoarded outside the banking system by Muslims who abide by that prohibition (estimated at $40 billion by the Islamic Banking Association in 1982) have prompted action aimed at adapting conventional modern banking to the fundamental tenets of Islam. Modern banking was introduced in many Muslim countries in the late nineteenth century as a result of political pressures by the European powers and against the wishes of large segments of the population. Such action has led to the establishment or the total or partial reorganization of a number of financial institutions to foster the development of an interest-free banking system.

The first such financial institution to be established was the Nasser Social Bank, set up in Egypt in 1971. Soon after that, at the Conference of Finance Ministers of Muslim Countries held in Jeddah, Saudi Arabia, in December 1973, a Declaration of Intent was issued relative to the establishment of the Islamic Development Bank. The inaugural meeting of the new institution took place in July 1975 and the Bank opened on 20 October 1975. According to its Articles of Agreement, the Bank, which has forty-two members, is "to participate in equity capital and grant loans for productive projects and enterprises besides providing financial assistance to Member countries in other forms for economic and social development" and "to establish and operate special funds for specific purposes." The Bank "is authorised to accept deposits and to raise funds in any other manner" and is "charged with the responsibility of assisting in the promotion of foreign trade, especially in capital goods, among member countries, providing technical assistance to member countries, extending training facilities for personnel engaged in development activities and undertaking research for enabling the economic, financial and banking activities in Muslim countries to conform to the Islamic shariah." To carry out its technical assistance and research functions, the Islamic Development Bank has set up the Islamic Research and Training Institute at the Bank's headquarters in Jeddah.

The year 1975 also witnessed the establishment of the Dubai Islamic Bank, owned jointly by the rulers of Dubai and Kuwait (20 percent) and private citizens (80 percent). The Bank subsequently opened a branch in Abu Dhabi in 1983 and in 1984 was granted permission to open another branch in the United Arab Emirates. The contribution by private citizens to the capital of the Dubai Islamic Bank took place following the 1973 oil price increases, which led to a considerable rise in individual incomes in the oil-exporting countries, particularly the Middle Eastern countries. That increase in the wealth of Muslims and the recognized need to channel their savings away from hoarding and investment in physical assets and into financial assets that could be used for productive investment led Prince Mohamed Al-Faisal Al-Saoud, the second son of the late King Faisal of Saudi Arabia, to seek as broad a consensus of *shariah* experts as possible on ways in which Muslims could entrust their savings to financial institutions and receive appropriate remuneration without infringing the Koranic injunction against *riba*. After studying the question, a number of *ulema* decided that it was legal under the *shariah* for the lender to share in the profits the borrower obtained from a venture financed with the lender's funds, but that it was forbidden to invest in ventures involving gambling, alcoholic beverages, or pork and pork products.

On the basis of the studies carried out by the *ulema*, Prince Mohamed Al-Faisal Al-Saoud and his associates established in 1977 two banks named after the late King Faisal: the Faisal Islamic Bank of Egypt (51 percent owned by Egyptians and 49 percent owned by Saudi Arabians and others) and the Faisal Islamic Bank of the Sudan (owned 60 percent by investors from Saudi Arabia and other Middle Eastern nations and 40 percent by Sudanese, including members of the Muslim Brotherhood). In the same year, they also founded the Islamic Investment Company of the Gulf (owned by Middle Eastern nationals, mostly Saudi Arabians), which is incorporated in the Bahamas to benefit from the tax and other advantages available to foreign investors in that country. In 1978 the Islamic Investment Company of the Gulf set up a wholly owned subsidiary, the Islamic Investment Company Ltd., at Sharjah in the United Arab Emirates, which engages in all investment operations complying with Islamic principles. In the same year, a number of Jordanians joined with the Housing Bank of Jordan to establish the Jordan Islamic Bank for Finance and Investment, which finances trade (mainly exports); the Jordanians contributed 98.7 percent of the capital and the Housing Bank of Jordan 1.3 percent.

In 1981 the Islamic Investment Company of the Gulf submitted an inquiry to the Committee of the Organization of Supreme Scholars of the Al Dawa and Iftaa and Irshad and Scientific Research Directorate of the Kingdom of Saudi Arabia to make doubly sure that the activities carried out by the company with the approval of its *shariah* advisers were indeed in conformity with the tenets of the *shariah*. The committee ruled by a majority that nothing in the activities reviewed appeared to "contravene Islamic *shariah*." The committee recommended

to Muslims in general and to those with the power of "Solving and Tieing" the authorities in particular, to do their utmost to protect their societies from *riba* (interest and/or usury) and exposure to war from Allah and his Prophet, and they should act to set up Islamic banks and Masaret (financial institutions) and render them active to allow people through them (the institutions) to deposit their funds and investments in the ways authorized by Allah, and diminish the activities of the insurance companies and *riba* banks existing today among the shoulders of Muslims.

In the same year, on the basis of the committee's decision, Prince Mohamed Al-Faisal Al-Saoud, together with "Rulers and prestigious personalities of the Islamic Community," founded Dar Al Maal Al-Islami (DMI) as a trust registered in the Bahamas to "operate investment, solidarity (Islam alternative to Western insurance) as well as Islamic banking through its subsidiaries in all Muslim States on a world-wide basis." The DMI's authorized capital was set at $1,000 million, of which $250 million was raised by private subscription, and the remaining $750 million was to be raised "by public subscription throughout the Muslim world." The DMI, which is based in Geneva, has an eighteen-member board of supervisors and a religious board. It has established or brought under its umbrella more than twenty companies in Africa (Guinea, Niger, Senegal and the Sudan), the Caribbean (Bahamas), Europe (Jersey, Channel Islands, Luxembourg, Switzerland and the United Kingdom) and the Middle East (Bahrain and the United Arab Emirates). In a decree published in the official gazette on 5 August 1984, Turkey authorized the DMI to establish the Faisal Finans Kurumu, a finance house, with a capital of TL 5 billion ($13.5 million). The DMI had hoped to open that bank in 1982, but the enactment of the necessary legislation took longer than expected. The DMI has close links with the International Association of Islamic Banks, which is likewise presided over by Prince Mohamed Al-Faisal Al-Saoud, is based in Jeddah and has twenty-eight members.

Another major Islamic umbrella organization is the Al-Baraka Group, based in Jeddah. The principal shareholders in the Group's companies (directly or indirectly) are Sheikh Saleh Abdullah Kamel and his brother-in-law Sheikh Hussein Mohsen al-Harithi. The Group includes:

— The Al-Baraka Investment and Development Company, set up in Jeddah in 1982 with a paid-up capital equivalent to about $56.8 million.

— The Al-Baraka Investment Company, incorporated in the Isle of Man (United Kingdom) in 1983, which has a paid-up capital equivalent to $13.9 million and whose purpose is to carry out international investment for the banks and finance companies of the Al-Baraka Group. Its four main areas of activity are commodity trading, trade finance, inventory funding and real-estate development.

— The Al-Baraka International, which was set up in London in 1983, when Sheikh Saleh Kamel acquired Hargrave Securities, poured fresh capital into the firm and gave it a new name. It is a licensed deposit taker with an authorized capital of £100 million, of which £5 million have been paid up. It plans to focus at first on trade finance and subsequently to become involved in leasing and inventory financing.

— The Saudi Tunisian Finance House, which was established in Tunis in January 1984 as an Islamic financial institution for the purpose of carrying out banking, investment and development-related activities. Classified as an "off-shore bank" under the Tunisian Banking Act, it has an authorized capital equivalent to $50.0 million, of which $12.5 million have been paid up. The Tunisian Central Bank has contributed 20 percent of the capital.

— The Al-Baraka Islamic Investment Bank, established in Bahrain in February 1984 with an investment banking license. Of the bank's capital, 50 percent has been contributed by the Al-Baraka Group and 50 percent by Sheikh Saleh Kamel (directly), the Bahrain Islamic Bank, the Dubai Islamic Bank, the Bahrain Islamic Investment Company and Al-Rajhi Company for Currency Exchange and Commerce. The Bank has an authorized capital of $200 million, of which $50 million have been paid up.

— The Al-Baraka Bank, Sudan, an Islamic investment bank established in Khartoum in March 1984. It has an authorized capital of $200 million, of which $50 million have been paid up. Of the capital, 80 percent is owned by the Al-Baraka Group and Sheikh Saleh Kamel, and 20 percent is owned by Sudanese businessmen.

— The Al-Baraka Finans Kurumu, whose establishment as a finance house with a capital of TL 5 billion ($13.5 million) was authorized in a decree published in the Turkish official gazette on 5 August 1984.

Other important privately promoted Islamic financial organizations include the Kuwait Finance House, the Islamic Banking System International of Luxembourg, the Al-Rajhi Company for Currency Exchange and Commerce, the African Arabian Islamic Bank and the Arab Agriculture Investment Company.

The Kuwait Finance House (KFH) was established in 1979; 51 percent of its capital is owned by Kuwaiti nationals and 49 percent by Kuwaiti Government agencies. At one point it collected 10 percent of all new deposits in Kuwait, but in 1983 its earnings and profits declined, and it ceased taking new deposits. Subsequently, the government reportedly began assisting the KFH by authorizing it to invest in mixed portfolios, notably in leasing and venture capital.

The Islamic Banking System International (IBSI) was established as a holding company in Luxembourg in 1978, reportedly to serve as a window on the West for a consortium of Islamic institutions and individuals. It has an authorized capital of $100 million, of which $34 million is paid up, and its shareholders include the Ministries of Awqaf of Kuwait and Abu Dhabi, the Al-Baraka Group, the Al-Rajhi Group, the Tadamon Islamic Bank of Sudan and the Kuwait Finance House. It has twelve subsidiaries including the Islamic Bank International in Denmark, the first Islamic bank in Europe, which began operations in 1983. The Islamic Bank International (IBI) is an investment bank whose purpose is to promote joint ventures between European and Muslim businessmen. Although established to function according to Islamic law, the IBI must also comply with Danish law, and each of its transactions must be approved by the Danish authorities. As part of its efforts to diversify its operations, the IBSI has reportedly been working out of the modalities of a fund consisting of short-term investments constantly coming to maturity that can be used for overnight money.

The Al-Rajhi Company for Currency Exchange and Commerce, which specializes in trade finance, was reported in mid–1984 to be in the process of being transformed into the Al-Rajhi Investment Banking Corporation, which will be the first Saudi Arabian Islamic Bank and will have a capital equivalent to $212.9 million, with more than 40 percent of its shares being for sale to the public. The aim of the transformation is to give Saudi Arabian Muslims an opportunity to obtain a fair return on their funds without contravening *shariah* principles and incidentally to attract funds currently deposited with Saudi commercial banks in interest-free accounts. Forty-three percent of the shares of the Al-Rajhi Investment Banking Corporation will be earmarked for public offering.

The African Arabian Islamic Bank, registered in the Bahamas, was set up in 1981; one of its purposes is said to be to channel capital from the Middle East to Africa for investment in development projects, trade financing and commodity trading in accordance with the Islamic *shariah*. It is reported to be particularly interested in technology investment and technology transfer projects.

The Arab Agriculture Investment Company, whose establishment was decided at a conference of Arab businessmen and investors held in Morocco in 1983, is registered as a Bahrain off-shore company. It will reportedly manage agricultural projects for third parties, market agricultural produce, promote research and participate directly in joint ventures in Arab countries.

Private Islamic investors and institutions have also promoted the establishment of Islamic banks in Bangladesh (the Islamic Bank Bangladesh, which began operations in August 1983) and in Malaysia (the Bank Islam Malaysia, which began operations in July 1983).

The spread of Islamic banking has also been facilitated by the fact that a growing number of Western-style banks in Muslim countries have been opening Islamic windows or branches to meet the demand for banking facilities that conform to the Islamic *shariah*. The banks that have set up Islamic windows include the United Commercial Bank of Malaysia, and those that have opened Islamic branches include a number of Egyptian banks such as Bank Misr, the National Bank for Development, the Principal Bank for Development and Agricultural Credit, and the Bank of Alexandria.

All of the cases of Islamization mentioned above involve solely the sporadic establishment of individual Islamic banks or the provision of Islamic banking facilities by existing individual Western-style banks. In other words, in all the cases cited thus far, Islamic banking has been fitted into banking systems that have remained essentially Western. However, in three countries—namely, in chronological order, Pakistan, Iran and the Sudan—

efforts are under way to Islamize the entire banking system or to make it predominantly Islamic.

In Pakistan the elimination of *riba* was one of the goals listed in the 1956 Constitution, and article 37 of the 1973 Constitution enjoined the state to eliminate *riba* as soon as possible. However, because of different views concerning the definition of *riba*, it was not until September 1977 that the President of Pakistan asked the Council of Islamic Ideology to prepare a plan for an interest-free economic system. In the following November, the Council set up a panel of bankers, economists and religious scholars to help Islamize the economic and financial system. One year later, in November 1978, the panel submitted an interim report suggesting a gradual approach, the first step being the elimination of interest from the operations of selected financial institutions. The panel's interim report, together with the Council's recommendations, was submitted to the Government, which implemented the recommendations effective 1 July 1979, when three institutions were instructed to do away with their interest-based business and switch to interest-free operations. Those institutions were the National Investment (Unit) Trust (an investment bank operating an open-ended mutual fund), the House Building Finance Corporation and the Mutual Funds of the Investment Corporation of Pakistan. In 1979 the Government also began introducing a scheme to provide farmers cultivating subsistence holdings with interest-free production loans. In January 1980 the panel submitted to the Council its final report, which after modification by the Council was submitted to the Government for consideration in June 1980.

From 1 July 1980, the Small Business Finance Corporation was fully converted to noninterest operations. Beginning on 1 January 1981, Pakistan's commercial banks began accepting, on a voluntary basis, savings and term deposit accounts on the basis of profit-and-loss sharing; the funds deposited in these accounts do not bear interest, and their use is restricted to noninterest-bearing investments. In June 1984 the Minister of Finance announced that interest-bearing operations would be phased out of the internal banking system by 1 July 1985, a step in the gradual process of establishing a comprehensive system of Islamic banking as part of a wholly Islamic society. In a number of stages between 1 January and 1 July 1985, Pakistan's twenty-two nationalized and foreign-owned banks that run a retail banking service were progressively to abandon the payment of interest on all new operations except international business operations. As regards the latter, the banks were to continue to pay interest to creditors, and foreign companies with affiliates in Pakistan were to continue to receive interest on loans to such affiliates. Since the banks— particularly the foreign banks—engage in foreign trade as well as retail banking, trade financing was also to be subject to procedural changes: the banks would be considered temporary owners of the imports and exports they deal with, and, implicitly, would be responsible for the delivery and quality of the goods. Moreover, all new corporate operations in both the private and public sector were to be carried out on a noninterest basis as of 1 January 1985, followed by operations by partnerships and individuals as of 1 April 1985 and by all other business operations as of 1 July 1985.

Beginning on 1 January 1981, the commodity financing operations of the federal and provincial governments and the purchase of export bills negotiated under letters of credit were converted to a markup basis with regulated rates of return. Beginning on 1 March 1981, the commodity operations of the Rice Export Corporation, the Trading Corporation of Pakistan and the Cotton Export Corporation and the purchase of import bills and inland acceptances drawn under letters of credit were likewise transferred to a regulated markup basis. In November 1981 the trading operations of the Government-owned Utility Stores Corporation were also converted to a markup basis. The rates of return established for the use of profit-and-loss sharing funds in all of those markup operations are very close to the interest rates formerly charged by the banks in connection with such transactions.

Under the Modaraba Companies and Modaraba (Floatation and Control) Ordinance, promulgated on 26 June 1980, Pakistan has also provided for the establishment of *modaraba companies*, or companies functioning on a profit-and-loss-sharing basis within the framework of partnerships. No business that is incompatible with the injunctions of Islam can be carried out by any company registered under the Modaraba Ordinance. A religious board and a tribunal were set up on 3 February 1981 to ensure that all of the operations carried out by a modaraba company are permissible under the *shariah*, and no modaraba company can be registered and authorized to begin business until the religious board has certified that its proposed activities do not violate any of the injunctions of Islam. In fact, virtually all Islamic financial institutions, irrespective of the country in which they are situated, operate under the guidance of religious advisors or boards that determine whether proposed operations are in conformity with the tenets of the *shariah*.

In March 1984 Iran began implementing an 18- to 36-month changeover to Islamic banking, during which the banks and their customers would gradually adapt their transactions to the tenets of the *shariah*. According to an article in the June 1984 issue of *South: The Third World Magazine*, the changeover "in theory . . . will improve the Iranian economy."

Ever since the collapse of the Shah's regime, substantial funds have been circulating outside the banking system. It is hoped that the security of the new system and its acceptability to devout Muslims will encourage people to use the banks more. But for the system to be really effective in mobilizing domestic savings, the Government will need radically to reduce inflation from its present official rate of 20 per cent, otherwise people with spare cash will continue to invest in valuables and property or lend within their family circle. Islamic banking will also assist development in that it tends to favour the small borrower and will be concentrated on the agricultural sector, particularly cooperatives, and the productive sector. But there are constraints that could limit the more dynamic role now expected of the banks. The latest figures on lending to farmers show that 72 per cent of loans cannot be recovered, and in business there may be resistance to the banks' greater participation.... One clear drawback to a completely Islamic economy is the lack of interest rates as a tool for managing the economy as a whole.... In practice, however, the Central Bank will be able to exercise some control on the economy by the level at which it sets the maximum and minimum repayment charges and returns to depositors (although these will not fluctuate). The Central Bank will also be able to call in special deposits from the banks.[32]

The Iranian Interest-Free Banking Act was approved by the Consultative Assembly on 30 August 1983 and ratified by the Guardianship Council on 1 September 1983. While the draft law was before the Consultative Assembly, training courses were organized to acquaint bank employees with the new system, and by mid-October 1983 about twenty thousand employees had attended such courses. Under the Interest-Free Banking Act, the objectives of the Iranian banking system include: the establishment of a monetary and credit system based on righteousness and justice (according to the *shariah*) to systematize a correct circulation of money and credit for a healthy and developing economy in the country; and the creation of necessary facilities to expand public cooperatives and interest-free lending by attracting free funds, savings, and deposits and mobilizing them to provide conditions and possibilities of work and investment.

According to the act, the functions of the Iranian banking system are, among other things: to open various interest-free accounts (current and savings) and long-term investment deposits and to issue relevant documents in accordance with rules and regulations; to give loans and credits without interest according to rules and regulations; and to give loans and credits and extend other banking services to legal cooperatives in order to realize paragraph 2 of article 43 of the Constitution.

According to article 43, the economy of the Islamic Republic of Iran is to aim at:

Securing opportunities and possibilities for employment for all in order to achieve full employment, offering employment opportunities to all who are able to work but lack the means, making use of the co-operative system in providing interest-free loans and other legitimate means, so that capital is not concentrated and is not circulated in the hands of specific individuals or groups, and in a way so that the Government does not become a major absolute employer.

In the Sudan, prior to 1983, there were two Islamic banks, the Faisal Islamic Bank mentioned above, which has opened a branch in Omdurman to promote investment in small and medium-sized projects, and the Islamic Co-operative Development Bank, a government-owned institution set up in 1982 to help the cooperative societies, which were not in a position to borrow at commercial interest rates, and to provide collateral for their borrowing. By mid-1984 there were six Islamic banks and one Islamic insurance company; two commercial banks, including the National Bank of Sudan, were reported to be in the process of Islamizing their operations. Besides the Al-Baraka Bank, Sudan, the Islamic banks established since 1983 include the Bank al-Tadmun al-Islami (Islamic Solidarity Bank), the Sudan Islamic Bank and the Islamic Bank for Western Sudan. The Islamic Solidarity Bank has an authorized capital of $20 million, and its owners include members of the Kuwarta tribe, one of the richest in the northern region. The Sudan Islamic Bank likewise has an authorized capital of $20 million. Sixty percent of its shareholders are Sudanese based in the Sudan, and the rest are Sudanese working abroad or citizens of Arab states, especially Saudi Arabia and the United Arab Emirates. The Islamic Bank for Western Sudan was established by the inhabitants of that region, where Islam is considered to be particularly strong.

The International Association of Islamic Banks was founded in August 1977 and acts as technical advisor to those banks and other Islamic financial institutions; it promotes cooperation among national Islamic banks, assists in training their personnel, and represents the common interests of the Islamic financial institutions.[33] In addition to having a Board of Directors (its highest authority), the Association has a Supreme Legal Supervisory Board, consisting of leading Muslim scholars, that follows the Association's activities from the standpoint of the Islamic *shariah*.

Generally, Muslim countries face a number of practical constraints regarding the Islamization of the entire banking system. These constraints, which vary from country to country, include: the presence of large non-Muslim minorities with a substantial savings capacity, which might seek to place their savings abroad if national banks offered no interest; the need to attract the savings of large numbers of nationals working abroad who accept the liberal interpretation of the term *riba* and who out of patriotism would prefer to deposit their savings with banks in their own countries, provided that they would receive some interest; the high degree of interlocking between international banking and national banking; the limited absorptive capacity of the domestic economy, which combined with the substantial volume of bank deposits considerably restricts the scope of internal banking activity and makes it necessary for deposit-taking institutions to look for outlets abroad for the large sums of money available to them; and the need to borrow on international capital markets for development purposes, which entails paying interest to foreigners.

Modes of Remuneration Permissible under the Islamic *Shariah*

The main modes of remuneration permissible under the Islamic *shariah* are profit-and-loss sharing, awards of nonpredetermined value, reduction of or exemption from bank service fees, markup, administrative fees or service charges, and profits from dealings in future markets.

Profit-and-Loss Sharing. Profit-and-loss sharing involves three parties: savers, who entrust to banks the savings they want to hold primarily as a source of income or as a means of meeting foreseeable expenditures in the relatively distant future; banks, which in turn invest the savers' funds, together with their own funds, either directly or jointly with entrepreneurs in ventures approved by their Islamic *shariah* advisers; and entrepreneurs, who manage and operate the ventures and share the profits or losses with the banks, which in turn share them with their depositors. In practice, the funds deposited with a bank form part of a general pool of funds, and the banks share with their depositors the overall profits or losses yielded by the general pool, since they do not usually earmark for investment in particular operations the funds deposited by specific savers. In March 1985 the way in which the profit-and-loss-sharing system was intended to work in Pakistan was described by the Chairman of the Banking Council, a government organization for Pakistan's nationalized banks: "A bank's profits, after deducting administrative costs, doubtful debts, and a management fee of up to 10 per cent, will be distributed between the bank's equity holders and its depositors on a five-to-one basis."[34]

An Islamic bank, whose earnings are linked to the profits and losses of the ventures it finances, naturally has to become more deeply involved than a *riba* bank in the affairs of the entrepreneurs who use its funds and to make an even more careful assessment of their business acumen, competence and honesty. Even so, an Islamic bank incurs greater risks than a *riba* bank, because it has to rely to a much greater extent on the good faith of the entrepreneurs to whom it entrusts its funds.

Profit-and-loss sharing generally occurs within the framework of *modaraba* or *musharaka*. In a footnote to the Iranian Interest-Free Banking Act, *modaraba* is defined as "handing over of capital to a party to work with the money in return for an agreed share in profits or losses," and *musharaka* is defined as an arrangement "in which profit and loss are shared on the basis of percentage capital of various parties to the investment." The footnote adds that in *musharaka*, "according to Islamic Law, there is no restriction whatsoever on any of the parties withdrawing his capital at any time." Thus in a *modaraba*, one party provides the funds and the other contributes his managerial skill and business acumen by operating the venture. Any profit will be shared between the provider of funds and the entrepreneur, usually on the basis of pre-agreed percentages. If the venture loses money or fails altogether, the provider of funds may lose some or all of his investment, while the entrepreneur will have lost the cost of his time, skill and effort. In the case of a *musharaka*, the funds are provided by both partners, but the venture is managed by one partner, whose share of any eventual profits will be based on his contribution of both skill and capital. If the venture fails, both parties will lose some or all of their capital. According to Islamic tradition, the outcome of any venture cannot be foreseen, for it is in the hands of Providence: Insha-Allah.

Although Islamic banks incur greater risks by lending on a profit-and-loss sharing basis, the yields they have obtained through partnership arrangements have been at least comparable with the returns *riba* banks obtain by charging conventional interest rates on their loans. To determine how profits will be shared between the bank and the entrepreneur, Islamic banks "often use the relevant interest rates charged by the traditional banks as a guideline."[35] An official of the Faisal Islamic Bank of the Sudan remarked:

We calculate the shares of profits in the light of the interest due to a lender for a similar purpose and duration. The figure is then adjusted to allow for the fact that an Islamic bank, unlike an interest-charging bank, is a co-bearer of risk. Other criteria we give weight to are things like the social benefits of a project, the profitability of the investment and its contribution to the economy.[36]

The profits savers receive when they deposit their money with Islamic banks or at Islamic windows of *riba* banks on a profit-and-loss sharing basis may be greater than those they would receive by depositing their funds in conventional savings accounts, since in most developing countries and many developed countries, interest rates are maintained at artificially low levels through an administered rate system. Moreover, savers may profit from competition among Islamic banks to attract funds by sharing their profits with their depositors in a manner more advantageous to the depositors. In fact, the returns savers earn on deposits in profit-and-loss sharing accounts seem to have been attractive compared with the rates paid on interest-bearing accounts by *riba* banks in Muslim and other countries. Thus in 1980 the Bahrain Islamic Bank paid dividends of 9.0 to 9.5 percent on deposit accounts and 5.25 percent on savings accounts, compared with the interest rates paid by other Bahraini banks (7.5 to 8.0 percent on deposits held for up to three months and 8.5 to 9.5 percent on deposits held from six to fifteen months). In the same year, the Jordan Islamic Bank paid 7.4 percent on one-year deposits, 5.8 percent on three-months-notice accounts and 4.1 percent on seven-days-notice accounts; other Jordanian banks were paying between 7.0 and 7.5 percent on one-year accounts during 1980. In Pakistan, where the five nationalized banks during the three-year period July 1981-July 1984 had accumulated about $1.6 billion in profit-and-loss accounts representing about 22 percent of total deposits as of July 1984, the returns yielded by the various types of account in the first half of 1981 were as follows:

	Interest-bearing Accounts	Profit-and-Loss-Sharing Accounts
Savings accounts	--	9.0 percent
Time-deposit accounts		
6 months to 1 year	9.5 percent	11.5 percent
1 to 2 years	10.5 percent	12.75 percent
2 to 3 years	11.0 percent	13.25 percent
3 to 4 years	11.75 percent	14.25 percent
4 to 5 years	12.25 percent	14.75 percent
Over 5 years	12.75 percent	15.25 percent

The difference between the returns on the two types of account has narrowed, but in mid-1984 returns on profit-and-loss-sharing accounts were still at least one percentage point higher than those on interest-bearing accounts. The ability of the Pakistani banks to pay higher returns on the profit-and-loss-sharing accounts was probably due to the fact that the money deposited in such accounts was channeled into commodity dealings, foreign-trade financing and instruments such as the participation term certificates introduced by a syndicate of six major banks in 1981 to replace debenture issues, which involve a fixed rate of repayment.

The difference between what savers earned on their time deposits with Islamic banks and administered interest rates in general may not be as great in the case of the Islamic Republic of Iran: article 20 of the 1983 Interest-Free Banking Act authorizes the Central Bank to fix "the minimum and maximum percentages of the share of a bank's possible profits in partnership and limited partnership activities." According to the article, "this minimum percentage of profit may differ in different fields," and the Central Bank may fix: "the minimum and maximum percentages of possible bank profit on instalment dealings and leases on condition of transfer of ownership on the basis of total cost of a deal . . . . The minimum and maximum percentages of bank service charges of various types . . . and agent's fee for utilization of investment deposits received by the banks."

Article 20 also empowers the Central Bank to fix the minimum and maximum amounts each bank may invest in partnership, limited partnership, hire-purchase operations and other types of operations. Any limitation on the banks' possible profits will also limit the returns to savers.

Awards of Nonpredetermined Value. Giving such awards to Islamic bank depositors is an acceptable mode of remuneration under the *shariah*. Thus the Iranian Interest-Free Banking Act states in article 6 that "with a view to attracting deposits" the banks can provide a number of "privileges to depositors by way of encouragement." The first privilege is giving "unfixed awards, in cash or kind, on interest-free deposits." Article 20 of the act empowers the Central Bank to fix the types and the minimum and maximum values of the awards that banks may offer to attract deposits. The emphasis on the "un-fixed" value of the awards is in keeping with the letter of the Islamic *shariah*. If the saver knew in advance the value of the award he might receive, the award would be tantamount to the paying of interest on his deposit.

Reduction of or Exemption from Bank Service Fees. Under the Islamic *shariah*, Islamic banks can charge fees for banking services similar to those provided by *riba* banks, including checking account facilities, letters of credit, bills of exchange or similar instruments, expert advice on the establishment or expansion of a business or the management of customers' portfolios and safe-deposit facilities. By reducing or waiving their service fees for eligible depositors, Islamic banks can provide those depositors with some indirect remuneration on their savings without contravening the tenets of the *shariah*. Thus the second privilege that Iranian banks offer savers under article 6 of the Iranian Interest-Free Banking Act is a "reduction of or exemption from service charges or agent's fees."

Markup. In the case of markup operations (also known as cost-plus operations), an Islamic bank, after negotiations with its clients, acquires the goods a client needs for trade or personal use, and assumes temporary ownership of the goods. It then puts the goods at the client's disposal on the basis of instalment payments that represent portions of the purchase price plus a surcharge, which is normally calculated to provide a reasonable return on the money invested by the bank during the period over which the instalments are spread. The State Bank of Pakistan has issued guidelines calling on the banks to negotiate with their clients a markup in the range of 10 to 20 percent. Markup bears a closer resemblance to traditional interest than does profit-and-loss sharing, in that it does not involve the managerial responsibilities or degree of risk for depositors' funds that the profit-and-loss-sharing system entails.

Some *shariah* experts think that markup does not conform to the tenets of the Islamic *shariah*, since the banks do not share any losses suffered by their clients in connection with markup transactions. However, the predominant view seems to be that the return earned through markup is in full conformity with the *shariah* since it is earned through trading. Although the Koranic ban on *riba* is interpreted as applying to transactions in which money is made directly out of money—that is, when a given sum of money is made available on the understanding that an equivalent amount plus an increase will be returned at a later date—it is generally agreed that the Koran, which was initially addressed to people engaged in commercial activities, encourages trading, since it specifically states: "God hath permitted trade and forbidden usury." The Prophet himself was a successful merchant and is believed to have said that "the trustworthy merchant will sit in the shade of God's throne at the Day of Judgement." Islam came into being in a city where political power was to a large extent exercised by a mercantile oligarchy. According to Islamic tradition, trade is a very honorable way of earning a living, and it is said that "a *dirham* lawfully gained from trade is worth more than 10 *dirhams* gained in any other way." Much early Islamic literature was written in a mercantile environment and encourages profit making.

Markup is used particularly in connection with hire-purchase, leasing and buy-back arrangements. Hire-purchase was originated by United States retailers in the nineteenth century. In Western commercial practice, a *hire-purchase transaction* involves the supplier of the goods and the buyer. The buyer makes a down payment and pays the balance of the purchase price plus interest in instalments over a given period. In contrast to a credit sale, the supplier of the goods retains the ownership until the last instalment is paid. In Islamic banking practice, on the other hand, a bank purchases the goods a prospective buyer needs, assumes temporary ownership and then transfers them to the buyer for his use. The buyer is usually expected to make a down payment and to pay the balance of the purchase price, plus a markup, in instalments over a given period, at the end of which ownership of the goods is transferred from the bank to the buyer. Hire-purchase is used for trade financing and for financing the purchase of housing, motor vehicles, furniture, and other consumer durables.

Markup in *leasing* is used in Islamic banking to enable bank customers to have at their disposal for personal or business use goods such as cars, equipment, machinery, buildings and land. In Western business practice, a leasing operation may involve three parties. The first party is the *lessee*, an entrepreneur who is unwilling or unable to buy the equipment he needs and who through leasing can obtain such equipment on more convenient financial terms. The second party is the *lessor*, an entrepreneur who is willing to accept the burden and risk of owning the equipment in order to benefit from the tax deductions that governments may grant to foster economic development, deductions that the lessor can use to offset his profits and reduce his tax liability; the lessor often buys on credit or secures partial financing from an external source and receives from the lessee rental fees set at levels that allow him to repay his loans and also to make a profit, the size of which will depend on the size of the tax relief he obtains. If the lessor borrows to buy the equipment, a third party is involved: a *bank*, from which the lessor borrows to finance the purchase, or the *supplier* of the equipment, who sells it to the lessor on instalment terms. In some cases, such as hire-purchase, ownership of the leased goods is transferred to the lessee at the end of the lease agreement for a nominal charge. In the United States, where leasing has been growing rapidly in recent years, there are two main reasons for its popularity with nonfinancial corporations: it allows firms to expand without showing large amounts of debts directly on their balance sheets (in most cases lease obligations are reported in the footnotes of financial statements); and it enables firms to avoid buying equipment that may become obsolete.[37]

In Islamic banking practice, two parties are involved in a leasing transaction: the *bank*, which is the owner of the property or the lessor, and the bank's *customer* or the *lessee*, who is granted the use of the property for a given period at a given rent payable monthly, quarterly or annually and calculated to cover depreciation, servicing and maintenance of the goods plus a reasonable markup to cover administrative and other overhead costs. In Islamic banking practice, in contrast to Western business practice, title to the leased goods is usually transferred to the lessee at the end of the lease for an agreed charge.

The 1983 Interest-Free Banking Act of the Islamic Republic of Iran provides in article 12 that:

The banks may, with a view to creating facilities for the expansion of services, agriculture, mining and industry, purchase properties (movable and immovable) at the request and agreement of the client that he shall take the purchased property on lease on condition of transfer of ownership and for his own utilization, and put it at the disposal of the client on lease on condition of transfer of ownership.

A footnote to the act further specifies that such transactions involve "the leasing of a property to a party on the condition that it shall be sold to him after an agreed period on the terms and conditions mentioned in the lease agreement."

Leasing has been used at the national level by various Islamic financial institutions, such as the Small Business Finance Corporation of Pakistan. It also has been used at the international level, in particular by the Islamic Development Bank. According to the Islamic Development Bank, the expansion of its lease financing in recent years is "a direct result of its simplicity and flexibility, which makes its use possible in various sectors and industries." From the Bank's viewpoint, leasing operations "are less risky, have a shorter repayment period and provide a reasonable return on investment." During 1403 H (1982–1983), the Bank's rentals were "fixed at between 8 and 9 per cent, depending upon cash flow, expected return and ability to pay."[38]

In a *buy-back arrangement* the owner of commercial property sells it to a financial institution and then buys it back at a repurchase price that consists of the original selling price plus a markup; the repurchase price is paid in instalments over an agreed period. The instalments and the repayment period are generally geared to estimates of production in the property and not to the overall operating profits and losses of the business of the original owner of the property. Buy-back arrangements enable entrepreneurs to free for business use the capital tied up in real estate. In particular, they enable Islamic financial institutions to provide long-term financing to customers in a manner consistent with the *shariah*.

Administrative Fees or Service Charges.   Most of the Muslim world abides by the decisions of schools of jurisprudence which allow Islamic banks to charge administrative fees or levy service charges on their loans to cover administrative costs and overhead. An Islamic bank that charges administrative fees that exceed the actual costs or overhead incurred in connection with its lending operations would naturally invite accusations that it was resorting to legal fictions or terminological subterfuges and was in fact charging interest under another name. Since Islamic banks make no profit on the funds they use for loans, such funds must be obtained from grants or interest-free loans from public or private sources, from deposits on which the banks pay no remuneration, or from the profits they obtain from other operations.

Interest-free lending on which only minimal charges or no charges are imposed is considered to be a form of *sadakat*, a voluntary charity that is recommended to the faithful by the Koran and the Hadith. The 1983 Interest-Free Banking Act of the Islamic Republic of Iran even makes it the duty of Iranian banks "to allocate a part of their resources to interest-free loans to applicants in order to fulfill the objectives of paragraphs 2 and 9 of article 43 of the Constitution."

The *sadakat* is not the only form of charity mentioned in the Koran; in fact, it supplements *zakat*, a regular charity, the payment of which to the poor and the needy is a religious duty.[39] The word *zakat* means "purification," because the payment of this charity is believed to purify the donors and their wealth and make their remaining property religiously and legally legitimate. *Zakat* must be paid in food grains, money, and so on each year after one year's possession of the assets in question. The annual rate depends on the type of assets involved: it is 10 percent on produce grown on lands watered by rainfall; 5 percent on produce grown on irrigated lands and on privately extracted minerals and buried treasure; 2.5 percent on gold, silver and money; and various percentages in the case of livestock for breeding or for sale and in the case of spoils of war.

In earlier times, the collection and expenditure of *zakat* were a function of the state. Today there are, generally, no formal arrangements for collecting *zakat*, the payment of which is left to the conscience of the individual. However, in certain countries it is currently a formal state levy.

Thus, in Pakistan, the Zakat and Ushr Ordinance, promulgated on 20 June 1980, on the recommendation of the Council of Islamic Ideology, empowers the government to make deductions for *zakat* at source for various types of assets (savings bank accounts, fixed-deposit-receipt accounts, notice-deposit-receipt accounts, and savings-deposit certificates; shares held in the National Investment Trust, the Investment Corporation of Pakistan and other companies, a majority of whose shares are owned by Muslims; government securities, annuities, life-insurance policies and benefits from Provident Funds; and other assets) at an annual rate of 2.5 percent of the face value, paid-up value, surrender value, and so on as appropriate. The amounts collected are deposited into the Central Zakat Fund, which is separate from the normal budgetary accounts of the government.

The provisions of the Ordinance of 20 June 1980 relating to *Ushr* did not come into effect until March 1983. *Ushr*, an annual tithing on the produce of the land, is collected in cash from every landowner, grantee, allottee, lessee, leaseholder or landholder at the rate of 5 percent of his share of the produce as on the valuation date, minus one-third of the total produce if the land is irrigated by pipes and wells and one-quarter if it is not.

Under the Pakistan Income-tax Ordinance, 1979, an individual's taxable income in a given assessment year is to be reduced by the amount paid by him to the *zakat* fund during the previous year. Under the Wealth-Tax Act 1983, assets for which *zakat* or a contribution in lieu thereof has been deducted at source are to be excluded from taxable wealth during the relevant assessment year. Finally, land-revenue and development taxes are not levied on land on the produce of which *Ushr*, or a contribution in lieu thereof, has been charged on a compulsory basis.

Zakat is also collected in Saudi Arabia, where the government collects it from Saudi individuals and Saudi firms. It is levied at the rate of 2.5 percent on local income and capital that has been held for one year or more. In the Sudan *zakat* was introduced in the budget presented to the National Assembly on 25 August 1984, two months later than usual in order to coordinate with the Islamic new year.

Profits from Dealing in Futures Markets. Many commodity exchanges, such as those for cotton, wheat and wool, have set up futures markets that allow producers, consumers and traders to hedge against unforeseeable variations in the price of the commodities they use or deal in. There are also futures markets that are intended to provide similar protection against price fluctuations in the stock market and the money market. A number of Islamic *shariah* scholars believe that Islamic banks can deal in such markets and buy and sell in the hope of selling and buying at a profit later when prices have changed. Islamic banks can also deal in the precious metals markets.

The concept of market dealing is fundamental to Islamic banking and indeed to Islamic economics, since it is the basic mechanism of commerce; trade, as noted above, is referred to approvingly in the Koran and has been encouraged in Islamic tradition. As the fourteenth-century Islamic scholar Ibn Khaldun observed:

It should be known that commerce means the attempt to make a profit by increasing capital, through buying goods at a low price then selling them at a high price.... The accrued amount is called profit. The attempt to make such a profit may be undertaken by storing goods and holding them until the market has fluctuated from low prices to high prices. Or the merchant may transport his goods to another country where they are more in demand than in his own.

Islamic Banking–Western Banking: A Comparative Analysis

All banks, both Western and Islamic, provide a link between economic units that spend less than they earn (surplus units or savers) and economic units that want to spend more than their expected receipts (potential deficit units or seekers of funds). In effect, savers may be unable to undertake production ventures because they lack the necessary technical skills or are unwilling to do so, either alone or with partners, because they fear uncertainty and the risk of loss. They may also consider it risky to place their funds directly at the disposal of ultimate borrowers. In the absence of any acceptable alternative way of putting their savings to remunerative use, they may increase their consumption or hoard precious metals or stocks of goods. Similarly, seekers of funds may want to undertake production ventures, to acquire houses or other durable goods, or simply to satisfy a desire for goods or services. However, they may find it difficult, if not impossible, to contact savers willing to lend them their savings or to obtain funds from savers on conditions that meet the requirements of both parties. Through the process of financial intermediation, banks provide an acceptable way for savers to make their funds available to those who need them and an acceptable way for borrowers to obtain the funds. By pooling risks and averaging the preferences of savers and the requirements of borrowers, both Western and Islamic banks can offer a range of financial instruments tailored to savers' preferences and a variety of arrangements geared to the needs of borrowers.

Although the contemporary Islamic revival has focused attention on the idea of interest-free banking, interest-free operations are widespread within the Western banking system in the case of both deposits and lending. Moreover, a number of specialized Western banks engage exclusively in noninterest bearing operations.

Current-account deposits, which constitute a very sizable proportion of a Western bank's deposit base, usually earn no interest and may be subject to charges, depending on the number of checks cleared through the account and the average credit balance maintained over a certain period. For example, in the United Kingdom, three-quarters of the banks' *sight deposits* (deposits in current accounts and deposits that are repayable on demand or at short notice or are placed overnight) are noninterest bearing, and if sight deposits are added to the time deposits, as much as one-third of the banks' sterling deposit base is noninterest bearing. The corresponding percentages are currently smaller in the United States, because the competition brought about by the recent deregulation of interest has forced banks to pay interest on eligible demand deposits. In other industrialized countries the corresponding percentages are at least as high as in the United Kingdom, and in developing countries they are generally much higher.

A number of banks endowed with government funds provide interest-free loans at the national level for specific areas of activity, specific categories of borrowers or specific purposes. At the international level, the International Development Agency (IDA) and regional development banks such as the African Development Bank, the Asian Development Bank and the Inter-American Development Bank offer interest-free loans, usually with long-term maturities. At the national level, the financial institutions that concentrate exclusively on interest-free banking operations within the framework of the Western banking system include investment trusts, *mutual funds* (the United States term for open-ended investment trusts, that is, investment trusts without issued capital stock and owned by those members that do business with them), unit trusts and other institutions of similar types. The sole purpose of an investment trust or a mutual fund is to invest its capital in the equity of other companies. It obtains its capital by issuing shares to savers, although it may also mobilize resources by issuing interest-bearing securities. It pays dividends to its shareholders out of the profits from its equity portfolio, after deductions for reserves. The unit trust uses its own funds to buy shares in other companies and then mobilizes capital by issuing units constituting holdings of shares; however, these units entitle their holders not to a portion of the profits of the company managing the trust but to a portion of the profits of the companies whose shares constitute the holding. Investors in investment trusts and unit trusts run the risk of loss if profit expectations fail to materialize. Nevertheless, both investment trusts and unit trusts offer savers two major advantages: expert management, since the trust can afford to carry out an in-depth assessment of the profit prospects of companies whose shares it is thinking of buying; and lower risks, since by investing in a larger number of companies than the average saver can afford to do, the trust can offset eventual losses in one area by profits in another.

Thus in Western banking interest-free deposits constitute a long-standing tradition, and specialized institutions engaging solely or essentially in investment operations yielding noninterest income have become increasingly common in recent decades. What is really novel is the emergence of the contemporary Islamic concept of a modern bank providing a full range of banking services that for religious reasons never engages in interest-bearing operations and does not provide financing for certain categories of ventures, namely, those involving alcoholic beverages, gambling, or pork and pork products. The notion of interest-free banking seems all the more intriguing against the background of the international debt crisis, which makes it advisable to encourage equity investment rather than borrowing from banks, particularly at floating interest rates. Equity funding entails no debt repayment as such and therefore does not create an obligation that must be met in the future as bank borrowing does. The funds that flow out of the host country will depend on the profitability of the venture, and in any event, some of the profits may be ploughed back into the venture.

It may be tempting to see a ripple effect of interest-free banking in the appearance on the international financial markets of zero coupon bonds, which some Islamic jurists might consider as not transgressing the tenets of the *shariah* because, if they are sold on a secondary market before maturity, their value is not predetermined. Unlike regular fixed-income securities, which carry coupons that are clipped periodically in order to obtain the interest payment, a zero coupon bond is issued at a substantial discount owing to its noninterest-bearing character, and it yields no income to the investor until it reaches maturity, when the investor is paid its full face, or par, value. The difference between the issue price and the bond's value at maturity is the return on the investment, known in the bond market as "yield to maturity." A zero coupon bond issue provides the borrower with an immediate cash flow, yet frees him from the burden of debt servicing and other related borrowing costs until the bonds reach maturity. Moreover, the borrower may be able to reduce the cost of borrowing in so far as the tax system permits the amortization over the life of the bonds of the discount at which they are issued. A possible disadvantage is that the imputed yield from the bond may be taxable every year, even though the bondholder has received no actual return on his investment.

There are various types of zero coupon bonds. They have been created by Wall Street investment firms that, seeking new ways of borrowing money while hedging against the risk of fluctuating interest rates, purchase long-term Treasury bonds, separate the principal from the coupon interest payment and sell certificates representing each part of the "stripped" bond as independent, noninterest-bearing obligations. Depending on the firm that issues them, the zero coupon bonds have been identified by acronyms such as CATS (Certificates of Accrual on Treasury Securities) and TIGRS (Treasury Investment Growth Receipts). Canadian brokerage firms and financial institutions, like their United States counterparts, have begun to strip conventional bonds, and zero coupon bonds have also been attracting increasing attention elsewhere.

In the United States, CATS, TIGRS, and other zero coupon bonds based on United States Treasury bonds and known as Treasury Receipts (TRs) are becoming increasingly popular with investors because of the interest guarantee provided by the full faith and credit of the federal government and because TRs, unlike proprietary zero coupon bonds, can be traded through numerous investment firms. Furthermore, TRs may be available in units as small as $1,000, and even if an investment firm sets the minimum purchase at $5,000 or $10,000, these amounts are within reach of the typical bond buyer. When the Treasury pays interest on TRs or repays their principal, the custodian bank transfers the sums involved to the appropriate TR holder. More than $50 billion worth of TRs were purchased in 1984, and the amount invested in such securities is expected to continue increasing.

Although interest-free operations are widespread in Western banking, the fact that an Islamic bank can engage solely in such operations means that there is a fundamental difference between the two concepts of banking that is one of nature and not merely one of degree. This explains why Islamic banks established in Muslim countries that want to be able to provide a broad range of banking services—and not to be confined, like the Islamic financial institutions in Western European countries and other non-Muslim countries, to specific activities that conform to both Islamic *shariah* and Western banking laws—have usually had to be granted exemption from certain provisions contained in the general banking legislation, which is based on conventional Western banking principles and practices. A case in point is that of Egypt, where in 1977 a special law had to be passed to pave the way for the establishment of the Faisal Islamic Bank, which wanted to engage in operations involving, among other things, the buying and selling of real estate and shares; the general banking legislation, passed in 1957, had prohibited banks from dealing in real estate other than their own premises and from owning more than 25 percent of the equity in any company. The 1977 legislation placed the Faisal Islamic Bank under the supervision of the Ministry of Awqaf to emphasize the special character of that bank, just as the Nasser Social Bank, established in 1971, which likewise provided an interest-free banking service, had been placed under the supervision of the Ministry of Social Affairs. The 1977 legislation also granted the Faisal Islamic Bank a fifteen-year period of tax exemption on its capital and profits. In 1981, however, the banking legislation was revised, and the Faisal Islamic Bank and the Nasser Social Bank were placed under the supervision of the Central Bank, and the Faisal Islamic Bank's period of tax exemption was reduced from fifteen to five years; moreover, the bank was made subject to local controls on foreign currency and credit.

The fundamental difference between Western and Islamic banking is reflected even more clearly in the extent to which the activities of Islamic banks are inhibited by the application to them of provisions of the general banking legislation concerning the liquidity position of deposit-taking institutions and the fact that Islamic banks remain subject to the monetary policy stipulations of the central bank.

In Muslim countries, as in virtually all other countries, the banking laws or banking practice requires that deposit-taking institutions always have at their disposal sufficient cash and assets that can be converted into cash, without significant loss of capital, to cover foreseeable withdrawals. They can meet this requirement by holding cash and other liquid assets and by borrowing from other banks with surplus cash or from the central bank. A *riba* bank's liquid assets may include cash, its balances with the central bank (other than noninterest-bearing special deposits where they are required), short-term government securities, money at call on the money market, and commercial bills and other bills eligible for rediscounting by the central bank. All of these assets except the first two earn income in the form of interest. An Islamic bank cannot hold such interest-bearing assets and thus has fewer opportunities for short-term investments than a *riba* bank; unless it is exempted from central bank reserve requirements, it can comply with them only by relying on cash and the short-term bills mostly issued in connection with its markup operations. An Islamic bank will be at an even greater disadvantage if these short-term bills are not eligible for refinancing by the central bank. The smaller the proportion of an Islamic bank's reserve assets constituted by short-term markup bills, the greater the amount of nonproductive cash the bank must hold to satisfy the reserve requirements, with a corresponding reduction in its ability to put its deposits to work. Furthermore, an Islamic bank, unlike a *riba* bank, cannot accommodate its short-term liquidity problems by borrowing in the interbank market unless it can borrow on a noninterest basis from another bank with surplus cash.

The question of bank liquidity is closely linked to that of the protection of customers' deposits. Although Muslim savers may be willing to invest their funds in profit-and-loss-sharing accounts, they undoubtedly assume, consciously or unconsciously, that as a result of the bank's managerial and investment expertise their savings will ultimately yield a profit and more importantly will not be lost. Consequently, Islamic banks—particularly newly-established ones—with no publicized affiliation with well-known wealthy promoters (which constitutes a form of insurance in savers' eyes) and no successful "track record" may find it difficult to attract savers' funds in competition with *riba* banks, with the exception of the savings of Muslims who believe that the term *riba* covers all interest irrespective of rates. Even the backing of wealthy and influential personalities and some years of experience may not be enough for an Islamic bank to lure savers away from *riba* banks. A comparison between the performance of the Dubai Islamic Bank, established in 1975, and the performance of a *riba* bank of comparable size established in the same area at about the same time showed that in the period 1978-1979 deposits with the *riba* bank increased more rapidly than those with the Dubai Islamic Bank.[40]

An Islamic bank is also at a disadvantage *vis à vis riba* banks because it cannot raise funds on the capital markets by issuing bonds, certificates of deposit or similar interest-bearing instruments. Islamic banks therefore have to devise ways and means of mobilizing resources on the international capital market that both conform with the Islamic *shariah* and appeal to Muslim and non-Muslim investors alike. In this connection the Islamic Development Bank (IDB) states in its Eighth Annual Report that its aim is "to formulate ways and means for raising resources which would be partially through subscription to paid-up capital, creation of funds, etc. which do not have to be compensated and to raise the balance through investment instruments both short-term and long-term which provide return to the investors in the form of profits." The Bank observed that:

Since a significant portion of IDB's investment is in equity, it could develop institutional arrangements for effecting disinvestments through selling the shares to the institutions in the country concerned on the basis of negotiations, selling them through the stock exchanges where it is possible, or through offers for sale or other arrangements. For new investments in equity, the IDB may consider buy-back arrangements and put options where possible with the Government or institutions in the country concerned. In addition, one other vehicle for effecting disinvestments which the IDB is examining would be through issue of Closed-end Mutual Funds.

The IDB would transfer from its portfolio to the Mutual Funds its shares in "those investments which have become profit yielding after having provided the bank adequate return on its investments." According to the IDB, "the funds so generated could be applied towards the fresh investment programmes of the Bank" and "in order to provide for liquidity of the Mutual Funds, it may be necessary to arrange listing of these Mutual Funds at stock exchanges in member countries."[41]

Despite the constraints discussed above, Islamic banks are not always at a disadvantage *vis à vis riba* banks. As noted earlier, their shares of the profits from partnership ventures compare very favorably with the interest rates charged by *riba* banks on their loans. Indeed, it is an open secret that Islamic banks often use those rates as guidelines when negotiating their shares of the profits in partnership ventures. This approach is facilitated by the fact that in most Muslim countries, as in most developing countries and many industrialized countries, the interest rates that *riba* banks can charge are fixed, either directly by administrative decision or indirectly by directives imposing limits on the interest rates payable on deposits; such limits eliminate competition among banks in the market for funds, thus making it possible for them to lend at artificially low rates. The goal of such controls on interest rates is usually the promotion of investment within the context of a policy aimed at stimulating economic growth and providing employment. It is doubtless the same goal that prompted the government of the Islamic Republic of Iran to empower the central bank to fix upper and lower limits for the shares of the profits banks may take in *modaraba* and *musharaka* ventures. This provision naturally reduces the overall profits the banks can share with savers, but the savers are protected by article 4 of the Interest-Free Banking Act, which states that banks can "undertake, guarantee and insure repayment of the principal of long-term investments." Generally, the net profits Islamic banks receive from their investments in partnership ventures may be reduced by the cost of the additional management burden they must bear by supervising or playing an active managerial role in ventures in the equity of which they participate.

The activities of an Islamic bank may be more constrained than those of a *riba* bank if the central bank applies monetary or credit controls such as a ceiling on participation in the equity of firms, a ceiling on credit bill holdings, and mandatory hire-purchase terms (minimum down payment and maximum repayment period). Since most of an Islamic bank's financing activities involves equity financing and the short-term and medium-term financing of trade, it will be affected more by the application of such instruments than will a *riba* bank, whose modes of financing encompass a wider range.

If Islamic banking is to develop in the West, Islamic bankers must try to demonstrate to Western banking authorities that Islamic banks can function simultaneously under the Islamic *shariah* and Western banking laws. That may not be easy, however, as is clear from a statement made in London by the Governor of the Bank of England to the Arab Bankers' Association on 2 October 1984:

There has been much debate about Islamic banking in the past year or two, but the practical implementation is as yet far from complete.

Even in those countries where Islamic banking is most developed, many details still do not seem to have been settled, nor have they been subjected to the test of large scale use in a variety of circumstances. A central feature of the UK banking system, and one which is now enshrined in our legal framework, is that of capital certainty for depositors.

One of the crucial principles underlying Islamic banking, as I understand it, is that depositors should share fully in the fortunes of the institution receiving their funds. Although detailed interpretations of the requirements may vary, there usually appears to be no capital certainty for the depositor as to his original deposit, for certainty as to the rate of return on it.

This is of course a perfectly acceptable mode of investment, but it does not fall within the long established and well understood definition of what constitutes banking in this country.

The bank of England is not legally able to authorize under the Banking Act an institution which carries on business in this way because it does not take deposits as defined under the Act; moreover, there would be numerous supervisory problems, including those involved in assessing the capital adequacy of an institution engaging in essentially capital-uncertain transactions.

It is also important not to risk misleading and confusing the general public by allowing two essentially different banking systems to operate in parallel. This is not to say, however, that such types of facility cannot be provided in this country; and it may well be possible for them to be accommodated within other areas of our financial system.

But the institutions covered cannot hold themselves out to be a bank, or use a banking name.

NOTES

1. In a typical African traditional mutual-help association, each participant pays a certain sum into a common fund at stipulated intervals, and the total amount received at the time of each collection is allocated to one participant, whose name is drawn by lot. That participant is not included in subsequent drawings, which continue at regular intervals until all participants in turn have received the same amount. Hence the first participant to receive the kitty gets a completely interest-free loan, the last participant to receive it is a lender who obtains no interest, and the other participants combine in varying degrees the status of noninterest-earning lender and noninterest-paying borrower.

2. The Tanach consists of the Pentateuch (comprising the first five Books of the Tanach—the Books of Genesis, Exodus, Leviticus, Numbers, and Deuteronomy), the Neveem (comprising the Books of the Prophets) and the Kettuvim (comprising the other books). The Pentateuch (a term of Greek origin) is known as the Torah in Hebrew and is believed by Orthodox Jews to have been handed down to Moses on Mount Sinai; it embodies basic laws of moral and physical conduct, interspersed with narratives.

The Talmud is a compilation of the Oral Law of the Jews (elucidations and commentaries on the Written Law contained in the Torah). It consists of two main parts, the Mishnah and the Gemara. The Mishnah, written in Hebrew, contains the authoritative corpus of Jewish oral law and tradition developed on the basis of the Torah. It was prepared by the sages who lived in Palestine before the destruction of the Second Temple (c.e. [Common Era] 70 or a.d. 70) and a century and a half thereafter. The Gemara, written in Aramaic (which replaced Hebrew as the language spoken by the Jews after the sixth century b.c.e. [Before the Common Era]) consists of commentaries on and interpretations of the Torah and the Mishnah. The legal parts of the Mishnah and the Gemara are known as the *Halakah*, and the literary parts, illustrating the application of legal and moral principles through parables, tales and anecdotes, are known as the *haggadah*.

3. In this work, usually known in English as the *Strong Hand*, Maimonides

compiled and organized the voluminous corpus of Jewish oral law, producing a reference work intended for use by rabbis, judges and laymen.

4. Maimonides, *Strong Hand*.

5. "And the Lord spoke unto Moses in Mount Sinai, saying: Speak unto the children of Israel, and say unto them: When ye come into the land which I give you, then shall the land keep a sabbath unto the Lord.

"Six years thou shalt sow thy field, and six years thou shalt prune thy vineyard and gather in the produce thereof.

"But in the seventh year shall be a sabbath of solemn rest for the land, a sabbath unto the Lord; thou shalt neither sow thy field, nor prune thy vineyard.

"That which groweth of itself of thy harvest thou shalt not reap, and the grapes of thy undressed vine thou shalt not gather; it shall be a year of solemn rest for the land.

"And the sabbath-produce of the land shall be food for you: for thee, and for thy servant and for thy maid, and for thy hired servant and for the settler by thy side that sojourns with thee;

"And for thy cattle, and for the beasts that are in thy land, shall all the increase thereof be for food.

"And thou shalt number seven sabbaths of years unto thee, seven times seven years; and there shall be unto thee the days of seven sabbaths of years, even forty and nine years" (Leviticus 25:1–8).

6. Mishnah Baba Metziah 5:8–9.

7. Baba Metziah 63b; 5:4, 6:2–5; and Yad, Malveh 5:9, 8:12.

8. Baba Metziah 5:10.

9. Baba Metziah 63b.

10. Baba Metziah 5:4, 5:6; 70a; and Yad, Malveh 5:9, 8:12.

11. Baba Metziah 5:1, 5:2; 64b.

12. Baba Metziah 5:10.

13. Yad, Malveh 5:13.

14. Baba Metziah 5:10; Yad, ibid.

15. Yad, Malveh 5:12.

16. Baba Metziah 5:11, 75b; and Yad, Malveh 4:2.

17. Baba Metziah 70b.

18. Makkot 24a.

19. Mechilta on Exodus 22:25.

20. Shabbat 63a; Deuteronomy 15:9; and Yad, Malveh Veloveh I, 1.

21. "The Principles of Jewish Law," edited by Menachem Elon, *Encyclopaedia Judaica*, p. 504.

22. Tosefta to Baba Metziah 70b.o.u. tashikh.

23. Anthony Burgess, *Shakespeare*, London: Penguin Books, 1972, p.137.

24. This passage from Pothier is quoted in *Capital and Interest* by Eugen von Böhm-Bawerk (New York: Augustus M. Kelley, Publishers, 1970), 52- 53.

25. See A.R.J. Turgot, *Mémoire sur les prêts d'argent* (1763).

26. This "time-distance" argument anticipated the theory of interest formulated by the Austrian economist Eugen von Böhm-Bawerk, who in *Capital and Interest* (1884) and *Positive Theory of Capital* (1889) sought to demonstrate that interest was not participation in the productivity of capital nor the price paid for renting capital nor a tribute extracted from an exploited borrower but simply the price of

time or the difference in the valuation of present goods and future goods. Subsequently, the United States economist Irving Fisher, in *The Rate of Interest* (New York: Macmillan Company, 1907), sought to rectify Böhm-Bawerk's theory by relating the concept of interest to an individual's preference for current as opposed to future consumption and to the individual's "willingness" or "impatience" concerning the sacrifice of present income for future income. "Time preference" (the expression invented by Fisher) varies according to each individual's assets and other circumstances.

27. See, for example, Abdullah Yusuf Ali, *The Holy Quran: Text, Translation, and Commentary*, New York: Hafner Publishing Company, 1938, from which the passages quoted in this study have been taken.

28. Ibn Kathir was a famous Koranic scholar of the fourteenth century.

29. *Shorter Encyclopaedia of Islam*, edited on behalf of the Royal Netherlands Academy by H.A.R. Gibb and J.H. Kramers, Ithaca, N.Y.: Cornell University Press, 1953, p. 471.

30. *Ulama* (sometimes *Ulema*) is the plural of the Arabic word *'Alim*, meaning a learned and respected teacher or lawyer.

31. *Shariah* is the general Arabic word for "law," its literal meaning being "the way to the watering place." In a religious sense it signifies the rules applicable to all aspects of life implicitly or explicitly made known by God. Early in the eighth century four jurists—Abu Hanifa al Noaman, Malik bin Anas, Mohamed bin Idris as Shafi and Ahmed bin Hanbal—began determining whether the law was being applied in conformity with the Koranic principles and drew up an Islamic legal code. They founded four schools of jurisprudence: the Hanifi, Maliki, Shafi and Hanbali schools. As formulated by these and other Muslim religious leaders, the *shariah* encompasses both doctrine and practice of the law with detailed guidance regarding religious rituals and the ethics of social behavior. The *shariah* is derived from four main sources: the Koran; the Sunna, a corpus of Islamic learning, consisting of the Hadith (the day-to-day actions and sayings of the Prophet as recounted by his companions and recorded in the two centuries following his death) and similar records of the actions and sayings of the Prophet's companions and of later authorities, including the founders of the four schools of Islamic jurisprudence; the Ijtihad, the opinions of the *ulemas*; and the Ijma or consensus of Muslims, which has played a major role in the definition of the meaning of the Koran and the Sunna.

32. William Pike, "Iran's Banks Go Back to the Roots," *South: The Third World Magazine*, June 1984, 39.

33. The members of the International Association of Islamic Banks are: Nasser Social Bank, Cairo, Egypt; Faisal Islamic Bank, Cairo, Egypt; Dubai Islamic Bank, U.A.E.; Faisal Islamic Bank, Khartoum, Sudan; Kuwait Islamic Finance House, Kuwait; Bahraini Islamic Bank, Bahrain; Gulf Islamic Investment Corporation, Bharain; International Islamic Bank of Investment and Development, Sharjah; Investment Corporation of Pakistan, Karachi, Pakistan; House Building Finance Corporation of Pakistan, Karachi, Pakistan; Small Business Financing Corporation of Pakistan, Karachi, Pakistan; Islamic Solidarity Bank of Sudan, Khartoum, Sudan; Faisal Islamic Bank, Bahrain; Faisal Islamic Bank, Guinea; Faisal Islamic Bank, Senegal; Faisal Islamic Bank, Niger; Faisal Islamic Bank, Bahamas; Faisal Islamic Bank, Cyprus; Islamic Investment Company, Khartoum, Sudan; Islamic

Investment Company, Bahrain; Islamic Investment Company, Conakry, Guinea; Islamic Investment Company, Dakar, Senegal; Islamic Investment Company, Niger; Islamic Bank of Sudan, Khartoum, Sudan.

34. *Financial Times*, 27 March 1985, 22.

35. *The Middle East*, August 1984, 44.

36. Ibid.

37. Michael J. Moran, "Recent Financial Activity of Nonfinancial Corporations," *Federal Reserve Bulletin*, May 1984, 407.

38. Islamic Development Bank, *Eighth Annual Report*, 1403 H (1982–1983), p. 70.

39. Paying *zakat* is one of the five basic duties of the Muslim, the others being: reciting in public at least once in a lifetime the *shahada*, or short creed: "There is no God but Allah, and Mohamed is His Prophet"; engaging in *salat* (worship or formal prayer) five times a day: at dawn, at noon, at mid-afternoon, at sunset and about two hours after sunset; practicing *sawm*, the fast observed during the lunar month of Ramadan "in which the Koran was sent down" and during which the Koran enjoins Muslims to refrain from all food and drink and other pleasures of the senses during daylight hours; and undertaking *hajj*, the pilgrimage to the *Kaaba*, the shrine in Mecca, once in a lifetime (provided that the person supports himself or herself during the journey and makes arrangements for his or her dependents to be taken care of during his or her absence).

40. See Z. Ahmed, M. Iqbal, and M.F. Kahn, *Money and Banking in Islam*, jointly published by the International Centre for Research in Islamic Economics of King Abdel Aziz University in Jeddah and the Institute of Policy Studies in Islamabad, 1983.

41. Islamic Development Bank, *Eighth Annual Report*, 1403 H (1982–1983), pp. 49, 50.

3   United States Interest Rates and the International Debt Imbroglio

THE 1982–1984 INTERNATIONAL DEBT CRISIS

The impact of United States interest levels on the developing world is demonstrated clearly by the role they played in the genesis of the 1982–1984 international debt crisis. The impact is also evident in the role that United States interest rates have been playing in its sequel, the continuing international debt imbroglio, and by the emphasis placed on those rates in the various proposals aimed at making the developing countries' debt more manageable.

The international debt crisis was triggered by Mexico's announcement on 20 August 1982 that it could no longer meet its debt servicing payments. In fact, the international debt situation had been deteriorating for a long time, particularly since the first oil price increase in 1973. However, most developing countries' debt-service ratios (the proportion of foreign exchange earnings from exports of merchandise and services that is used for interest and amortization payments) had remained within manageable limits until the second oil price increase, in 1979. Then, owing to the onset of a world-wide recession, which caused a fall in the prices paid for the debtor countries' exports, those countries found themselves increasingly unable to meet their debt-servicing payments. Their position was further aggravated by the effects of higher dollar interest rates, given the proportion of their debts bearing variable interest rates and the importance of roll-over credits and short-term liabilities in their external debts.

The external indebtedness of the developing countries—particularly the Latin American countries—had been rising at a rate that clearly could not have continued for long without becoming unsustainable, except in an extremely favorable world economic situation. The second oil price increase, the lingering recession and high dollar interest rates made the borrowing countries realize that they could no longer prevent their financial situation from worsening by borrowing more.

The Scope of the Crisis

According to the International Monetary Fund, the external debt of the developing countries (excluding the eight Middle Eastern oil exporters: the Islamic Republic of Iran, Iraq, Kuwait, the Libyan Arab Jamahiriya, Oman, Qatar, Saudi Arabia and the United Arab Emirates for which external debt statistics are either not available or are small in relation to external assets) grew at an average rate of 19 percent per annum in 1977–1981, amounting to $332.4 billion in 1977, $470.9 billion in 1979 and $660.5 billion in 1981. The rate of growth of developing countries' external debt subsequently slowed down, falling to 5.25 percent annually in 1983 and 1984. In the two latter years, the external debt of the developing countries amounted to $790.7 billion and $827.7 billion respectively. The growth of the external debt was projected to fall to about 4 percent annually in United States dollar terms in 1985 and 1986, when the external debt is expected to amount to $865.3 billion and $896.5 billion respectively.

The aggregate debt of the non-oil developing countries grew more than fivefold in nominal terms and more than doubled in real terms from 1973 to 1983. During that period, the cumulative current account deficit was financed as follows: nondebt-creating flows (official transfers, direct investment flows, allocations of special drawing rights (SDRs), valuation adjustments and gold monetization), 29 percent; long-term borrowing from official creditors, other than monetary institutions (mainly export credits and credits from international institutions), 22 percent; and borrowing from private markets (almost entirely from banks), 29 percent. In 1973, nondebt-creating flows to non-oil developing countries were almost as large as those countries' total external borrowing, but by 1978 and 1981 they were only one-half and one-third as large respectively, reflecting a definite shift in the pattern of financing current account deficits and a considerable increase in commercial bank borrowing. Much commercial bank borrowing consisted of loans contracted at variable interest rates; such loans accounted for an increasing share of the non-oil developing countries' aggregate debt, rising from 5 percent in 1972 to more than 40 percent in 1982 and even to over 75 percent for a number of major debtors.

Although reliance on variable interest rates benefited developing countries when interest rates declined, it meant that market interest rates affected their total debt servicing commitments more frequently than before, raised the cost of past debts as well as the cost of new borrowing, and introduced an element of unpredictability in the management of the maturity profile of their outstanding bank debts.

The upward trend in United States interest rates generated upward pressures on interest rates worldwide. That situation was compounded by the increase in the spreads over basic international rates charged by banks on loans to developing countries in order to compensate for what the banks perceived as higher credit risks. High real interest rates on a mounting debt combined with falling export revenues worsened the developing countries' external position and caused a serious decline in their ability to service their debts.

The developing countries' aggregate debt, which in the period 1973–1981 had represented an annual average of about 120 percent of the value of their exports of goods and services, climbed to 148 percent of that value in 1982 and to 157.9 percent in 1983 but fell to 151.3 percent in 1984; it was projected by the IMF to fall further to 148.5 percent in 1985 and 141.5 percent in 1986. The developing countries' debt-service ratio (covering all interest payments and amortization payments on debts with an initial maturity of over twelve months but excluding service payments on IMF drawings), which had never exceeded 20 percent before 1981, rose to 20.9 percent in 1981, jumped to 24.6 percent in 1982 and declined to 22.2 percent in 1983 and to 22.5 percent in 1984 as a result of substantial debt reschedulings; it was projected by the IMF to stand at 23.1 percent in 1985 and 22 percent in 1986. The debt-service ratios of a number of indebted developing countries, including the largest, were much higher than those averages. Interest payments alone absorbed 14.3 percent of the developing countries' export earnings in 1982, compared with 5.8 percent in 1977 and 8.9 percent in 1980; the interest payments ratio fell to 13.5 percent in 1983 and 13 percent in 1984, and according to IMF projections was expected to decline to 12.7 percent in 1985 and 11.4 percent in 1986.

Within these debt-service ratio and interest-payments ratio aggregates, the situation of the various regions has varied considerably. The debt-management problem became particularly critical for Latin America, and as a result the debt-service ratio of the developing countries of the Western hemisphere rose from 28.7 percent in 1977 to 41.5 percent in 1981 and 51.6 percent in 1982, but fell to 41.1 percent in 1983 and 39.4 percent in 1984; it was projected to stand at 40.5 percent in 1985 and 40 percent in 1986. The changes in the interest-payments ratio of the developing countries of the Western hemisphere were even more dramatic: the ratio almost tripled in six years, jumping from 10.4 percent in 1977 to 32.4 percent in 1982, but it fell to 30.5 percent in 1983 and to 28.9 percent in 1984 and was projected to fall further to 27.7 percent in 1985 and 24.9 percent in 1986. For many Latin American countries, debt-servicing payments reached levels that were not sustainable.

The debt-management problem of the developing countries of Africa, although less acute than that of Latin America, has been a source of great concern. The debt-service ratio of those countries as a whole doubled in seven years, rising from 11.9 percent in 1977 to 23.7 percent in 1983, and rising again to 28.3 percent in 1984; it was projected by the IMF to rise even further to 30 percent in 1985 and to decline to 27.7 percent in 1986.

The situation was less disturbing in Asia, where the debt-service ratio increased from 7.6 percent in 1977 to 11.2 percent in 1982 but declined to 10 percent in 1983 and was projected to stay at about the same level in 1984 and 1985. The interest-payments ratio of the Asian countries as a whole rose from 2.9 percent in 1977 to 5.7 percent in 1982 but dropped to 5.1 percent in 1983 and was expected to remain at about the same level in 1984 and 1985.

The seriousness of the developing countries' debt difficulties is reflected in their increasing use of IMF resources to support programs of balance-of-payments adjustment. While the number of industrialized countries that borrowed from the IMF rose from one in 1971 to six in 1982, the number of non-oil developing countries that had recourse to the IMF facilities jumped from thirty-two in 1971 to eighty-six in 1982. Given the increasing demand placed on IMF resources as a result of the debt crisis, a number of steps were taken in 1983 to strengthen its capacity to continue meeting its members' needs. Under the Eighth General Review of Quotas, aggregate quotas were increased from SDR 61.1 billion to SDR 89.2 billion. The General Arrangements to Borrow—a line of credit extended to the IMF by the major Western countries (Belgium, Canada, the Federal Republic of Germany, France, Italy, Japan, the Netherlands, Sweden, Switzerland, the United Kingdom and the United States)—was enlarged from SDR 6.4 billion to SDR 17 billion. An SDR 1.5 billion associated arrangement between Saudi Arabia and the General Arrangements to Borrow was completed. Also completed were other borrowing arrangements totaling SDR 6 billion with the Saudi Arabian Monetary Agency, the Bank for International Settlements, Japan and the National Bank of Belgium. From mid-1982 to mid-1985, the IMF lent some $27 billion to nearly seventy member countries experiencing balance-of-payments problems.

The seriousness of the debt-servicing difficulties facing developing countries is likewise reflected in the large increase in their external payments arrears and particularly in the record number of countries that have negotiated reschedulings of their debts with both official creditors and commercial banks. In the early 1960s, debt reschedulings tended to be arranged mostly on a bilateral basis. Since then, official debts and officially guaranteed debts have been increasingly renegotiated within the framework of "creditor clubs" (informal forums comprising official representatives of creditor countries) and sometimes within the framework of aid consortia, whose negotiation procedures are similar to those of the creditor clubs. The most important and well known of the "creditor clubs" is the Paris Club, set up in 1956 at a meeting of European countries convened to renegotiate outstanding balances in their bilateral accounts with Argentina.

The Paris Club, which is chaired by a senior official of the French Treasury, provides a forum for negotiating the rescheduling of loans granted or guaranteed by official agencies of creditor countries that are members of the Development Assistance Committee of the Organisation for Economic

Co-operation and Development. Although the Club has no formal rules, it operates on the basis of a number of generally accepted guidelines that have emerged over the years. First, to qualify for rescheduling, a debtor country that is a member of the IMF must have an IMF stabilization program in force before the rescheduling can become effective, and in most cases the continuing validity of the Paris Club rescheduling agreement depends on the country's continuing adherence to the terms of that program. The classic IMF stabilization program provides, as appropriate, for devaluation, wage freezes or limitation of wage increases, the ending of price controls, reduction of public spending and reduction of imports. Second, the debtor country should not grant more favored treatment to debts rescheduled outside the framework of the Paris Club. Third, the rescheduling should not encompass short-term debts which have already been rescheduled, although there have been some exceptions to this guideline in special circumstances. Fourth, the reschedulings should cover 85 to 90 percent of the debt falling due in the period to be covered by the rescheduling and should allow for a grace period of as much as five years with repayments being made in an additional period of up to five years, the nonrescheduled portion of the debt usually being repayable during the grace period. Fifth, the rescheduling agreement should cover any payment in arrears and the payments falling due in a specified period of twelve months and in some cases a longer period. The Paris Club usually meets for two days to discuss each rescheduling and the results of the meeting are set forth in Agreed Minutes which enumerate the general guidelines for the rescheduling and provide a basis for subsequent bilateral agreements between the debtor country and its creditors. Only when the bilateral agreements have been reached does the rescheduling achieve legal status.

The number of IMF member countries undertaking a multilateral rescheduling of their debts owed to official creditors under the auspices of the Paris Club rose from three in 1980 to eight in 1981 but fell to six in 1982. However, in the sixteen-month period January 1983–April 1984, there were eighteen such reschedulings, involving an estimated aggregate debt of $10.9 billion. One debt rescheduling, that of Mexico, was conducted at a meeting of creditors held at the Organisation for Economic Co-operation and Development and not under the auspices of the Paris Club. Of the twenty-four rescheduling agreements concluded in the period January 1982–April 1984, two-thirds covered debts owed by African countries.

Commercial bank debts are renegotiated within the framework of informal groupings consisting of banks from various countries with a number of "lead banks," frequently the principal lenders, conducting the negotiations. Because it is difficult, if not impossible, to bring representatives of all the creditor banks to participate in the negotiations, a negotiating or steering committee may be formed to represent the creditor banks in the negotiations with the debtor country. The latter may, for its part, engage an investment firm to negotiate for it or advise it during the negotiating process. The majority of commercial rescheduling arrangements encompass medium-term debts contracted by the public sector in the debtor country, which are not backed by official guarantees in the home countries of the creditor banks. The arrangements may also deal with long-term debts, either through rescheduling or by rolling over earlier liabilities. They may likewise deal with arrears on debt-service obligations.

Commercial bank reschedulings are based on two fundamental principles. First, if a creditor bank seeks to circumvent the agreement by trying to obtain repayment of its loans on a bilateral basis, a "cross default clause" frees the other banks from complying with the terms of the common agreement with the debtor country. The second principle is that, generally speaking, the debtor country must continue making its interest payments while the rescheduling of the principal is being negotiated, and interest arrears must be paid before the rescheduling agreement is signed. Like the Paris Club, the creditor banks involved in a rescheduling usually require the debtor country to have concluded a stabilization program with the IMF before negotiations can begin, or before the end of the consolidation period. The rescheduling usually covers 80 percent of the debt due during that period, in some cases the whole amount, and encompasses loans falling due within the next two years, with a shorter moratorium in the case of arrears. In the period 1978–1982, fourteen countries rescheduled their commercial bank debts, some of them more than once. With the intensification of the debt crisis, the number of countries seeking rescheduling increased sharply and seventeen countries entered into rescheduling agreements in 1983 alone. Between 1978 and 1983, some forty developing countries restructured or requested the restructuring of their external commercial debts. Those countries included the eight countries (Argentina, Brazil, Chile, Mexico, the Philippines, Yugoslavia and Venezuela) which accounted for 70 percent of the credits granted to developing countries by commercial banks. Four of those countries (Argentina, Brazil, Mexico and Venezuela) accounted for over 50 percent of those credits, so that default by any one of them would have a ripple effect throughout the international banking system, frightening depositors and shareholders alike.

The Causes of the Crisis

The international debt crisis was preceded by nine years of accelerated borrowing by developing countries, mostly middle-income and high-income countries, primarily on the international capital markets. Indeed, the high-income developing countries were deriving more than half of their non-equity external capital flows from those markets, mostly in the form of medium-term loans from commercial banks. A limited number of developing countries also managed to raise funds by floating debt obligations on the international bond markets.[1] Following the first oil price rise in 1973 and the elimination in the United States of all controls on capital movements[2] the international capital markets became the major financial intermediaries between the deficit countries and the new surplus countries (that is, the OPEC countries) as well as the traditional surplus countries such as the Federal Republic of Germany, Japan and Switzerland.

Eager to recycle their deposits from the OPEC payment surpluses, which had enlarged their loanable resources to a point where they far exceeded credit demand from domestic customers, the Western banks actively or even aggressively sought lending opportunities in the third world and Eastern Europe, with the overt or tacit approval of their governments. These governments did not wish to impose further burdens on their budgets and their taxpayers by increasing their official development assistance to developing countries but realized that unless those countries' urgent need for additional finance was met, important foreign policy goals and economic interests would be jeopardized. Through roll-over credits Western banks were able to transform relatively short-term deposits into relatively long-term lending. Until mid-1982, the Western banks, like official and commercial circles in Western countries, held the view that recycling through the international banking network was consistent with the promotion of world trade and economic growth and did not pose any serious problem. As the international lending policies of Western banks become more optimistic, increasingly aggressive competition for international business led in a number of cases to loans being extended to sovereign borrowers without due attention to their internal situation and policies or the economic feasibility of investment projects. The lending banks probably assumed that they would eventually be reimbursed in any event, since a sovereign borrower, unlike a commercial borrower, inevitably continues to exist even in default and cannot go into liquidation. They also assumed that foreign policy considerations would lead their governments to assume the role of ultimate underwriters if the borrowers defaulted.

Developing countries, taking advantage of the easy availability of credit and of the very low or even negative real interest rates (measured in relation to the dollar unit value of the borrowing country's exports) resulting from inflation, not only entered into loan contracts based on excessively optimistic premises but were also tempted to over-borrow. In Latin American countries with rapidly expanding economies and very promising export potential, foreign borrowing was in many cases used to implement a strategy of building up domestic industries to supply internal markets, which also entailed maintaining high protective tariffs on imports with a consequent overvaluation of national currencies. Such overvaluation, which made the dollar appear cheap, encouraged private firms to borrow abroad. The Latin American approach thus differed markedly from that adopted by the East Asian countries, which by and large used foreign capital to expand their export industries and thereby increased their inflows of foreign exchange, while at the same time imposing relatively few restrictions on imports. The East Asian countries' approach obliged them to enhance their competitiveness on world markets and prevented them from allowing their currencies to become overvalued. Hence, they have been able to accumulate foreign exchange reserves which have allowed them to cope with unfavorable developments in international capital markets.

Many developing countries resorted to commercial borrowing on the over-confident assumption that they could generate the trading surpluses required to service their debts without any significant decline in the real living standards of their peoples. In fact, between 1973 and 1980, the export earnings of the non-oil developing countries did indeed more or less keep pace with the growth of their debts. However, that assumption was subsequently invalidated by the second oil price increase in 1979, the protracted world-wide recession and the rise in real interest rates.

Throughout the debt crisis there were two questions relevant to the formulation of future lending and borrowing policies that were rarely, if ever, asked and never comprehensively answered. The first question was whether commercial lending is an appropriate method of transferring financial resources to developing countries. That question was all the more relevant because the debt crisis affected most borrowing developing countries to a greater or lesser degree, irrespective of their political and economic systems, the efficiency of their public and private sectors, the size of their per capita GNPs, or whether they were importers or exporters of oil. This would seem to indicate that the debt crisis was created at least partially by the terms of the borrowing, a hypothesis apparently substantiated by the fact that the crisis was least acute in the poorest borrowing developing countries, which have never been lent large sums by commercial banks, and most acute in the wealthiest developing countries, whose commercial bank debt constitutes a large part of their aggregate foreign debt. There would therefore seem to be reasonable grounds for concluding that commercial bank lending is not the most appropriate method of transferring financial resources to developing countries. It may, of course, be an acceptable or even constructive method of financing so long as the borrowing country manages its debt maturity profile with great prudence and provided that:

—The proceeds of borrowing are used to finance productive investment that yields a return commensurate with the real cost of borrowing

—The proceeds of borrowing are used to build up the borrowing country's export potential and/or its import substitution capacity to a point where the external

debt can be serviced without any serious adverse effect on the country's terms of trade
—The proceeds of borrowing are not used to finance food imports in order to alleviate nonemergency shortages brought about by inadequate agricultural policies
—The proceeds of borrowing are not used to finance budget deficits resulting from inadequate tax efforts
—Recourse to external borrowing does not become a substitute for efforts aimed at the mobilization and productive use of domestic savings and the maximization and productive use of foreign exchange earnings
—Recourse to external borrowing does not foster unethical use of domestic savings or of the proceeds of borrowing

If these conditions are not fulfilled, borrowing from foreign sources, whether banks or individual investors, may end in default even when the borrower is a sovereign state. In fact, the incapacity of states to pay their debts is an age-old problem. Of the thirteen Greek states which borrowed from the temple of Apollo at Delos in the fourth century B.C., eleven defaulted and four-fifths of the loans were never repaid. Thereafter, the temple became somewhat disinclined to lend to sovereign borrowers, opting instead to make loans to individuals who could pledge land as collateral.

The intervening centuries provide innumerable examples of default by sovereign borrowers, but perhaps not surprisingly the default rate has been particularly high among developing countries in the nineteenth and twentieth centuries. In the 1820s, Gran Colombia (which in 1830 separated into Bolivia, Colombia and Ecuador) defaulted on the loans it had floated in London. In the nineteenth century, Haiti defaulted on the loans it had contracted in Paris to help pay the 150 million franc indemnity France had demanded as compensation for property lost by French colonists when Haiti became independent in 1804. In 1892 the difficulties experienced by Argentina in repaying its debts created serious problems for Baring Brothers, the British merchant bank, which was finally bailed out by the Bank of England. United States lenders fared no better than their British and French counterparts; by the end of the 1930s, Latin American countries had defaulted on almost 80 percent of the debts they had contracted in the United States.

However, the defaults have not been confined to developing countries. Gaston Jèze observed in 1935 in his course at the Academy of International Law:

With the exception of a few small States (Switzerland, Holland), all the others have failed more or less seriously to meet their obligations. . . . The example of default by debtors comes from higher up. . . . The most powerful States, which prided themselves on having always met their obligations, have defaulted: England,

Germany, Belgium, France, the United States and so on. Following in their footsteps, most States have done the same.[3]

Indeed, at a 1932 meeting in Lausanne, debtor industrialized countries had agreed to waive the debts owed to them provided that the United States would waive the debts owed to it. The United States had refused to do so, and the other debtor countries with the exception of Finland had announced that they considered their war debts cancelled. In response, the United States had in 1934 enacted federal legislation under which it became an offense to sell in the United States bonds issued by any foreign government that had defaulted on its commitments toward the United States government. At the same time, a number of state legislatures had enacted legislation forbidding institutional investors from acquiring bonds of foreign governments. That prohibition, which stemmed in part from an isolationist tendency in the United States and from its lack of a tradition of foreign lending, was, according to Sir Arthur Lewis, "a blow at international investment." He recalled that when the International Bank for Reconstruction and Development was formed at the end of the Second World War, "its President had to spend nearly two years touring the state legislatures and persuading them to pass Acts permitting institutional investors to hold bonds issued by this Bank."[4]

Although the United States Congress and state legislatures had reacted sharply to the failure of foreign governments to honor their war debts, defaults and debt repudiations were at the origin of current state constitutional restrictions on state borrowing. Because of mounting debt requirements and declining revenues resulting from the depression of 1837, nine states—Mississippi, Florida, Arkansas, Indiana, Illinois, Michigan, Maryland, Pennsylvania and Louisiana—had defaulted on their obligations in 1841 and 1842, and several others narrowly missed defaulting. Four of those states—Arkansas, Florida, Michigan and Mississippi—subsequently repudiated part of their debts. Public disapproval eventually led to the adoption of state constitutional provisions limiting the power of state legislatures to incur debt. Today forty-three states have significant constitutional debt restrictions. In twenty of them a constitutional amendment is a prerequisite for borrowing. In twenty others, borrowing is allowed only after a referendum. There are no constitutional restrictions on borrowing at the federal level, but borrowing by the Treasury Department has long been limited by Congress. Specific congressional authorization for federal borrowing was required before 1917; from 1917 to 1938 Congress set maximum figures for each type of loan, and since 1938 Congress has set a maximum figure for overall federal borrowing.

The second and even more crucial question raised by the debt crisis was: what use has been made of the money borrowed? Admittedly, much of the borrowing was used to finance unprecedented deficits in the balance-of-trade accounts of the oil-importing countries resulting from increases in the price of oil and, to some extent, from the continued importation of other essential goods. Before 1973 the structural deficits on current external accounts of the developing countries, which were relatively small, had been financed mainly through official capital transfers, direct investment and import finance. The greatly increased use by oil-importing developing countries of international bank loans to meet their growing external financing requirements after 1973 contrasted sharply with the course followed by the industrialized countries. The industrialized nations were in a position to finance their balance-of-payments deficits, caused by the oil price increases, by attracting direct inflows of funds from the members of the Organization of Petroleum Exporting Countries (OPEC) and by borrowing in the international bond markets. It is also true that some of the funds borrowed by developing countries were invested in projects that have increased the debtor country's ability to produce and to export, either directly or indirectly.

On the other hand, developing countries have often resorted to external borrowing for less urgent or less worthwhile purposes. First, the proceeds of external borrowing have sometimes been used to overexpand the public sector, despite obvious inefficiency and mismanagement of public enterprises. Although some public enterprises have been able to generate substantial financial surpluses, many have not yet done so. The average rate of return yielded by some successful public enterprises has often been significantly lower than the cost of borrowing, and administered prices combined with rising operating costs have often led to a profit squeeze. Some public enterprises earn just enough to maintain themselves in a state of borderline solvency, and others have been financing their investment programs by simply enjoying preferential tax treatment or refraining—with the tacit consent of the tax authorities—from meeting their tax liabilities, thus reducing the funds available for allocation in the government budget and making the optimal allocation of investment resources more difficult.

Many public enterprises have consistently had a deficit and have survived only with the help of direct budget transfers, discretionary government subsidies, wholly or partially earmarked taxes and so on. Generally, public enterprises, particularly those that are potentially able to operate competitively, should not be supported by taxpayers and should be able to generate sufficient income to cover their expenses and finance their future expansion. Despite the shortcomings of the public sector, the international debt crisis has indirectly enhanced the importance of that sector in some Latin American countries, where governments have had to help pay off the foreign debts of some private firms to prevent them from being forced into bankruptcy, thus bringing them under the wing of the state.[5]

Second, the money borrowed has often been used to finance projects selected not because they were potentially profitable or corresponded to the country's priority needs but because they were aggressively pushed by foreign promotors or suppliers. The eagerness of suppliers to get orders very often made it difficult to carry out a sufficiently cautious assessment of a project's profitability or of the country's ability to repay the new credit, taking into account its overall debt-repayment capacity.

Third, the money borrowed was sometimes used to purchase arms, although the borrowing countries were facing no external threat. Fourth, the money borrowed was often used to support national currencies through intervention on foreign exchange markets. This lowered the price of imports and made it easier for the well off to buy imported luxury goods such as cars, television sets and refrigerators.

Fifth, the money borrowed or equivalent amounts often found their way into foreign bank accounts or were used to finance the purchase of foreign property. A former Secretary of Information of Costa Rica observed:

Here in Latin America, a large part of what gets in through the front door gets out through the back. In the last three years, some $15 billion was invested in real estate or deposited in foreign banks by Central Americans. This is nearly twice the sum that the Kissinger Commission proposed for the region—$8 billion in five years. . . . Assistance programs are clearly not the key. Political reform is urgent and indispensable. Without it nothing will help.[6]

According to the fifty-fourth annual report of the Bank for International Settlements, capital flight from Latin America as a whole may be estimated to have amounted to at least $50 billion during 1978–1982. The report contains the following comments:

Those Latin American countries whose residents have been exporting capital on a massive scale would be well advised to put their house in order so as to end this capital outflow and even, hopefully, to draw some of the flight capital back. It is too much to expect the rest of the world—whether multilateral institutions, governments, banks or corporations—to perform the development functions that these countries' own nationals refuse to assume. Clearly, the burden of interest charges would look much less frightening if it could be calculated in terms of net interest owed to the rest of the world, i.e. the interest to be paid on external debt minus the income received (but not necessarily repatriated) by the owners of the exported capital.[7]

According to the 2 July 1984 issue of *Time* magazine, experts believe that between 1979 and mid-1984 as much as $70 billion left Latin America, an amount well over one-third of the debt accumulated by Latin America in the same period. This has prompted the magazine to observe: "Is the money lost for good? In the case of funds that went into foreign bank accounts, there is hope that some will return home if currency rates are corrected and investment opportunities improve. But the money that was wasted or stolen is undoubtedly gone for ever."[8]

A former minister of finance and director of national planning in Colombia, who is currently Director of the IMF's Western Hemisphere Department, has analyzed the situation in the following terms:

One of the most surprising results of any analysis of Latin America's external debt data is the lack of a direct correlation between the aggregate debt and the deficit on current account and changes in reserves. Theoretically, a country or a region taken as a whole cannot accumulate external debt in excess of the total of its deficits on current account and the changes in its international reserves. It is assumed that external liabilities cannot be greater than the amount of the deficit less the losses in reserves. In the case of Latin America, however, external liabilities exceeded estimated external financing needs. The reason is well known: capital flight. . . . The thrust of the foregoing analysis is that the countries in question did not follow the correct policies to take advantage of the increase in external financing made available to them. The surprising fact is that in most of the cases the increased inflow of external funds was accompanied by a drop in domestic savings as a percentage of GDP. Thus, given the imbalance created between the growth of external debt and domestic capital accumulation, a debt crisis was virtually inevitable. In sum, the region lacked not funds but better policies for the use of these funds.[9]

Unfortunately, governments that lack foresight or even are profligate or corrupt, were only too often granted loans by banks that studiously refrained from inquiring what they planned to do with the money or from applying any of the criteria routinely applied to domestic borrowers: capacity, character and collateral. The resulting debts may be inherited by more efficient and more honest governments, which will then be forced to assume the burden of repaying funds that never benefited their countries and for which they have nothing or little to show. In short, the money has in many cases been carelessly lent, carelessly borrowed and carelessly used.

Jeremy Bentham observed almost two centuries ago:

The business of a money-lender has nowhere nor at any time been a popular one. Those who have the resolution to sacrifice the present to the future are natural objects of envy to those who have sacrificed the future to the present. The children who have eaten their cake are the natural enemies of the children who have theirs.[10]

In many cases the burden of repaying the funds lent to developing countries does not fall upon "those who have sacrificed the future to the present," that is, the ruling cliques that have been mainly responsible for those countries' indebtedness. The depressing reality is that in many cases the members of those cliques have—to pursue Bentham's image—not only "eaten their cake" but have also managed to have "cake" securely stored in the form of foreign bank accounts and foreign property. If the debts are to be repaid, they will be repaid through the sacrifice of those who have never had any "cake" and will have to postpone indefinitely any hope of "cake" not only for themselves but also for their children.

Strategies in the Search for a Solution

As it became increasingly clear that the international debt crisis would seriously affect all of the parties involved—the creditor banks, the debtor countries and the countries of the creditor banks—each party began developing its own self-defense strategy to deal with the crisis.

The Strategy of the Creditor Banks. In international banking, as in domestic banking, the risk of loss is evaluated in relation to a bank's capital, and the larger that capital, the greater the safeguard of a bank's solvency. At the end of 1981, eight months before the onset of the international debt crisis, the collective exposure of the banks reporting to the Bank for International Settlements (BIS) relative to their capital was 17.1 percent for Mexico; 15.8 percent for Brazil; 7.9 percent for Venezuela; and 7.5 percent for Argentina (See table 4). The consolidated developing–country exposure of banks registered in the United States in relation to their capital was 34.2 percent for Mexico, 28.5 percent for Brazil, 15.9 percent for Venezuela and 13.3 percent for Argentina. The corresponding exposure of banks registered in the United Kingdom was 21.4 percent for Mexico, 18.5 percent for Brazil, 9.5 percent for Argentina and 8.6 percent for Venezuela (see Table 5). At the end of 1982, the nine largest banks in the United States had a combined debt exposure to Argentina, Brazil, Chile, Mexico and Venezuela equivalent to 1.6 times their capital; the exposure was higher in the case of three of those banks: Manufacturers Hanover Trust (2.6), Citibank (1.7) and Chemical Bank (1.7). In Brazil alone, the exposure of Citibank, Chase Manhattan Bank, Morgan Guaranty, Manufacturers Hanover and Chemical Bank exceeded 50 percent of their capital, the highest percentages being those of Manufacturers Hanover (77.7 percent) and Citibank (73.5 percent). Similarly, the exposure of Citibank, Bank of America, Manufacturers Hanover, Chemical Bank and First National Chicago in Mexico exceeded 50 percent of their capital, the greatest exposures being those of Manufacturers Hanover (66.7 percent) and Chemical Bank (60.0 percent). However, the exposure of United States banks to non-oil developing countries fell from about 170 percent of their capital in 1982 to 130 percent at the end of 1984 and thus returned to the level of the late 1970s.

Information on the country exposure of United States banks has been made available to the public since 1977 when, amid growing concern about the rising indebtedness of oil-importing developing countries, the three federal agencies that supervise bank lending and other bank activities, namely, the Federal Reserve System, the Comptroller of the Currency and the Federal Deposit Insurance Corporation, began conducting a country

Table 4
International Banks: Developing Country Exposure at the End of 1981

Country	Loans In billion $U.S.	Loans as Percentage of Bank Capital [a]
Algeria	8.4	2.5
Argentina	24.8	7.5
Brazil	52.7	15.8
Chile	10.5	3.2
Colombia	5.4	1.6
Indonesia	7.2	2.2
Israel	6.0	1.8
Korea	19.9	6.0
Mexico	56.9	17.1
Nigeria	6.0	1.8
Philippines	10.2	3.1
Thailand	5.1	1.5
Venezuela	26.2	7.9

Source: Bank for International Settlements, Maturity Distribution of International Bank Lending, July 1982; and the IMF staff estimates.

Note: Figures represent aggregate claims of BIS reporting banks on countries outside the BIS reporting area.

a. Capital of banks in the BIS reporting area amounted to about $335 billion U.S. at the end of 1981.

exposure lending survey.[11] In 1979 the survey was supplemented by the introduction of a uniform system for the examination of country risk which is operated by the InterAgency Country Exposure Review Committee, consisting of members from the three federal supervisory agencies. The debt-servicing difficulties experienced by Mexico, Argentina and Brazil in 1982 and 1983 prompted the United States Congress to question whether foreign lending by United States banks was effectively supervised. The Congress therefore enacted in late 1983 the International Lending Supervisory Act, which required the federal supervisory agencies to strengthen the existing system for supervising foreign lending.

The country exposure lending survey, currently carried out on a quarterly basis, covers banks with a foreign office and over $30 million in outstanding foreign loans. It contains information on bank claims on individual countries, the maturity distribution of those claims and the type of borrower. Banks are required to list claims on a country when the claims exceed 1

Table 5
Consolidated Developing Country Exposure of Banks Registered in the United States and the United Kingdom at the End of 1981

| Country | U.S. Bank Claims | | U.K. Bank Claims | |
	In Billion $U.S.	Percentage of Bank Capital[a]	In Billion $U.S.	Percentage of Bank Capital[a]
Algeria	1.2	1.9	0.6	1.7
Argentina	8.4	13.3	3.5	9.5
Brazil	18.2	28.5	6.5	18.0
Chile	5.7	9.0	1.5	4.2
Colombia	3.0	4.8	0.6	1.7
Indonesia	2.1	3.4	0.5	1.5
Israel	2.5	3.9	0.6	1.6
Korea	9.0	14.1	2.5	7.0
Mexico	21.4	34.2	7.8	21.4
Nigeria	1.1	1.7	1.2	3.3
Philippines	5.1	7.9	1.2	3.4
Thailand	1.8	2.9	0.6	1.6
Venezuela	10.1	15.9	3.1	8.6

Source: Federal Financial Institutions Examination Council, Country Exposure Lending Survey, n.d.; and Bank of England, Quarterly Bulletin, n.d.

a. Bank capital estimated by the IMF staff on the basis of published data in the Federal Reserve Bulletin and the Bank of England, Quarterly Bulletin, is $63.7 billion for the United States and $36.2 billion for the United Kingdom.

percent of their assets or 20 percent of their capital. They are also required to list countries whose claims represent between 0.75 percent and 1.0 percent of their assets or between 15 percent and 20 percent of their capital, together with their aggregate claims on those countries.

The uniform system for the examination of country risk currently classifies loans adversely affected by country risk in three main categories: "loss" for loans regarded as uncollectible; "value-impaired" for loans whose quality is considered impaired by the debtor's protracted inability to make payments and by the lack of any reasonable assurance that regular debt service will be resumed in the near future; and "substandard" for loans for which the debtor country has not been fulfilling its debt-servicing obligations, as shown by arrearages or forced restructurings. There is a fourth category, "other transfer risk problems," for loans considered to be adversely affected by country risk problems but not badly enough to be classified as "substandard." The Internal Lending Supervision Act is also aimed at alleviating debt-servicing burdens on debtor countries and at discouraging foreign lending made to increase a bank's current income. It provides that the fees banks receive for originating and restructuring foreign loans should not be absorbed into income immediately but should be deferred and amortized over the effective life of the loan. The size of foreign loan fees may be gauged from the fact that at the 1983 Hearings of the Committee on Banking, Finance and Urban Affairs of the House of Representatives it was revealed that the banks involved in the 1982 restructuring of Mexico's debt had been paid some $200 million in fees.

United States banks have not been the only ones facing high levels of exposure. For example, in the United Kingdom at the end of 1983, Lloyds Bank had an exposure to Latin American countries (excluding Mexico) equivalent to 2.3 times its shareholders' funds, and the corresponding exposure of Midland Bank was 2.1 times. The average capital-to-assets ratio for the world's 100 largest banks fell from 4.5 percent in the early 1970s to less than 3.5 percent in mid-1984, the corresponding figures for the 34 largest banks were 5.3 percent in the early 1970s and just over 3.5 percent in mid-1984.

The Western banks' high degree of exposure resulted from lending that, in the words of Lord Lever, economic and financial adviser in the cabinets of the British Prime Ministers Harold Wilson and James Callaghan, "was approved and then encouraged by Western Governments because they recognized that without the provision of new funds, political and economic interests of the highest importance would be at risk."[12] Because of such official encouragement, which often led the banks to give little serious thought to the ability of the borrowing country to pay the interest on its debt or make payments on the principal, the banks have been unwilling to write down their assets to reflect potential losses on their own initiative, although they have had to write off a number of loans to private Latin American firms that were forced into bankruptcy.

The creditor banks reasoned that since their governments had helped to get them into their predicament, they should also, if necessary, help them to get out of it. Banks are well aware that, unlike other economic agents, they will not be left to suffer the full consequences of their imprudence or be abandoned to the merciless verdict of the market because that might damage the overall financial and economic system, which cannot be allowed to disintegrate. They therefore have adopted a strategy with the ultimate objective of having their governments bail them out should their borrowers eventually default. They tried to secure protection for their depositors for all of their deposits—and not only to the maximum insured, as is the case in the United States—and protection for their managers and shareholders as well. Being bailed out by the government means being bailed out by the taxpayers, who are also savers and depositors, a fact wittily emphasized in a cartoon published in *The New York Times* on 24 June 1984, which depicts a glib banker saying to a bemused depositor: "How's this for a deal? You deposit your money in our bank; we lend the money to the third world; if the third world goes bust, you pay us back?"

In earlier times, the creditor banks would have relied on their governments to help them recover their loans by sending official demands for repayment, intervening to take control of the debtor country's finances, or dispatching naval forces to blockade the debtor country or even military forces to occupy it. Thus when Tunisia defaulted on its foreign loans, France, Great Britain and Italy intervened in 1869, took over the country's finances and set up an international commission empowered to collect all revenues and distribute them among Tunisia's creditors. In 1876, when Egypt's ordinary revenues proved insufficient to service the foreign debts contracted in connection with, among other things, the construction of the Suez Canal, its finances were placed under British-French control, with a British official supervising Egypt's revenue and a French official supervising its expenditures.

In the twentieth century, failure to repay debts owed to European and United States creditors led to overt foreign intervention in the affairs of Latin American countries. Thus in 1902 Great Britain, Germany and Italy, acting to collect unpaid loans owed to their nationals in Venezuela, dispatched a joint naval expedition that blockaded and shelled Venezuelan ports and captured Venezuelan gunboats. That intervention led to the formulation in 1902 by Luis Drago, Minister for Foreign Affairs of Argentina, of the Drago doctrine, which called for acceptance of the principle that for the common safety of the South American republics, the collection of pecuniary claims of citizens of any country against the government of any of those republics should not be effected by armed force. The fundamental principle of the Drago doctrine was subsequently embodied in the *Convention Respecting the Limitation of the Employment of Force for the Recovery of Contract Debts*, signed at The Hague on 18 October 1907. The Convention stated that "the contracting powers agree not to have recourse to armed force for the recovery of contract debts claimed from the government of one country by the government of another country as being due to its nationals." However, the Convention also stated that the foregoing provision would not be applicable "when the debtor State refuses or neglects to reply to an offer of arbitration, or after accepting the offer, prevents any compromise from being agreed on, or after the arbitration fails to submit to the award."

Despite the principle of the nonuse of force embodied in the Drago doctrine, the United States intervened in 1905 in the Dominican Republic in the name of the Monroe Doctrine and the even more controversial Roosevelt corollary to it to ensure that Dominican customs revenues were used to repay the debts owed to foreign creditors.[13] In a statement to the Dominican Congress, the Minister of Finance described his country's view of the situation in the following terms: "The payment of interest [*usura*] is threatening to absorb the financial resources of the State and keep the country for ever subservient to foreign creditors, who receive five, ten or more pesos for every peso they lend, despite the guarantees they demand. This snowball is bound before long to become an avalanche that will wipe out the Republic." That critical financial situation, aggravated by chronic political troubles and the competing claims of foreign creditors, gave the United States the pretext to intervene and assume control of the Dominican Republic's finances in 1905.

Under a treaty signed by representatives of the Dominican Republic and the United States in February 1905, the United States was to assume responsibility for the collection of the customs duties of the Dominican Republic and endeavour to negotiate a settlement with the latter's creditors. Pending action on the treaty by the United States Senate, the two governments entered into a *modus vivendi* under which the President of the Dominican Republic resolved:

To name a person to receive the revenues of all the custom-houses of the Republic, and, for the better guaranteeing of the latter's creditors, to leave to the President of the United States the designation of the person who will receive said revenues, the Dominican Executive conferring upon him the office, providing always that the designation shall be satisfactory to it.

The 1905 treaty was not approved by the United States Senate, but the latter subsequently consented to the ratification of a convention between the Dominican Republic and the United States on the collection and application of customs revenues that entered into force on 8 July 1907. The convention provided:

That the President of the United States shall appoint a General Receiver of Dominican Customs who, with such Assistant Receivers and other employees of the Receivership as shall be appointed by the President of the United States in his discretion, shall collect all the customs duties accruing at the several customs houses of the Dominican Republic until the payment or retirement of any and all bonds issued by the Dominican Government . . . , and said General Receiver shall apply the sums so collected, as follows:

First, to paying the expenses of the receivership; second, to the payment of interest upon said bonds; third, to the payment of the annual sums provided for amortization of said bonds including interest upon all bonds held in sinking fund; fourth, to the purchase and cancellation or the retirement and cancellation pursuant to the term thereof of any of said bonds as may be directed by the Dominican Government; fifth, the remainder to be paid to the Dominican Government.

The Convention also provided that: "Until the Dominican Republic has paid the whole amount of the bonds of the debt its public debt shall not be increased except by previous agreement between the Dominican Government and the United States. A like agreement shall be necessary to modify the import duties."

Recalling that period of his country's history, the President of the Dominican Republic observed in a statement made on 7 February 1985 at the Third Ministerial Meeting of the Consultation and Follow-up Machinery of the Cartagena Consensus:

The problem of the external debt has been a determining factor in our country's historical and political existence for the past one hundred years. As a result of that problem, we first lost control of our customs service early in the century, because our creditors insisted on it in order to ensure that their loans were repaid. Next, our sovereignty was violated when foreign troops occupied our territory. That occupation lasted for many years, the aim being to guarantee the fulfillment of our international financial obligations.

The Drago doctrine and the Hague Convention notwithstanding, the United States also sent the marines to Haiti in 1915 to seize that country's gold after it had failed to repay its foreign debt. Haiti was at that time experiencing a financial and political crisis whose roots could be traced to the Haitian Revolution, the successful slave revolt that, in the words of Sir Arthur Lewis, had "destroyed a prosperity based upon slavery and substituted for it poverty and freedom,"[14] but had also left Haiti under the constant threat of invasion by France, the former colonial power. To eliminate that threat, Haiti had agreed to pay the indemnity demanded by France as the price of recognizing Haiti's sovereignty and to that end had contracted loans in France in 1825, 1875, 1896 and 1910. Haiti's situation thus contrasts sharply with that of the countries that have acceded to independence since the Second World War; these countries have often received substantial assistance not only from the former colonial power but from the international community, which in the early nineteenth century treated the newly independent Negro state of Haiti as an outcast.

The servicing of the French loans imposed a heavy financial burden on Haiti for nearly a hundred years. Nord Alexis, who was President of Haiti from 1902 to 1908, rightly summed up the situation in the following terms:

It is pointless to talk to me about borrowing. I am opposed to borrowing, both in Haiti and abroad. What has the country ever gained from our foreign loans? Not one cent of the 1875 loan found its way to our treasury. It was a real scandal! The same thing happened in 1896. The country derived very little benefit from the millions borrowed. The final result of the borrowing was to enrich foreign bankers at our expense. We ourselves remain as poor as ever or even poorer. These two loans combined cost us enormous amounts every year for servicing and in addition burden us with a never-ending debt. I do not want my name to be associated with such operations. I am above all the guardian of our heritage, no matter how much it may have been dilapidated by others.

The money borrowed was often stolen by unscrupulous Haitian officials in collusion with foreign lenders. In 1903, President Alexis had appointed a commission which concluded that from 1901 to 1903 the equivalent of about $2 million had been embezzled from the treasury. That sum represented almost half of total annual government revenue during the same period.

The situation created by the servicing of the French loans led to the United States invasion of Haiti and the subsequent forced conclusion of the treaty of 16 September 1915 between the United States and Haiti, which provided in article II:

The President of Haiti shall appoint, upon nomination by the President of the United States, a General Receiver and such aides and employees as may be necessary, who shall collect, receive and apply all customs duties on imports and exports accruing at the several customs houses and ports of entry of the Republic of Haiti.

The President of Haiti shall appoint, upon nomination by the President of the United States, a Financial Adviser, who shall be an officer attached to the Ministry of Finance, to give effect to whose proposals and labors the Ministers will lend efficient aid. The Financial Adviser shall devise an adequate system of public accounting, aid in increasing the revenues and adjusting them to the expenses, inquire into the validity of the debts of the Republic, enlighten both Governments with reference to all eventual debts, recommend improved methods of collecting and applying the revenues, and make such other recommendations to the Minister of Finance as may be deemed necessary for the welfare and prosperity of Haiti.

The treaty stated in article V:

All sums collected and received by the General Receiver shall be applied, first, to the payment of the salaries and allowances of the General Receiver, his assistants and employees and expenses of the Receivership, including the salary and expenses of the Financial Adviser, which salaries will be determined by previous agreement; second, to the interest and sinking fund of the public debt of the Republic of Haiti; and third to the maintenance of the constabulary referred to in Article X, and then the remainder to the Haitian Government for purposes of current expenses.

The treaty stated in article VIII:

The Republic of Haiti shall not increase its public debt except by previous agreement with the President of the United States, and shall not contract any debt or assume any financial obligation unless the ordinary revenues of the Republic available for that purpose, after defraying the expenses of the Government, shall be adequate to pay the interest and provide a sinking fund for the final discharge of such debt.

Thus Haiti, like the Dominican Republic, saw its sovereignty infringed upon as a result of its external debt problem, a situation that tarnished the image created by its heroic and successful struggle to win independence more than a century earlier. Subsequently, a protocol between Haiti and the United States signed on 3 October 1919 provided for the establishment of a claims commission "to examine and pass upon all pecuniary claims against Haiti" with certain specific exceptions that included "the indebtedness represented by the three bond issues of 1875, 1896 and 1910." The protocol also provided for Haiti's issuance of a $40 million loan "to make possible the settlement of the awards rendered by the Claims Commission and the refunding of those obligations mentioned . . . in Article III, and otherwise to establish the finances of Haiti on a firm and solid basis." The loan was floated in 1922, but in 1947 the Haitian government decided to redeem the outstanding portion of the loan to regain Haiti's financial independence.

Today, some creditor banks probably wish that the international climate of opinion would still permit their governments to enforce their claims against debtors in the developing world by military means. Resigned to the fact that a military solution is no longer politically feasible, those banks have envisaged another scenario to achieve the same end by legal means. According to this scenario, legal authorization would be sought to seize all assets in foreign countries belonging to the government of a country that has repudiated its external debts and to natural and juridical persons that are nationals of that country. In particular, all accounts in foreign banks would be blocked, and all ships and aircraft in foreign harbors and airports would be impounded. These banks have allegedly argued that if it were not for the possibility of such a vigorous legal riposte, some debtor countries would already have repudiated their debts.

Most banks realize, however, that although this scenario may have a deterrent effect, its actual implementation would be too fraught with political and legal complications to make it a realistic option. Consequently, their basic strategy is still to rely on their governments to bail them out. Their confidence that their governments will do this was bolstered by the rescue operation mounted in favor of the Continental Illinois Bank and Trust Company by the Federal Deposit Insurance Corporation (FDIC) and the Federal Reserve System, with the participation of a syndicate of United States banks, informally arranged by the Morgan Guaranty Trust. Continental Illinois had outstanding loans to Argentina, Brazil, Mexico and Venezuela that as of 31 December 1983 represented 4.7 percent of its total assets. It was the ninth largest United States lender to Latin America, but its troubles were caused not so much by its Latin American exposure as by shaky loans for domestic oil and gas ventures exceeding $1 billion that it had taken over from Penn Square, an Oklahoma city bank that had collapsed in July 1982.

Following a run by Continental Illinois foreign investors and depositors and the subsequent organization of a rescue package by other United States banks, the federal regulators announced on 18 May 1984 that to safeguard the stability of the financial system, all depositors and all general creditors of Continental Illinois would be protected against any loss irrespective of amount, although the FDIC is legally obligated to insure deposits only up to $100,000 (under that rule, only about 14 percent of the funds deposited with Continental would have been insured by the FDIC). Furthermore, the Federal Reserve explicitly pledged to continue to back up Continental Illinois. The banks' confidence that the authorities would not let them go bankrupt was strengthened further on 28 May 1984 when the Vice-Chairman of the Federral Reserve Board stated in a television interview in Washington that the Federal Reserve was ready to "lend, lend boldly, and keep on lending" should any more major United States banks encounter liquidity problems. Indeed, the central banks of most countries, fearing disruption of financial intermediation and the social consequences of bank failures, have recognized the need to act as lenders of last resort for their domestic banking systems by providing sufficient funds to individual banks whose solvency is threatened by liquidity problems. That need is all the more acute where banks are engaged in international operations. In the aftermath of the collapse of the Herstatt in the Federal Republic of Germany and of the London subsidiary of the Israel–British Bank of Tel Aviv, the Bank for International Settlements had issued on 11 September 1974 the following communiqué on behalf of the Central Bank Governors from the countries of the Group of Ten (Belgium, Canada, the Federal Republic of Germany, France, Italy, Japan, the Netherlands, Sweden, the United Kingdom and the United States) plus Switzerland: "The Governors had an exchange of views on the problem of lender of last resort in the Euromarket. They recognized that it would not be practical to lay down in advance detailed rules and procedures for the provision of temporary liquidity. But they were satisfied that means are available for that purpose and will be used if and when necessary."

The provision by central banks of lender of last resort services is in keeping with the "last resort" doctrine originated by Walter Bagehot in *Lombard Street: A Description of the Money Market* (1873). According to Bagehot, who believed that the lender of last resort should make every effort to ensure the liquidity of the banking system: "Whatever bank or banks keep the ultimate banking reserve of the country must lend that reserve most freely in time of apprehension, for that is one of the charateristic uses of the bank reserve, and the mode in which it attains one of the main ends for which it is kept."[15]

The rescue package initiated in May 1984 proved inadequate, and since no other bank was willing to buy Continental Illinois without substantial government assistance, the federal government on 26 July 1984 committed itself to a $4.5 billion rescue of the bank. The FDIC not only took over the bad loans of Continental Illinois but also assumed ownership of the bank and was expected to continue owning it until it could be returned to ownership by the public. The assumption of temporary ownership by the FDIC represented an unusual development, for in almost 70 percent of the bank failures that had occurred since the Second World War, the FDIC had taken over the bad loans, and another bank had taken over the failed bank itself. In the case of the other failures, the FDIC had reimbursed the insured depositors and had sold the failed bank's assets, with any proceeds remaining after the FDIC had recovered its outlay going to the uninsured creditors and the stockholders.

As part of their strategy, the creditor banks showed great willingness to cooperate with their governments and the IMF. They not only refrained from providing fresh loans unless the borrowing country accepted an IMF austerity program but were even willing to accept certain cuts in their earnings. At an international financial conference in Philadelphia in June 1984, attended by private bankers and government finance officials from twenty-two countries, the Managing Director of the IMF and the Chairman of the Federal Reserve Bank urged bankers to reward debtor countries accepting the IMF austerity recommendations with *lower spreads* (the percentages charged above the United States prime rate), small front-end fees and longer repayment periods.

The Strategy of the Debtor Countries. The strategy of the creditor banks, which realize that their countries' foreign policy interests and economic interests are at stake, has been aimed at ensuring increased involvement of their governments in resolving the crisis. The debtor countries, too, are eager to see the countries of the creditor banks become more involved in efforts to solve their debt problems. Their strategy has therefore been aimed at getting the creditor countries to acknowledge that they share with the creditor banks the major responsibility for the debtor countries' inability to service their debts. To that end, they have adduced three main arguments:

1. The debt crisis has been created partly by the actions of creditor banks and industrialized countries, especially the raising of interest rates, the lowering of commodity prices, and the adoption of protectionist measures that restrict market access for products from developing countries.
2. No matter how much debtor countries cut public spending, reduce real wages, or devalue their currencies, they will be unable to generate the resources they need to keep up with principal and interest payments, but in the process they will be destroying their economies, starving their populations and risking major political upheavals.
3. The creditor banks and their shareholders have already benefited greatly from their lending to developing countries and should therefore resign themselves to writing down the value of their assets and/or seeking financial assistance from their governments.

In a declaration published in the January-February 1984 issue of *World of Banking*, the Federation of Latin American Bankers Associations made the following comments on the external indebtedness of Latin America:

All the parties involved in the problem can be said to have an interest in ignoring it: the creditors to avoid shocking their depositors, and the debtor governments so as not to reveal weaknesses in their economic policies and to avoid the spread of pessimism. . . .

The experience of this first year of attempts at solutions demonstrates two things: first, that the external debt of Latin America, at least as contracted, cannot be paid; second, that creative formulas are necessary, demanding probably very harsh solutions and an immediate application. This first year of negotiations has made the internal situation of the debtors much more difficult and at the same time the possibilities of payment more remote. The debt is too great compared to the Gross National Product of each country and it is overwhelming in relation to the net balance of the foreign exchange rates. . . . Therefore the problem has no other solution except for making the burden compatible with the ability for payment of these countries based on their generating power of net currency.[16]

The Latin American countries have played the leading role in the developing countries' efforts to involve the industrialized countries in the search for a solution to their debt problem; they have met on a number of occasions to coordinate their actions and thereby lend greater weight to their proposals.

In September 1983 the Organization of American States convened a special conference in Caracas to discuss the Latin American debt situation. The international banking community's fear that the conference might establish a "debtor's club" to pressure creditor banks to ease their debt-repayment terms was allayed when the conference ruled out cartel-like action and decided to set up a commission to study ways to ease the region's foreign-debt burden. The United States, while stressing that each country must tighten its belt if the rapid deterioration in the region's balance-of-payments position was to be stopped, committed itself to examining ways of bringing debt-service payments "into line with a country's payment capacity and economic development needs."

In January 1984, a Latin American Economic Conference was convened by the President of Ecuador: it was attended by the heads of state or government of Latin America and the Caribbean or their personal representatives, who adopted the Quito Declaration and Plan of Action. In the Declaration, the participants asserted:

The attitude of the Latin American and Caribbean Governments in recognizing and assuming their obligations calls for an attitude of shared responsibility by the Governments of the creditor countries, the international financing organizations and the international private banks in the solution of the external debt problem, bearing in mind, furthermore, its political and social implications. Therefore, flexible and realistic criteria are required in the renegotiation of the debt, including repayment periods, grace periods, and interest rates compatible with the recovery of economic growth.

The participants also pointed out "that the maladjustment between the fiscal and monetary policies of certain industrialized countries is the cause of the rise in real interest rates which has persisted despite the fact that inflation has been diminished, thereby very seriously exacerbating the present situation." They therefore asked "that the international community make the adjustments necessary to eliminate the causes of this distortion." They reaffirmed "the urgent need to take measures designed to reform the international monetary and financial system."

The Quito Plan of Action calls for a "balanced set of commitments and measures" by both lenders and debtors. With regard to the external debt, the Plan of Action states:

Responsibility for the external debt problem must be shared by the debtor and the developed countries, the international private banking system and the multilateral finance organizations.

The Latin American and Caribbean countries have already assumed their responsibility by making extraordinary adjustments in their economies and enormous efforts to meet their international obligations, despite the high social, political and economic cost involved. Because of these circumstances and the need to maintain adequate levels of development in Latin America and the Caribbean and to avoid greater crises in the international economic and financial system, it is to the mutual benefit of those concerned that an urgent solution be found to the problem of the region's external debt.

Furthermore, the close relationship between trade and financing also requires any solution of the payments problem to take both into consideration and be of a permanent nature.

The adjustment process should operate in the future through an increase in the volume and price of exports and a decrease in real interest rates, and not through additional restrictions of imports vital to the internal economic recovery.

The magnitude of the regional economic recession and the persistence of adverse external factors make it imperative that any external debt arrangements and negotiations, which our countries enter into individually in the future, should harmonize the requirements of debt servicing with the development needs and objectives of each country, by minimizing the social cost of the adjustment processes already under way.

Based on those considerations, the participants adopted the following basic criteria:

(i) In renegotiating the external debt, export earnings income should not be committed beyond reasonable percentages consistent with the maintenance of adequate levels of internal productive activity, taking into account the characteristics of the economies of each country;

(ii) Formulas should be devised to reduce debt service payments, by drastically reducing interest rates, commissions and spreads which substantially increase refinancing costs. Moreover, mechanisms should be explored to stabilize over time the amount of resources annually allocated to debt servicing in accordance with the payments profile of each country;

(iii) Terms and maturities must be substantially longer than at the present time, and grace periods must be broadened; and the possibility of converting a part of the accumulated debt into long-term obligations should be urgently explored, which will require the cooperation of the Governments of developed countries and of international finance agencies;

(iv) The maintenance of a net, adequate and increasing flow of new public and private financial resources for all the countries of the region as an essential component of external debt renegotiations and as a guarantee of social and economic development, should be assured by granting additional commercial and financial credits;

(v) Likewise, in order to enhance our countries' ability to pay, debt renegotiation should be accompanied by commercial measures essential to improving the terms of access for exports from Latin America and the Caribbean in world markets and eliminating increasing protectionism by the developed countries.

The Latin American countries' strategy of seeking to solve their debt problems through concerted action also took the form of mutual self-help measures. Early in 1984 Mexico provided Costa Rica with a short term $50 million bail-out loan to keep that country from defaulting on interest payments on its foreign debt and later, at the end of March 1984, played the leading role in organizing a debt-rescue package for Argentina in the form of a loan for thirty days or so, the aim being to prevent Argentina from becoming the first major Latin American borrower in recent times to shift into a nonaccrual status on its foreign debt.[17] The package consisted of $300 million contributed by the monetary authorities of Brazil, Colombia, Venezuela and Mexico, $100 million put up by the eleven United States commercial banks on the eleven-bank advisory committee of creditor banks, and $100 million contributed by Argentina from its own reserves. At the same time, the United States Treasury promised to lend Argentina $300 million from the Treasury's Exchange Stabilization Fund (ESF) to be used to repay the loans from Brazil, Colombia, Mexico and Venezuela, once Argentina had signed a letter agreeing to an IMF adjustment program. At the request of the parties to the agreement on the rescue package, the United States Federal Reserve System participated as agent in implementing the agreement through the Federal Reserve Bank of New York. The involvement of the Federal Reserve System stemmed from the fact that the Federal Reserve Bank of New York is the agent for foreign central banks and as part of its normal functions holds their deposits and makes payments from their accounts.

By using their own funds to help Argentina meet the 1 April 1984 deadline for interest payments, thus bailing it out before it agreed with the IMF on a program of economic reforms, Mexico, Brazil, Colombia and Venezuela reportedly acted out of a willingness to cooperate in devising ways to meet their debt commitments and to maintain a negotiated approach to the solution of the international-debt problem. In the words of Mexico's Minister of Finance, the four Latin American countries have constituted "a cartel that organized itself to pay, not to not pay." On the other hand, there was some indication that creditor banks, while welcoming that development, were worried that debtor countries might henceforth be more inclined to propose to pay on their own terms instead of those of their creditors or the IMF.

The creditors' fear that a Latin American debtors' cartel would be formed was revived by a declaration issued on 19 May 1984 in which the Presidents of Argentina, Brazil, Colombia and Mexico stated:

We . . . express our concern at the fact that the aspirations of our peoples for development, the progress of democratic trends in the region and the economic security of our continent are seriously affected by events beyond and outside the control of our Governments. We note that the successive increases in interest rates, the prospect of possible further increases and the proliferation and intensity of protectionist measures have cast a pall of darkness over our countries and the region as a whole.

They warned that they would not be "thrust into a situation of enforced insolvency and continued economic stagnation." Apparently frustrated by the austerity programs imposed on the Latin American countries as a condition for bail-out loans, they proposed:

the adoption of specific measures for bringing about substantial transformations in international financial and trade policy that will enhance the possibilities for our products to have acccess to the markets of the developed countries, will substantially and effectively relieve the burden of indebtedness, and will ensure that the flows of financing for development are restored.

In particular, they stated that it was "necessary to establish adequate amortization and grace periods and to achieve reductions in interest rates, margins, commissions and other financial charges."

Concern about the external indebtedness of Latin America intensified on 30 May 1984, when Bolivia announced that it was "temporarily" suspending payments on its $1.05 billion debt to foreign commercial banks and limiting repayments to international lending agencies to 25 percent of its earnings from exports. The following day, economists and government officials at a conference of the Latin American Economic System (Sistema Economico Latinoamericano) (SELA), in Caracas, Venezuela, warned that Bolivia's action would be only "the first rock to roll down the mountain" and might be followed by a landslide if no steps were taken to lighten Latin America's debt burden. A few days later, on 4 June, Ecuador followed in Bolivia's footsteps and announced that it had suspended payments on $247.5 million of debts owed to foreign governments and banks falling due between June 1984 and the end of 1985. Ecuadorian officials said that they had approached bankers about rescheduling the debts in question over seven years, with three years' grace on the repayment of principal.

The movement toward concerted efforts by Latin American debtor countries to bring diplomatic and political pressure to bear on the industrialized countries gained added momentum on 6 June 1984, when the Presidents of Ecuador, Peru and Venezuela joined the four signatories of the 19 May declaration to send a joint communication to the participants in the international economic summit in London. The seven signatories of the communication stressed that "higher interest rates, problems in obtaining additional financial resources and the strengthening of protectionist activities are factors which have prevented the benefits of the recovery in industrialized countries from reaching our economies." They reiterated "the Latin American conviction that there is an urgent need for the international community to tackle the problems of the world economy in an integrated and coherent manner, recognizing the inter-relationships which link them, and to find satisfactory solutions in an interdependent world." They put particular emphasis on "the urgent need for concerted action . . . in the case of indebtedness," since "it is unthinkable that the problems could be solved solely through contacts with banks or with the isolated participation of the international financial agencies." They urged that "a constructive dialogue . . . be held between creditor and debtor countries, in order to identify specific measures for relieving the external debt burden, taking into account the interests of all the parties involved."

The communication of the seven Latin American Presidents was followed on 7 June by a letter addressed to the participants in the London summit meeting from the President of Panama, who was acting both in that capacity and as President of the thirty-eighth session of the General Assembly of the United Nations. He associated himself with the plea of the seven Presidents and emphasized the importance of giving consideration, at the London summit, to the Quito Declaration and Plan of Action.

Following their strategy of taking a regional position *vis à vis* their creditors, but without creating fear of a possible confrontation between debtors and lenders, the ministers for foreign affairs and ministers of finance of eleven Latin American countries (Argentina, Bolivia, Brazil, Chile, Colombia, the Dominican Republic, Ecuador, Mexico, Peru, Uruguay and Venezuela) met in Cartagena, Colombia, on 21 and 22 June 1984 to continue consideration of the international economic situation, particularly external debt issues and external debt as an obstacle to the reactivation of the economic development of their countries, and in order to propose initiatives and appropriate types of action leading to solutions acceptable to all the parties concerned.

The meeting took place in the shadow of two events—Argentina's continuing refusal to accept the IMF traditional stabilization proposals and its unilateral announcement of an economic program meant to be negotiated with the IMF—and in the aftermath of the partial suspension of payments by Bolivia and Ecuador. It also took place against the background of Brazil and Mexico's contention that, in an international context of rising interest rates and trade protectionism, austerity programs constituted a serious threat to their economic recovery, although they had agreed to the IMF stabilization programs and had not been in arrears on interest payments on their external debts.

In an opening address at the Cartagena Meeting, the President of Colombia, criticizing the present international framework for debt repayment, observed that "Latin America's foreign debt service has become so burdensome" that it "threatens the very stability of the international monetary system and the survival of the democratic process in various countries." After stating that "the developing countries should not be made to pay for the consequences derived from economic imbalances in the industrialized countries, and particularly the United States fiscal deficit," and noting that "it has been assumed so far that each country must get out of its predicament by adjusting its economy to the formulas of the International Monetary Fund," he said: "What we are learning now is that this will not suffice, that the industrialized countries where the banks have their headquarters . . . must acccept responsibility."

The Cartagena meeting ended with the adoption of an agreement, formally called the "Cartagena Consensus," that dissipated the fear in industrialized countries that the Latin American countries would paralyze the international financial system by deciding to repudiate their debts. Nevertheless, the Consensus was widely viewed as moving the Latin American countries closer to the constitution of a united front for debt negotiations. In effect, the participants decided to set up regional consultation and follow–up machinery in which all of the other countries of the region could participate. The purpose of that machinery would be to facilitate, at the regional level, the exchange of information and experience and to provide support for requests for technical assistance in connection with debt, financing and other related issues; to promote contacts with other developing countries outside Latin America; and to promote the dialogue with the governments of the creditor countries and, under appropriate conditions, with the multilateral financial agencies and the international banks.

The participants in the Cartagena Conference indicated their readiness to meet with the governments of industrialized countries to carry out a joint examination of the many aspects of Latin America's external debt and its economic, social and political implications. They emphasized the need for a solution to the excessive burden that the external debt constituted and for conditions conducive to the reactivation of the debtor countries' development and the steady expansion of the world economy and world trade, while safeguarding the interests of all parties involved.

The participants in the Cartagena Conference noted that the Latin American countries' external debt exceeded one-half of their gross domestic product and was equivalent to three times the region's annual exports. They pointed out that debt service payments had exceeded $173 billion in the past eight years and that the most negative consequence of such a situation was that the Latin American region had become a net exporter of financial resources, with the estimated loss amounting to $30 billion in 1983. They stressed that, to a great extent, the crisis was due to external factors beyond the control of the Latin American countries. From 1980 to 1983 those factors had led to a drop in the volume of exports and an unavoidable reduction in the volume of imports, which would have a serious impact on the development process.

The participants further emphasized that the international recession in the period in question and the stagnation of the industrialized countries' economies, the deterioration in the terms of trade and the resurgence of protectionist and restrictive trade policies in the industrialized economies had led to a serious shrinkage in the volume of the region's exports. Those factors had also led to considerable changes in the pattern of exports and, combined with the constant increases in interest rates, had produced a somber external debt picture for the countries of the region.

The participants thought that the Latin American debt problem was due largely to drastic changes in the conditions under which the credits were originally negotiated, particularly regarding liquidity and interest rates, the level of involvement of multilateral credit agencies in the debt structure, and economic growth prospects. They believed that those changes, which had originated in the industrial countries and were entirely outside the region's decision-making sphere, indicated that debtors and creditors were jointly responsible.

The participants in the Cartagena Conference reaffirmed their desire to fulfill their external debt commitments and reiterated that the conduct of external debt negotiations was the responsibility of each individual country. However, they pointed out that recent experience had shown that the external debt problem in developing countries could not be solved solely through a dialogue with the banks, through isolated action taken by the multilateral financial agencies or through the free play of market forces.

The participants therefore proposed:

—That when agreements were renegotiated and new credit operations were carried

out, the international banks should charge base interest rates that did not exceed
the actual cost of raising funds on the market and were not based on administered
rates

—That net interest margins and other costs should be reduced to a minimum, that
commissions should be eliminated and that penalty interest payments on arrears
should be cancelled during debt renegotiations

—That in the interim, temporary mechanisms such as official loans and the extension of repayment periods should be provided to compensate debtors for any
increase in interest rates

—That in renegotiation operations, account should be taken of the debt profile
and the capacity for economic recovery and that maturity terms and periods of
grace should be lengthened

—That in the case of countries with extreme balance-of-payments difficulties, consideration should be given to clauses permitting the postponement of payment
of a portion of the interest, upon which no further interest would be payable
and which would be paid through the use of a set proportion of the resources
derived from an increase in export volume

—That renegotiated debt payments should be limited to a reasonable percentage
of export earnings, compatible with the maintenance of adequate growth

—That creditors should eliminate demands that governments guarantee private-
sector debts indiscriminately and involuntarily

—That funding of the IMF, the World Bank and the Inter-American Development
Bank should be increased and that at the same time the IMF should proceed
with a new allocation of SDRs compatible with the liquidity needs of the developing countries and extend the deadlines on its adjustment programs

—That recognition should be given to the special status of sovereign nations as
debtors to the international financial community and that regulations that acknowledge such a status should be adopted.

The Cartagena Consensus also included a provision, reportedly proposed
by Argentina, calling on the IMF to relax the adjustment programs by
giving priority to countries' needs for the growth of production and employment. As the developing countries have been called upon to grapple
with increasingly serious financial difficulties, they have been demonstrating an increasing tendency to vent their anger and frustration on the IMF,
to which they have been turning for help in overcoming their problems.
In Latin America, where the debt problem has given rise to "the politics
of debt," recession and the lowering of living standards have been denounced as reflecting the "submission" of a government that has agreed
to an IMF adjustment program to what are called "the dictates of IMF."
Thus in Brazil nationalist demand that the Government reassert control
over the management of the economy was illustrated by the fact that during
the 1984 carnival parade one of the most popular floats was one satirizing
the officials responsible for Brazil's economy; the float was preceded by a

girl dressed in the national colors who was chained to a man symbolizing the IMF.

Prior to the Cartagena Conference, debtors from other regions were less inclined than the Latin American countries to place their debt problems within the context of a North-South polarization, leaving the Latin American countries to fight the battle for debt concessions but hoping nevertheless to benefit from any advantages that might be won. However, at Addis Ababa from 18 to 20 June 1984, the ministers of finance of the African countries, discussing for the first time as a group the debt payment difficulties of the African countries, approved a document on Africa's foreign debt that was presented to the July 1984 session of the United Nations Economic and Social Council. The document contained an appeal to the members of the Group of 77 (composed of the developing countries) for a rapid and equitable application of their undertaking to encourage long-term rescheduling of African trade debts. While recognizing the responsibility of African countries for their current debts, the document stressed that the problem was largely due to external factors. The Ministers proposed, among other things, total and partial cancellation of some debts, an immediate reduction of interest rates and an agreement to cap them, greater resources flows to Africa on concessionary terms, less harsh debt-rescheduling terms and a review of IMF conditionality. Conditionality means that IMF financial assistance is provided on the condition that it will be used to support economic policies aimed at restoring a viable balance of payments within a reasonable period of time. The IMF guidelines on conditionality state that in working out adjustment programs the IMF must take into consideration the domestic social and political objectives of member countries as well as their economic priorities and circumstances.

With a view to consolidating the common front constituted at the Cartagena meeting, ministers for foreign affairs and ministers of finance from Argentina, Bolivia, Brazil, Chile, Colombia, the Dominican Republic, Ecuador, Mexico, Peru, Uruguay and Venezuela met at Mar del Plata on 13 and 14 September 1984. The meeting formed part of the continuing effort by the Latin American countries to coordinate their responses to what they continued to view as the international debt problem. Opening the Mar del Plata Meeting, the President of Argentina called on the countries of the region to make "more concrete what until now has shown itself only as a potential capacity for negotiation," but in so doing he emphasized that "unity is not confrontation."

In the Mar del Plata Communiqué, issued on 14 September 1984, the Ministers "reaffirmed the need for dialogue as a way to promote understanding." On the matter of indebtedness, they concluded that dialogue between creditors and debtors was essential for proper comprehension of the problem and reaching such an understanding. The absence of dialogue would make it more difficult to initiate the cooperation among the parties

needed to resolve the crisis jointly. In a letter dated 3 October 1984 trans-
mitting the Mar del Plata Communiqué to the Secretary-General of the
United Nations, the Permanent Representatives to the United Nations of
the countries that had issued that Communiqué elaborated on the need
for such dialogue in the following terms:

The problem of the external indebtedness of the developing countries should be
tackled in the light of the joint responsibility currently borne by all the parties
involved: the Governments of both debtor and creditor countries, the multilateral
financial agencies and the international banking system. This responsibility makes
it essential that all the parties participate actively in the search for lasting solutions
to the problem.

The necessary understandings may be achieved only through dialogue, which
constitutes the appropriate procedure for comprehending the problem and making
progress in the search for solutions.

Accordingly, there is a need for direct political dialogue between the Governments of industrialized countries and the Governments of debtor countries. It is
clear that the problem of indebtedness cannot be resolved only through negotiation
with the banks and through discussions with the multilateral financial agencies,
since the latter are unable to grasp the full scope of the political and social implications of this serious problem.

Direct political dialogue between Governments will make it possible to define
the necessary guidelines for seeking solutions more in keeping with the long-term
interests of all the parties concerned. Without such guidelines, which only Governments can formulate, there will be a continuation of partial, limited approaches,
which until now have scarcely been conducive to dealing even inadequately with
some of the aspects of the problem.

In the Mar del Plata Communiqué, the ministers for foreign affairs and
ministers of finance of the eleven participating countries emphasized the
need for a global approach to the debt crisis. To that end, they reaffirmed
"their concern about the one-sidedness of adjustment efforts, which was
incompatible with the joint responsibility of creditors and debtors to seek
a solution to the debt problem." They pointed out "that it was of fundamental importance to continue to seek appropriate and lasting solutions
to all the external-debt problems . . . so that the Governments of the creditor countries, the multilateral financial agencies and the banking community would make contributions comparable to the efforts exerted by the
debtor countries in their adjustment process." They stated that "they felt
that it was essential to invite Governments of industrialized countries to
participate in a direct political dialogue" and "drew attention to the co-
ordination achieved by their countries."

In the Communiqué, the participants also pointed out that "the increase
in interest rates which had occurred shortly after the conclusion of the
Cartagena meeting had aggravated the adverse impact of their already
excessively high level." They noted that "signs of economic recovery were

still concentrated in a few developed countries, and that those countries continued to implement policies which adversely affected the growth prospects of most countries of the international community." They emphasized that "as long as the recovery did not extend to all countries, it would be a precarious one, threatening to bring on an international crisis whose size, depth and impact could not be predicted." They expressed the view that

except in isolated cases, protectionist trends and other restrictive measures had intensified, thus accentuating the adverse effects of those actions on the level of export earnings, import capacity, the ability to service the external debt and the prospects for development program in the countries of the region.

They also noted that "there had not been a satisfactory resumption of financial flows capable of promoting economic growth, or of short-term commercial credits."

After months of protracted negotiations, an agreement was reached on 2 December 1984 between Argentina and its creditor banks, which by the fourth quarter of 1984 had already classified 40 to 60 percent of their Argentine loans as nonaccrual. On 28 December 1984, the IMF approved a loan package for Argentina. Those developments were considered all the more significant because Argentina is not only one of the major debtors but was also the debtor most unwilling to agree to an IMF-sponsored austerity program. The IMF package was viewed by the banks and the creditor countries as confirming that the international debt crisis was indeed over. However, that assessment continued to be challenged in the developing world. In Argentina itself, a confederation of labor unions, fearing potentially recessionary effects of the terms of the IMF aid package, issued a statement that contained the warning: "We workers will not pay the foreign debt."

By early 1985 deals negotiated with Argentina, Brazil, Mexico and Venezuela gave the creditor countries and the creditor banks a new reason for believing that the debt crisis had been defused and that there was no longer any danger of the formation of cartels of debtor countries that would repudiate their foreign debts. However, that optimism contrasted sharply with the pessimism prevailing in the debtor countries and could be interpreted as hiding a deep-seated fear of eventually being forced to accept the global political solution advocated at the series of Latin American conferences, the participants in which had formed a *de facto* cartel whose ostensible purpose was not to repudiate foreign debts but to plan joint action. That fear was in no way allayed by the Third Ministerial Meeting of the Cartagena Consensus countries, held in the Dominican Republic on 7 and 8 February 1985.

Inaugurating that meeting, the President of the Dominican Republic admitted frankly that part of the funds borrowed by the Latin American countries had not been used for productive purposes. Specifically, he acknowledged that the funds had been used, among other purposes, "to maintain subsidies which distort their economies," to finance "imports of luxury goods or weapons" or "to maintain unrealistic exchange rates." However, he reaffirmed that responsibility for the debt problem lay not only with the debtor countries but also with the international private banks, the multilateral financial institutions and the industrialized countries. Noting that there was "an unjustified and dangerous generalized feeling of relief in some international circles because some progress had been made with regard to debt renegotiation," he reiterated the call for a constructive political dialogue involving not only the debtor countries and the creditor banks but also the governments of the industrialized countries. Such a dialogue was necessary because "the industrialized countries would have to provide financial resources, which cannot and should not be provided solely by private banks, . . . and should grant greater access to their markets for the debtor countries' exports, especially agricultural and agro-industrial exports."

At the end of the Santo Domingo Meeting, the participants issued a communiqué in which, after noting that some Latin American countries had recently "concluded with the international financial community programs for the restructuring of their external debts," they observed:

these debt restructurings are not sufficient and merely postpone the problem, since negotiations with the commercial banks, by their very nature, provide no opportunity to take up questions of broader scope such as the joint responsibility of debtors and creditors, balanced adjustment, the implications for the development of the debtor countries and the evolution of the international economy, international trade and international finance, which would make it possible to find a permanent solution to the debt problem.

The persistent application of stringent adjustment program has continued to entail, in general, a drastic reduction of the material levels of living and well-being of the broad mass of the Latin American population.

In many countries, it has not been possible to reduce unemployment and the level of domestic economic activity has declined. Social tensions have reached critical levels, owing to the scope and rapidity of the adjustment processes applied. In many cases, the efforts of the coming years will only make it possible to regain the levels of per capita output and income and the quality of life already achieved 10 years before.

The economic recovery of the industrialized countries has not spread to the Latin American countries; on the contrary, it has acccentuated in the former countries the application of protectionist measures and the restriction of trade and financing.

The transfer of financial resources has become negative for the region, amounting to an estimated $55,000 million in the past two years.

Interest rates have recently declined, but this trend has not been consolidated, since in many countries there still exist the factors which create an increased demand for credit and inflationary pressures that can produce a new rise in interest rate levels.

The Strategy of the Countries of the Creditor Banks (Creditor Countries). Following the outbreak of the international debt crisis, the Reagan administration developed a strategy for coping with it that was subsequently endorsed in broad terms at the May 1983 Williamsburg economic summit. In the Williamsburg Declaration on Recovery, the participants in the summit (the heads of state or government of Canada, the Federal Republic of Germany, France, Italy, Japan, the United Kingdom and the United States) stated:

We view with concern the international financial situation, and especially the debt burdens of many developing nations. We agree to a strategy based on effective adjustment and development policies by debtor nations; adequate private and official financing; more open markets; and worldwide economic recovery We will seek early ratification of the increases in resources for the International Monetary Fund and the General Arrangements to Borrow. We encourage closer cooperation and timely sharing of information among countries and the international institutions, in particular between the International Monetary Fund, the International Bank for Reconstruction and Development, and the GATT [General Agreement on Tariffs and Trade].

However, the Western European countries, while going along with that approach, continued to emphasize that the debt crisis stemmed largely from the United States federal budget deficit. By driving up interest rates and the exchange rate of the United States dollar, it added to the developing countries' debt burdens and weakened their debt-carrying capacity, thus threatening sustained Western economic recovery. Consequently, before the London summit in 1984, the approach to the debt crisis most commonly advocated in Western Europe in both nongovernmental and governmental circles was a drastic reduction in the size of the United States budget deficit. In the United States, on the other hand, despite the recognition in Federal Reserve circles of the effects of the budget deficit on the debt crisis, the Reagan administration continued to assert that the debt crisis was nothing more than a temporary liquidity squeeze that would fade away as the economic recovery in the United States spread to the other Western countries and the developing world. In the view of the Reagan administration, the crisis should be tackled on a case-by-case basis with the traditional institutional remedies used since the creation of the IMF to help countries remain solvent. These remedies include granting emergency credits to debtor countries and implementing appropriate adjustment measures by those countries.

The United States position was that the debtor countries should implement domestic belt-tightening measures aimed at demonstrating that they qualify to receive immediate relief and are eligible for further borrowing. According to the United States, responsibility for resolving the debt crisis lay entirely with the debtors, the private banks and the IMF. In fact, the United States government plays the leading role whenever the IMF is involved, because the policies of the IMF on basic issues are essentially the policies of the Western industrialized countries with the United States at their head. This indirect involvement enables the United States, in particular, to exert its influence without having to face the political consequences that direct involvement would entail.

Despite the official position taken by the Reagan administration, the Federal Reserve recognized that high United States interest rates affected the developing countries' debt burden. Its officials therefore proposed alternative approaches to the debt crisis. The most publicized alternative was the idea that a maximum interest rate should be set for debtor countries. On 3 May 1984, at Senate Banking Committee hearings into the rescue package for Argentina, the President of the New York Federal Reserve Bank said that countries and banks involved in international debt negotiations should consider mechanisms such as putting a limit on how far interest rates could move above current rates to sidestep the problems that rising interest rates posed in implementing the economic adjustment programs worked out by borrowing countries with the IMF and the creditor banks.

Later in the month, the idea of a cap on interest rates charged on loans to developing countries was advocated by the Chairman of the Federal Reserve Board at a seminar of central bankers held in New York under the auspices of the Board. The cap proposal would involve a two-tier interest rate structure under which the creditor banks would probably lend to developing countries at interest rates lower than the cost at which they acquire their funds. It would provide a way out of the dilemma created by the fact that monetary policy aimed at containing inflation in the United States causes interest rates to rise to levels that are so high that repayment difficulties are created for developing countries.

It was suggested in United States financial circles that in exchange for voluntary interest rate capping by creditor banks, the governments of the creditor banks' countries might offer some form of guarantee on outstanding loans granted by those banks. That would reduce the risk in such lending and enable the banks to cut the risk premium customarily included in the interest rates on loans to countries not enjoying a high credit rating, thus making the cap more bearable for the banks. Without a government guarantee of the outstanding loans or some similar compensatory formula, the financial burden imposed by the cap would be borne exclusively by the banks that, after all, exist to make a profit and may not be eager to accept any cut in their earnings.

The idea of a cap on interest rates was not accepted in all circles. Thus on 8 May 1984 *The Times* of London, in the editorial "Leaving the Debt Game While You're Ahead," recalled that a cap on mortgage rates had been proposed by Margaret Thatcher in the 1974 general election and observed that the idea of a cap on interest rates on foreign lending "makes as little sense in the international market place as it did in the British context." *The Times* said that although "American enthusiasm is understandable," it was not "clear why other governments—through the international institutions—or the private banks should be asked to pay for the consequences of American economic policy by stumping up their share of interest-rate subsidies." *The Times* concluded: Much planning for the future should take the unpopular form of resisting protectionism in the industrial world and encouraging direct investment in the developing world. Neither process needs seminars in New York to prove its necessity, only political will in the two halves of the world."[18]

The Reagan administration displayed an equally unenthusiastic attitude toward the interest-capping proposal. It indicated at both the May 1984 ministerial meeting of the Organization for Economic Co-operation and Development in Paris and the June 1984 international economic summit in London (attended by the heads of state or government of seven major Western industrialized countries) that it did not see any need for any major new government initiative to tackle the debt crisis and that it would continue to support the case-by-case approach, under which a debtor country must adopt appropriate economic and financial adjustment policies in order to be eligible for assistance. In fact, the Reagan administration had originally wanted to exclude the international debt crisis from the agenda of the London summit but had refrained from belaboring that point too hard in the face of intensified pressure from the Latin American countries, which were appealing to the creditor countries for a discussion of the debt crisis at the political level. Latin American countries have consistently argued that democratic governments are now being called upon to repay debts contracted by authoritarian and repressive regimes, at higher interest rates and from reduced revenue, and that there is a direct link between economic growth and viable democracy, because, as history has amply demonstrated, destitute people are an easy prey for both the extreme right and the extreme left. The Reagan administration's agreement to include the debt crisis in the agenda for the London summit was also prompted by growing international concern about the soundness of the United States banking system following the near collapse of Continental Illinois, which had made foreign depositors in United States banks extremely nervous.

The Reagan administration made a further concession by joining the governments of the other participating countries in recognizing in the London summit communiqué that "continuously high or even further growing levels of international interest rates could . . . exacerbate the problems of the debtor countries" and agreeing "to continue with and where necessary strengthen policies to reduce inflation and interest rates, to control and where necessary reduce budgetary deficits."

In October 1985, as the Latin American countries continued to call for a new approach to the debt problem, the Reagan administration suggested that the countries of the creditor banks should play a more active role. At the fortieth annual IMF—World Bank meeting, the Secretary of the Treasury proposed that over three years the commercial banks should lend an additional $20 billion and the multilateral lending institutions an additional $9 billion to debtor countries that streamlined their economies. On 28 October 1985 that proposal was examined at a working party of the Institute of International Finance, which acts as an information clearing house for nearly two hundred of the largest banks from thirty-eight countries. The working party was attended by fifty-eight banks from the United States, Western Europe and Japan. The European banks, which are less heavily committed in Latin America than United States banks, expressed doubts about the wisdom of increasing their holdings of shaky loans. They reportedly felt that the governments of the United States and other creditor countries should lend more money to developing countries (either by granting direct loans or by guaranteeing commercial bank loans) before the banks committed themselves to making the additional loans proposed by the United States Government.

Those changes in certain positions of the Reagan administration made it possible for the participants in the London summit to agree, in the terms of the communiqué, "to confirm the strategy on debt and continue to implement and develop it flexibly case by case," while promising to encourage "more extended multi-year rescheduling of commercial debts" and to stand "ready to negotiate similarly in respect of debts to governments and government agencies," especially "in cases where debtor countries are themselves making successful efforts to improve their position." The participants even promised to attach "particular importance" to "helping debtor countries to make necessary economic and financial changes, taking due account of political and social difficulties," an undertaking that was vague enough to be interpreted in some circles as meaning that they would consider multiyear rescheduling of debts, many of which are one- and two-year loans, not only for the countries that have adjusted their economic policies but also for those that are reluctant to atone for the irresponsible borrowing of the past and to accept economic stagnation as the price of the financing. The participants also agreed "to maintain and wherever possible increase flows of resources, including official development assistance through the international financial and development institutions, to the developing countries and particularly to the poorest countries." The latter provision reflected a more detailed commitment than the corresponding provision of the Williamsburg Declaration, which referred only to "adequate private and official financing."

FROM THE INTERNATIONAL DEBT CRISIS TO THE INTERNATIONAL DEBT IMBROGLIO

The Case-by-Case Approach to the Debt Crisis Versus the Global Approach

As is clearly evident in the various communiqués and statements they have issued since 1982, the Latin American countries consider that a global approach is the only one capable of solving the international debt problem. The global approach was also emphasized in the July 1984 report by a Commonwealth Group of Experts, *The Debt Crisis and the World Economy*. After stressing that "the debt crisis threatens not only development in developing countries but also the stability of the banking system of industrial countries," the report observed:

The message is clear. The present situation is not sustainable. The world's financial safety is balanced on a knife-edge. The greatest immediate danger of disruption is posed by the risk that interest will not be paid on the existing debts of the major developing country borrowers. The erosion in the living standards of developing countries has pushed their peoples to the margin of tolerance. There is thus an urgent need to organise an adequate collective response to the situation. . . . There is no room for complacency. We sense rather that a recognition of the gravity of the issues and of the dangers posed by the debt crisis in an interdependent world is growing. Full expression is not always given to this recognition, perhaps because of fear of seeming to aggravate matters. But the situation has now been reached where collective determination to take action is imperative. The knowledge that such determination has been mustered will itself be a factor for greater stability.[19]

Even in industrialized countries, there are economists, financiers and politicians who share the view that only a global approach to the developing countries' debt problem can pave the way to a resumption of normal flows of development finance and imports to developing countries from industrialized countries. For example, Lord Lever observed:

Western Governments must recognize that lending on this scale to poor countries cannot be repaid in real terms within a commercial time scale. They should have been involved from the outset in the lending, to support it, to determine its size and terms realistically and to prevent the misdirection that was the fate of too much of it. . . . The banks face far more than a liquidity problem. The pretense that hundreds of billions of their assets are "performing" is being only precariously maintained. Until these questionable assets are genuinely strengthened, the solvency and stability of the great banks will remain in peril. . . . We must not attempt to maintain the pretense that purely commercial lending is adequate for our purposes. It is defective in that it requires premature attempts at balance-of-payments surplus by the debtors not compatible with our political interests or theirs. Recent net transfers of resources from the debtors have been bought at the cost of economic setback and grave risk to political stability. They are too small to restore confidence but large enough to do serious damage to the debtor's economy and society. They are neither desirable nor sustainable. . . . The patchwork response to the difficulties of the banking system is breaking down. Confidence in the banks has not been restored by a charade of debt service and the debtors' present real contribution to that service is unsustainable.[20]

A similar view is held by Henry Kissinger, who wrote:

None of the major debtor countries will be able simultaneously to pay its debt, achieve economic growth and maintain its political and social equilibrium. When debtors have to borrow to pay even interest we have reached the historically unprecedented and politically unsustainable condition in which developing countries are being turned into capital exporters. . . . Statesmanship must be able to transcend formal theory: the time has come to bring the professed goals of the international financial system into line with political realities.[21]

Some of the experts in industrialized countries who advocate a global approach have made specific proposals in that regard:

—The replacement of existing debts, through the intermediation of national monetary authorities, by a consolidated debt of no fixed redemption dates whose capital would be subordinated to claims under future loans. The interest on the consolidated debt would be concessionary, or indexed, or a mixture of the two, and existing lenders could hold the bonds representing the consolidated debt in their portfolios or sell them for what they would fetch.

—The establishment of a world development agency that would take the bad debts from developing countries in exchange for long-term bonds yielding lower returns. This would enable the creditor banks to restructure their balance sheets without recording loan defaults while at the same time absorbing part of the real losses on nonperforming loans.

—The guaranteeing by the export credit insurance agencies of the creditor countries, on the advice of the IMF, of new lending equal to the total interest payments required combined with the provision of new funds to debtor developing countries to enable them to achieve some economic growth on the condition that such funds should be used productively to strengthen the debtor countries' economies.

—The creation and allocation by the IMF of 34 billion Special Drawing Rights to strengthen the depleted or exhausted reserves of the debtor countries.

—The issuance of "exchange participation notes" by the central banks of the debtor countries that would give the lenders proportionate rights to some agreed-upon percentage of the debtor countries' gross annual current account foreign exchange receipts. Interest payments would be maintained in accordance with the original loan documentation, and the central banks of the debtor countries would assume responsibility for redeeming the notes and would act as collection and paying agents.

—The repackaging of the loans with a view to selling them as negotiable instruments at their proper market value, thus putting an end to the fiction that the loans are really worth the amounts indicated in the balance sheets of the creditor banks.

—The establishment of a new international mechanism that would enable debtor countries to exchange short-term debt for long-term debt or equity as private firms do, thus reducing their dependence on fluctuations in the cost and availability of short-term credit.

—The conversion by creditor banks of part of their loans into equity investments in private and government-owned companies and

—The swapping by creditor banks of one country's debt for that of another so that a creditor bank could concentrate on helping one country.

There have been proposals that, like some of the preceding suggestions, involve a large writing down of the developing countries' debts and the creation of new institutions to take over the loans from the creditor banks and in exchange issue to them long-term, low-interest or noninterest-bearing bonds of their own.

On the other hand, most officials and bankers in industrialized countries, brushing aside all proposals involving a global solution to the developing countries' debt problem, the cost of which would have to be paid by taxpayers in industrialized countries, have consistently maintained that there is no feasible alternative to the case-by-case approach that has been applied so far, the ultimate success of which depends on the ability of debtor countries to make their economies more competitive and to reduce inflation through traditional belt-tightening methods. A number of reasons for considering the global approach unworkable are set forth in the fifty-fourth annual report of the Bank for International Settlements covering the period 1 April 1983–31 March 1984:

The most important of these is that the events of the last twelve months have demonstrated beyond any doubt that what may have looked like a global, fairly homogeneous debt problem in the autumn of 1982 in fact masks a great diversity of situations among the debtors. There are one or two very difficult cases in eastern Europe and Asia, alongside a majority of countries that have shown their willingness and ability to undertake external adjustment and which are in the process of reaping the benefits of the recovery in the industrial world. While Latin America contains a high concentration of the most difficult cases, diversity exists there too, in terms of the degree of adjustment achieved, of export diversification, of the position in relation to oil and of the amount of domestic capital that has been exported. As for the heavily indebted countries of Africa, their situation is altogether different from that of the indebted medium-income LDCs; most of them could not afford to take on new loans at market rates even if they were available; they need soft loans or grants. How could any global surgery be brought to apply to such a diversity of situations?

Moreover, it would be quite wrong to consider the indebted countries "insolvent" simply because as a group they are unlikely to be able, even in the longer run, to repay the principal owed. It is a simple economic fact—an inherent part of the savings/investment process—that total outstanding debt continues to grow. What matters is that each individual debtor country should (a) in the longer run keep the growth of its debt in line with its ability to service it, and (b) in the shorter run demonstrate (for the benefit of its watchful creditors) its control over its indebtedness by bringing its growth periodically to a halt, or even by paying off part of it. The number of countries that satisfy one or both of these criteria has grown encouragingly since the beginning of 1983. This does not mean that the international debt problems are behind us; they clearly are not. But it does mean that the passage of time has, so far, borne out the validity of the current way of handling them.

Through close co-operation between the borrowers, the lending banks, governments and international institutions, this approach has successfully encouraged the formulation of mutually agreed programmes in which adjustment and financing have gone hand in hand. While this co-operation will have to be continued and developed, it would be wrong to try to replace it by unworkable global schemes.

The diversity of situations among the various debtor countries is likewise considered by the IMF as precluding any "meaningful alternative" to the case-by-case approach. The Managing Director of the IMF, in his opening address to the 1984 annual meetings of the IMF and the World Bank, observed that "the differences among countries are such that a case-by-case approach offers the only realistic hope of continued progress."

The Conflicting Assessments of the Debt Crisis and the Resulting Imbroglio

The conviction that the case-by-case approach was bringing about a cure for the international debt crisis was reflected in the assessments of the situation made by the IMF Interim Committee on 22 September 1984 and at the 1984 annual meetings of the IMF and the World Bank. The Interim Committee stated:

While the external debt problems of many developing countries remain serious, the Committee felt that good progress had been made in the implementation of the co-ordinated strategy of debtors and creditors to tackle these problems within the framework of adjustment programs—a development that has been facilitated by the recovery in world trade.

The Managing Director of the IMF, in his opening address to the 1984 annual meetings, observed:

This case-by-case approach has already yielded positive results. Several major indebted countries have made significant progress towards restoring their creditworthiness while improving the basis for domestic growth. If the adjustment programs which these countries have adopted are continued, there is every prospect that further progress will be made in the period ahead.

In his concluding remarks on 27 September, the Managing Director further observed:

Recent developments in the economic situation of many developing countries were welcomed. Governors noted that the aggregate current account deficit of non-oil developing countries, in relation to exports, has fallen to its lowest level in many years. At the same time, output growth has been picking up in a number of countries.... We can take satisfaction from the fact that a willingness to work together enabled the crisis of 1982 to be surmounted and has laid the basis for a medium-term approach to debt problems.

The Managing Director's assessment of the situation was reportedly endorsed by the United States and other industrialized countries.

Like the IMF, the commercial banks consider that past efforts on complex rescue packages for Mexico and Brazil have been a success and prove that the case-by-case approach works. The September 1984 issue of *World Financial Markets*, published by the Morgan Guaranty Trust Company of New York, commented:

Much has been accomplished in overcoming the crisis aspects of Latin America's debt troubles. The region's external adjustment has been remarkably fast, at first thanks to import compression and substitution but this year helped greatly by strong U.S. demand for Latin America's exports. The challenge now lies in getting Latin America's economic growth back up to a pace that will reverse its continuing decline in per capita incomes and employment. Growth will not be possible without the support of foreign creditors, but their ability to furnish new credit is strictly limited, especially on the part of capital-constrained commercial banks. Latin America's long-term growth potential is best pursued by domestic reforms to create a favorable climate for investment and exports. That would attract resources from abroad, including both repatriated flight capital and new capital inflows from foreign direct investors, the latter adding the bonus of modern technology."

In the October 1984 issue of *World Financial Markets*, the analysts of the Morgan Guaranty Trust Company noted that impressive progress had been recorded by a number of major debtor countries in the previous two years and cited improvements in the trade and current account balances of countries such as Mexico and Brazil, as well as a resumption of economic growth. The analysts said that as a result, the international financial community had reached the half-way point in constructing an "enduring solution" to the developing countries' debt problem.

These optimistic assessments are at variance with the developing countries' insistence that the debt situation remains critical. Almost at the very time when the Managing Director of the IMF was expressing optimistic views concerning the international debt crisis, heads of state and ministers for foreign affairs of debtor countries were expressing very different opinions in their statements to the General Assembly of the United Nations.

On 24 September 1984, the President of Argentina stated:

We in Latin America have proposed a dialogue between the richer countries and our countries about one of the questions that most upsets the financial order and stability of our countries: the question of the foreign debt. We believe that this debt not only affects the debtor countries, but, because of its political impact, also directly involves the creditors. We think that if everything depended on the manner in which the problem is being dealt with at present, we would not find a permanent and safe solution.

On the same day, the Minister for Foreign Affairs of Mexico observed:

Foreign debt is now the most burdensome economic problem for developing countries, particularly those of Latin America. . . . The Latin American countries have in recent months begun a process of negotiations to reschedule payments on their foreign debt, lessen capital amortization and reduce the costs of financing. . . . These negotiations, however, require the political framework essential for a fruitful dialogue among debtor Governments, creditor countries, the international banking network and multilateral financing institutions. The problem of debt must be attacked at its roots and in all its complexity.

The following day, the President of Venezuela commented:

We are faced today with an extremely serious situation, perhaps the most serious in recent history. The amount of foreign debt of the developing nations is so overwhelming that its consequences affect their very political and social stability; the dimensions of the debt problems alone require the most far-reaching understanding. We are dealing here with issues which, because of their intimate links to the price collapses in the raw materials export market, the increasing protectionism of the industrialized countries, the irrational rise in interest rates—whose slight variations, a result of manipulations by the world financial market, undermine our social programmes—all contribute to the weakening of efforts toward national recovery, denying work to millions of Latin Americans and condemning them to a marginal existence. . . . The foreign debt problem is part of a gradual breakdown of the world economic situation, a process of decay whose most vivid expression is the debt situation in Latin America today. The problem has ramifications which branch out beyond the countries of Latin America and other developing countries. Therefore, if we do not address ourselves to this issue in a timely manner, with political sensitivity to the problems of these countries, the whole world could founder in a crisis of unfathomable magnitude.

In February 1985 the Latin American ministers of finance participating in the Third Ministerial Meeting of the Consultation and Follow-up Machinery established by the countries signatories to the Cartagena Consensus, after reviewing the developments that had taken place since their meeting in Mar del Plata, stated that they considered it essential

to reiterate firmly their belief that there can be no stable and permanent solution to the external debt problem unless the Governments of debtor and creditor countries agree on an appropriate political framework for these questions as a whole; and to overcome certain reservations expressed by some Governments in order to engage in a political dialogue. If this dialogue is not accepted, there will be a serious risk not only of financial and economic instability but also of social and political instability throughout the region.

The risk of social and political instability arising from debt-servicing arrangements led the President of Peru to announce in his inaugural address on 28 July 1985 that his country would limit its external debt payments to no more than 10 percent of its export earnings over the following twelve months, while it tried to renegotiate the debt. Although the eleven countries of the Cartagena group had proposed in the Cartagena Consensus that "renegotiated debt payments should be limited to a reasonable percentage of export earnings, compatible with the maintenance of adequate growth," the Peruvian decision was the first attempt to put that idea into practice and the first real challenge to the existing debt-management *modus vivendi*. However, in a meeting early in July 1985 with representatives of Citibank, Manufacturers Hanover Trust Company and Chase Manhattan Bank aimed at paving the way for the announcement of the debt-payment capping decision, the President of Peru asked the banks not to regard that decision as reflecting a confrontational approach.

On 30 July 1985, the representatives of twenty Latin American countries (Argentina, Bolivia, Brazil, Chile, Colombia, Costa Rica, Cuba, the Dominican Republic, Ecuador, El Salvador, Guatemala, Haiti, Honduras, Mexico, Nicaragua, Panama, Paraguay, Peru, Uruguay and Venezuela) issued in Lima, Peru, a declaration calling for repayments on their debts to be linked to the growth of their export earnings. The declaration stressed the need for creditors to be more flexible and realistic about the debts so as to help revive the economies of the Latin American countries.

The growing frustration felt in those countries at the alleged failure of IMF-sponsored stabilization programs to bring about a speedy economic recovery lay at the root of another challenge to the debt-management *modus vivendi* by the President of Peru. Describing the IMF as an "accomplice" that must share the responsibility for Peru's economic difficulties, the President rejected the IMF's involvement in Peru's talks with its creditors. The IMF had up to then taken part in every Latin American debt rescheduling because the creditor banks had insisted that the debtor country should first work out a stabilization program with the IMF. The only exception had been Venezuela, which had not needed a package of new loans to help to pay its old debt.

The frustration at the alleged failure of the IMF-sponsored programs to reactivate the Latin American economies had also been reflected in the publicity given in the region to a proposal made by the President of Cuba, Fidel Castro, in an address marking the thirty-second anniversary of the Cuban revolution. Referring to the debt crisis as "a battle for the new economic order in Latin America, a battle for the economic integration of Latin America," he insisted that the way to solve the crisis was for the Latin American countries to join forces and suspend all debt payments.

The concern repeatedly voiced by the Latin American countries over their external debt problems contrasts sharply with the relatively optimistic views expressed by creditor banks and Western governments. Those conflicting assessments epitomize the radically different ways in which the international debt situation has been perceived by debtors and creditors.

While the creditor banks and their governments, disregarding the social and political implications of the debt crisis in the debtor countries, are talking about finance and are taking a short-term approach to the problem, the debtor countries are talking about their economies and demanding recognition of their particular circumstances and of the fact that nations cannot be reduced to balance sheets. Where the creditor banks and their governments see the success of the stabilization programs worked out with the IMF, the debtor countries see long-term austerity with accompanying prospects of increased social and political tensions. Although the creditor banks and their governments are convinced that the debt crisis is virtually over and see their relations with debtor countries entering a less turbulent phase devoid of periodic threats of an imminent moratorium, the debtor countries insist that their debt situation remains critical and see the prospect of confrontation persisting because fundamental issues have not been resolved.

The international debt crisis can be considered resolved only in so far as its resolution is defined in terms of the ability of the debtor countries, and particularly the major ones, to roll over their maturing debts, thus staving off, but not eliminating, the possibility of financial disaster. However, it is difficult to see how the crisis can be regarded as resolved if resolution is construed as meaning that the debtor countries must be able to earn enough foreign exchange not only to catch up with their interest payments but also to amortize the principal and achieve economic growth so as to reduce unemployment and raise levels of living. Similarly, it is difficult to view the debt crisis as resolved, even in the most economically advanced debtor countries such as Brazil and Mexico. Despite modest economic growth since 1984, much remains to be done before those countries can regain the rate of growth they attained in the past and any improvement in their current accounts that has occurred has been achieved at the cost of high inflation and high unemployment. In fact, there are a number of ominous factors that indicate that the underlying debt situation remains serious and that facile optimism is unwarranted:

—The difficulties being experienced by debtors such as Bolivia, Chile, the Ivory Coast, Nigeria, Peru and the Sudan.

—The likelihood that revenue shortfalls resulting from declining oil prices and/or voluntary oil production cuts aimed at helping to sustain those prices could substantially further weaken the economies of oil-exporting countries such as Algeria, Ecuador, Mexico, Nigeria and Venezuela. (Although the trade balance of Brazil, for example, benefited greatly from the decline in oil prices—Brazil paid $9.0 billion for imported oil in 1982 but only $4.6 billion in 1984—Mexico, as an oil-exporting country, lost $550.0 million for every dollar fall in the price of oil.)

—The possibility that a recession in the United States and a slowdown in the economic recovery that began in the United Kingdom in 1982 and subsequently spread to other Western European countries could jeopardize the expansion of the developing countries' export markets.

—The possibility that in a number of debtor countries excessive budget deficits that induce monetary expansion and hyperinflation may impede continued implementation of the debt-rescheduling programs that are conditional on certain targets being met by the countries involved.

To sum up, the international debt crisis has developed into an international debt imbroglio. The fear of widespread default by major debtor countries has receded, but the underlying causes of the recent crisis remain largely unaddressed, so that another crisis could erupt at any time. Moreover, the parties involved seem to be deliberately or involuntarily talking at cross-purposes, thus adding to the confusion.

The Way Out of the Imbroglio

The International Debt Problem: A Perennial Problem. The international debt problem can, of course, be managed by periodic rescue packages and/or ingenious reschedulings but cannot be solved in that way, as is shown by the fact that between 1975 and 1983 seven countries rescheduled their debts more than once: for example, Zaire rescheduled its debt six times between 1975 and 1983, Peru rescheduled its debt twice in 1978 and Turkey rescheduled its debt twice in 1979. The harsh reality is that many debtor countries cannot repay most of their loans within a commercial time frame. A few debtor countries can manage to repay but only by dint of adopting very stringent measures. Generally, many if not most developing countries will be unable to achieve the large trade surpluses they need to service their recently rescheduled debts.

In fact, the external indebtedness of the developing countries has been a perennial problem. In 1968 a United Nations report observed:

While the proportion of outright donations to developing countries in the total flow of external resources has been declining fairly steadily, interest rates on official loans have tended to rise in some countries and, as the expansion of official transfers has slowed down developing countries have been obliged to make increasing use of private export credits at commercial rates. Transfers from developing countries in connection with the servicing of their external debts have become an increasing burden on their balance of payments. Unless measures designed to reduce the cost to developing countries of external borrowing are put into effect, the growth of debt-service obligations might become a serious obstacle to economic growth in the 1970s.[23]

Another United Nations report issued in 1968 stated:

For many developing countries, the indebtedness problem has in fact reached a point where there is a serious question as to whether they will be able to continue servicing their existing debts and whether they will be able to secure or reasonably to accept additional external financing. ... Even when consolidation credits are obtained, the method of repaying urgent debts by contracting other debts, the payment of which will soon become equally urgent, merely postpones the crisis, does not provide any debt relief, and may prove particularly onerous in terms of its impact on economic growth.[24]

In November 1976, at the Paris Conference on International Economic Co-operation, the Group of 19, representing the developing countries, submitted proposals on "the problems of indebtedness of developing countries." They urged

that as an extraordinary and one-shot operation, relief on official debt should be provided forthwith by developed countries to all most seriously affected countries, least developed, developing land-locked, developing island countries, and other interested developing countries in order to alleviate their existing debt burden, to restore the momentum of growth lost during the recent economic crisis and to facilitate the achievement of the International Development Strategy target.

With regard to commercial debts, it was proposed that:

—International agreement should be reached to consolidate the debts of interested developing countries and to reschedule payments over a period of at least twenty-five years.
—The consolidation of commercial debts and the rescheduling of payments should be achieved by funding the commercial debts of the interested developing countries.
—A financial facility to refinance the burdensome short-term loans contracted in

recent years should be established for the use of interested developing countries, perhaps under the aegis of the World Bank and the IMF.[25]

The generalized "relief on official debt" proposed by the developing countries at the Paris Conference was not accepted on the ground that generalization might create inequities. However, a compromise agreement was reached in March 1978 at the ninth special session of the Trade and Development Board of the United Nations Conference on Trade and Development (UNCTAD), which was embodied in resolution 165 (S-IX): "Debt and Development Problems of Developing Countries." In that resolution, the Trade and Development Board, after "noting the pledge given by developed countries to respond promptly and constructively, in a multilateral framework, to individual requests from developing countries with debt-servicing difficulties, in particular the least developed and most seriously affected among these countries," agreed to the following decision:

Developed donor countries will seek to adopt measures for such adjustment of terms of past bilateral official development assistance, or other equivalent measures, as a means of improving the net flows of official development assistance in order to enhance the development efforts of those developing countries in the light of internationally agreed objectives and conclusions on aid.

The decision was not binding, however, and has been implemented by donor countries in varying degrees. According to the UNCTAD Secretariat, the total debt relief granted amounted to $5.7 billion, of which $3.3 billion took the form of debt cancellation. About half of the debt for which relief was granted was owed by "least developed countries." More than half of the total debt of eight of those countries was written off, as was more than one-fifth of the debt of seven others.

Clearly, the developing countries' debt problem can be solved permanently only by repaying the debts or by cancelling them. Any realistic effort to find a way out of the current international debt imbroglio will necessitate an end to the continuing North-South debt dialogue of the deaf, in which industrialized countries and developing countries are passing the buck back and forth, and the initiation of a good-faith, comprehensive discussion of the issues involved. Unless those issues are dealt with realistically, the stage will be set for another debt crisis. On the other hand, as the *Financial Times* rightly noted in the editorial "The Shadow Over Latin America," published on 30 October 1984:

Trade surpluses and IMF agreements cannot guarantee a country's willingness to service debts for years, and even decades, ahead. Only if it can service its debts and improve economic conditions for its citizens at the same time, can a country be deemed genuinely creditworthy, for sooner or later, the people's readiness for sacrifice on behalf of foreign bankers will run out. The ability to generate higher per capita incomes is the litmus test by which economic policy must ultimately be judged.[26]

The Bleak Outlook for Capital Flows to Developing Countries.   There is no doubt that for the foreseeable future, the outlook is not very promising for flows of capital to developing countries, whether in the form of commercial bank lending, official development assistance or foreign private direct investment.

Commercial bank lending to developing countries has been drastically curtailed since the onset of the debt crisis, owing to the anxiety inspired by the crisis and the uncertain future of the world economy. The banks have been disinclined to make loans to countries that are already heavily in debt. Furthermore, the banks' liquidity has dwindled, notably due to a reduction in the income of the OPEC countries and to widespread concern about the strength of the international banking system. This concern has led investors everywhere to purchase United States government and corporate bonds and bonds issued in other industrialized countries instead of placing their funds with the banks. These developments mean that developing countries will not be able to rely on commercial loans as a source of financing to any significant extent.

The aggregate volume of official development assistance (ODA) from all sources combined has more than doubled in both nominal and real terms during the past twenty years. However, this increase masks a declining trend in ODA as a percentage of the gross national product of donor countries. This is the yardstick against which ODA should be measured according to paragraph 43 of the International Development Stategy for the Second United Nations Development Decade, which set an ODA target of 0.70 percent of the GNP of the industrialized countries. The net flow of ODA from the countries that are members of the Development Assistance Committee of the Organisation for Economic Co-operation and Development (OECD) declined from 0.51 percent of their GNP in 1960 to 0.36 percent in 1983 and has in fact remained at the level of roughly half the United Nations target since the early 1970s. Because of the decline in the earnings of the oil-exporting countries, the ODA disbursed by the OPEC aid donors has in the past few years fallen to its lowest levels since 1973, although the reduced OPEC aid still amounts to roughly 1.4 percent of the donor countries' GNP. In mid-1985 available budgetary data indicated that 1985 might be the third consecutive year in which there would be no significant growth in total real ODA flows.

There seems to be little immediate prospect of a reversal in the decline in ODA in terms of GNP at a time when the governments of Western industrialized countries are reconsidering their role in domestic social welfare. For one thing, the governments of donor countries are currently in a parsimonious mood, because on the whole their economies—with the striking exception of the United States economy—are currently growing at a slower pace than in the 1950s and the 1960s, a situation that is projected to continue throughout the rest of the 1980s and 1990s: at the end of 1984 there were in the European countries that are OECD members some 20 million unemployed compared with 10 million in 1979 and 5 million in 1970. Perhaps more important is the fact that the pressure of high tax levels, coupled with actual or threatened reductions in civilian government spending, has been making foreign aid a favorite target of antitax movements, groups concerned about the effect of cuts in domestic social welfare programs, and legislators of all persuasions seeking to reduce budget deficits. Those who do not actually oppose foreign aid tend to be indifferent to it, an indifference that extends even to those idealistic taxpayers who have traditionally constituted a counterpoise to the critics of foreign aid.

Even former staunch supporters of foreign aid have changed their minds. Thus Gunnar Myrdal is so disappointed with foreign aid performance that he now thinks aid should be channeled as directly as possible to increasing the supply of basic needs and not to industrial projects. Myrdal also believes that aid should be firmly policed and not given by established aid agencies. According to an article in the March 1985 issue of *Finance and Development*, Myrdal added the latter condition "presumably because they [the established aid agencies] have been contaminated by those corrupt elites of the developing countries that have caused Myrdal to change his mind."[27] It was concern about corruption in developing countries that led a United States congressman, James Scheuer, to observe in 1981 that "foreign governments can do nothing for people whose own governments ignore their basic needs" and to suggest that most foreign assistance should be reserved "for third world leaders who use it to attack joblessness, hunger, ignorance and disease" and that "the developed countries should require Southern leaders seeking foreign help to demonstrate their commitment to worthy goals."[28]

On the whole, three decades of foreign aid have produced disappointing results: three-quarters of the world's illiterates are in Africa (54 percent of the population), Asia (56.8 percent) and Latin America (34.6 percent); famine, disease and unemployment are still widespread in the Third World; 70 percent of the world's population receive only 30 percent of the world's income; at the end of 1983, GDP growth in developing countries had fallen to 1.0 percent, well below the 1965–1980 average and below the rate of population increase; and many developing countries are deeply in debt. Furthermore, there is sometimes a tendency in developing countries for the poor to become poorer while the powerful become richer; not infrequently, the poorer the country, the richer the powerful and the wider the gap between the rich and the poor.

The failure of foreign aid to produce results commensurate with the resources invested and the expectations originally aroused may be due to some extent to deviations from the original concept of foreign aid as a gesture of goodwill among peoples, which underlay the 1949 Point IV program of President Truman. In a world in which the developing countries have become almost pawns in an ideological chess game strategic and geopolitical considerations have come to carry more weight than morality in the decisions of certain donor countries. These considerations have often been so dominant that foreign aid has tended to become a reward to ruling cliques for "good" political conduct rather than a generous manifestation of human solidarity. The attitude which has given rise to this approach to foreign aid is reflected in the words of the Chairman of the Senate Appropriation Committee's Subcommittee on Foreign Operations, who has observed:

The second annual State Department study of United Nations voting patterns, required under legislation, is distressing, particularly if one attempts to correlate the United States' assistance to other countries with their support of our positions in the General Assembly. . . . Our foreign policy ought to be directed at making improvements in this situation. Again this year, Congress should keep this widespread lack of support for our positions at the United Nations in mind as we review requests for foreign assistance. The American people are entitled to expect more from many of those who call themselves friends and allies and who are quick to line up for a slice of our tax dollars.[29]

Moreover, so-called security aid, which has come increasingly to take precedence over development and humanitarian aid, has in certain instances been used to maintain the political and social *status quo* through repression. Although certain donor countries allocate their ODA more evenhandedly than others, the weight often accorded to strategic and geopolitical considerations, historical, religious and cultural ties, and the commercial interests of donors has created a situation in which low-income developing countries on the average receive on a per capita basis less than one-half of the ODA being channeled to middle-income countries. At the extreme ends of the scale, the available per capita annual ODA can range from as low as $3 to $15 in some of the most densely populated low-income countries to more than $1,500 in some of the smallest middle-income countries. It is difficult to resist the temptation to link these figures to the aforementioned article by the Chairman of the Senate Appropriation Committee's Subcommittee on Foreign Operations in which he noted: "African nations opposed us in almost 80 per cent of the votes—in fact, support we got from the bloc dropped by one-third last year. Asian and Pacific nations supported our side on less than 15 percent of the issues—again, a substantial drop from 1983."[30]

To sum up, high tax burdens and the fear of renewed tax protests in industrialized countries combined with large budget deficits that are forcing cuts even in domestic social programs and disillusionment at the results achieved by foreign aid, make it unlikely that legislatures and governments in donor countries will make the necessary effort to reverse the decline of official development assistance in terms of GNP.

As for foreign private direct investment, although the debate on such investment throughout the years—both within and outside the United Nations—may at times have tended to create an appearance of strongly divergent views on the subject, few developing countries do not welcome, or indeed actively seek, such investment. As the Chinese leader Deng Xiaoping remarked in October 1984 when explaining his overture to the West: "No country can now develop by closing its doors." After observing that "isolation landed China in poverty, backwardness and ignorance," he emphasized that China could achieve its goal of quadrupling its gross national product only through foreign investment and trade. Efforts are being made to attract multinational corporations to China through the adoption of new legislation that permits foreign investment in more cities, simplifies the approval process for such investment and protects patents.

Despite the more welcoming attitude of developing countries toward multinational corporations resulting from their reassessment of the advantages and disadvantages of investment by such corporations, there seems to be little prospect that the flow of foreign private direct investment into developing countries will increase to anywhere near the level that could enable those countries to make significant economic progress. In fact, private direct investment, as a proportion of net capital flows to developing countries, fell from 19.8 percent in the early 1960s to 12.9 percent in the early 1980s. This decline is largely due to the belief of potential investors that business prospects in developing countries are becoming increasingly less attractive.

In the Caribbean, for example, decreased profitability has led Reynolds Metals Company, hurt by falling prices caused by abundant supplies of aluminum from other sources, to end all bauxite mining in Haiti, allegedly because deposits of commercially exploitable ore have been exhausted. Across the border in the Dominican Republic, the Aluminum Company of America (Alcoa) has decided to terminate its bauxite-mining operations and return its concession to the government. Similarly, Gulf and Western, the largest private employer in the country, has divested itself of all Dominican assets, including not only those related to its main activity there, the production of sugar, but also cattle ranges, citrus plantations and hotels. Both Reynolds Metals and Alcoa have terminated their bauxite operations in Jamaica, where two-thirds of export earnings were derived from bauxite mining and refining. In Aruba, the oil refinery belonging to Lago Oil and Transport, a subsidiary of Exxon that has been providing 60 percent of the island's revenue, is to be closed. In Curaçao, Shell is reportedly thinking of closing its refinery, whose operation is said to be uneconomic. Economic considerations are likewise said to be prompting Texaco to sell its oil refinery in Trinidad and Tobago to the government of that country.

According to a study by the United States Department of Commerce, most of United States foreign investment has tended in recent years to flow to industrialized countries; Latin America (excluding the Caribbean) now accounts for only 14 percent of that investment, compared with 38 percent in 1950. A 1984 study by the Council of the Americas (the principal lobbying group in the United States for large firms operating in the region), which surveyed 52 miltinational companies active in Latin America, concluded that the companies were "having trouble ascertaining the future in Latin America." The council found that the four largest economies in the region—those of Argentina, Brazil, Mexico and Venezuela—were "becoming less significant for the responding companies" and that the companies were deterred by the prospect that those economies would not begin to grow significantly again until 1985 or later. The responding companies were also deterred by declining sales and an 11 percent drop in employment in the region since 1981. In many other developing countries there is little that foreign private direct investment can do unless the government steps in to establish the required basic infrastructure.

Foreign private direct investment in developing countries is likewise being deterred by increasing protectionism in the United States and other industrialized countries. This shields inefficient domestic industries from legitimate foreign competition and threatens a trading system that is vitally important to the developing countries' economic growth. The more protectionist tendencies and ad hoc restrictions increase, the more restricted the potential markets for the developing countries' products will be, whether commodities or manufactures, and the less incentive there will be for foreign businessmen to set up or participate in new ventures in those countries. In particular, protectionist trade measures adversely affect investment opportunities in those export sectors where developing countries have proved to have a comparative advantage.

The need to spur lagging foreign investment in developing countries has prompted the World Bank to propose the establishment of a Multilateral Investment Guarantee Agency. The agency would provide guarantees against noncommercial risks, including the risk of currency situations that prevent foreign investors from repatriating their profits as well as the risks of political violence and expropriation. The proposed new agency would thus supplement the coverage already offered by existing national and regional investment guarantee schemes. In a statement to the Foreign Policy Association on 30 May 1985, the President of the World Bank said that consultations with potential signatories to a convention setting up the proposed guarantee agency indicated growing support for it, and that a draft convention was to be discussed shortly by the World Bank's executive directors.

The Need for Greater Self-reliance on the Part of Developing Countries.
The history of the countries that are now industrialized shows that almost
all of them benefited from foreign capital in the early stages of their development. Britain, which in the nineteenth and twentieth centuries was
a lender to many other countries, borrowed in the seventeenth and eighteenth centuries from the Netherlands, which at that time had achieved
great prosperity and was financially in the vanguard. The United States,
before becoming the world's principal financier in the twentieth century,
borrowed so much abroad in the nineteenth century that its external debt
represented a greater proportion of its gross domestic product than do the
external debts of today's two largest debtor developing countries, Brazil
and Mexico. Foreign borrowing as a percentage of net capital formation
exceeded 50 percent in Sweden for long periods in the second half of the
nineteenth century and was as high as 40 percent in Canada in the first
two decades of this century. Nevertheless, the industrial development of
most industrialized countries has been based essentially on the full mobilization and efficient use of their own human and financial resources. Domestic resources have assumed the leading role in the development process
in those countries, with foreign capital playing only a supporting part.

The developing countries should always keep these precedents in mind
and would perhaps do well to ponder the words of Adam Smith in *An
Inquiry into the Nature and Causes of the Wealth of Nations*: "Nobody but
a beggar chooses to depend chiefly upon the benevolence of his fellow-
citizens. Even a beggar does not depend upon it entirely." The developing
countries should realize that only beggar countries would choose to depend
for their essential needs upon the benevolence of wealthier nations. The
developing countries must realize that they themselves bear the main responsibility for their own misfortunes and that no nation can be exploited
by another—no matter how powerful the latter may be—unless it is exploitable, that is, unless it acquiesces, through those in power, in that
exploitation. They must face the fact that nations, like people, are to a
large extent masters of their fate. As Cassius reminds us in Shakespeare's
Julius Caesar: "The fault, dear Brutus, is not in our stars / But in ourselves,
that we are underlings."

For the developing countries the best help is and will continue to be self-
help. Not only will self-help enable a developing country to limit its recourse
to foreign borrowing, but it will also facilitate such borrowing as is necessary
by enhancing the country's capacity to raise loans in foreign capital markets
and to service existing loans. The debt problem will continue to cast a dark
shadow over most developing countries unless they undertake the reforms
that will enable them to mobilize fully their own human and financial
resources and put them to the best possible use. Their failure to undertake
those reforms—despite their rhetorical claims to the contrary—has been
a major cause of their inability to service their foreign debt out of their

own income and to set off along the road to sustained economic growth: as Paul Valéry observed, "no nation likes to consider its misfortunes as being its legitimate children." That failure helps to provide an answer to a number of pertinent, albeit impertinent, questions. Why, with a volume of foreign capital comparable to that available to the United States and Canada in the initial stages of their development process, comparable human potential and natural resources, and political independence that dates back almost as far as that of the United States, do the countries of Latin America lag so far behind the two non-Latin countries of the North in economic development and human rights? Why is Haiti still the poorest country in the Americas, with the lowest wage scales—even if in answering that question due account is taken of the fact that the Revolution that made it the first Latin American country to win its independence also led to its *de facto* ostracization by the slave-owning powers in the nineteenth century? Why are so many African countries, after a quarter of a century of political independence, mired in economic and social immobilism?

Those in power in developing countries must finally face the harsh reality that development is impossible without self-denial and that self-reliant development is the only route to sustained economic progress that benefits all social strata. The plight of a number of developing countries, which in international forums is frequently blamed on colonialism or neocolonialism, is too often attributable primarily to what might be called autocolonialism, which involves the exploitation or neglect of the people not by foreigners but by their own egocentric compatriots, who seem to think they have almost a natural right to enrich themselves with impunity as quickly as possible by means of embezzlement, bribery, nepotism, influence peddling, awarding themselves lucrative public contracts and various other dishonest means.

It is true that public life in the countries that are now economically advanced was often corrupt in the past, and to a certain extent remains so today; but the destructive power of that corruption is limited by the force of public opinion and institutional curbs and by the strength and resilience of the national economy. Consequently, the results of that corruption are less catastrophic in those countries than in developing countries. In the developing countries it retards economic growth by siphoning off the scarce financial resources of the community and diverting them to foreign banks or nonproductive domestic uses and by stifling entrepreneurial initiative through the creation of an environment in which the powerful and their friends are above the law, honest entrepreneurs are subjected to harassment, and uncorruptible national technicians are killed or forced into exile.

Corruption is sometimes so pervasive that it creates a climate of uncertainty and insecurity that frightens off honest foreign investors, who do not want to become involved in bribery or to be the passive witnesses of, or accomplices in, the cynical exploitation of human misery. Perhaps even more depressing is the fact that corrupt government tends to perpetuate itself not only because the corrupt class seeks to retain a firm grip on the levers of power by whatever means but also because an extended period of such government lowers the ethical standards applied to the behavior of public officials, debases the moral values of the rising generation and renders the mass of the population resigned and apathetic.

The effects of corruption, of the failure to make sufficient efforts to reduce human misery and of the political persecution brought on by the fear of democratic change can be seen not only inside but also outside the countries concerned. The effects can be seen in the millions of starving people whose instinct of self-perservation, inherent in every living being, leads them to uproot themselves from their natural social, cultural and religious environment, thus deliberately condemning themselves to live as outcasts in foreign lands. The effects can be seen in the particularly dramatic plight of the thousands of desperate people who from time to time have braved the perils of the sea in frail boats, motivated by the hope that one day they would reach less cruel shores, where the concepts of human dignity and freedom are more than hollow ideological slogans.

Unless those in power in a number of developing countries change course and subject their egocentric desires to ethical control, those countries will find it increasingly difficult, if not impossible, to break the vicious circle of cumulative indebtedness resulting from rescheduling and the compounding of interest and to generate sufficient economic growth to improve the general level of living. Consequently, they will face continually declining real per capita incomes and the world in turn will face an endless series of debt renegotiations, with an ever-present threat of widespread default hanging over the international financial system like the sword of Damocles.

If the developing countries are to reestablish creditworthiness over the long term and at the same time create structural conditions for sustained economic and social development, they will have to enhance the probity of their public administration, increase the efficiency of their economic management, and practice monetary self-restraint to reduce inflation and budgetary self-restraint to curtail or eliminate waste and promote capital formation. In particular, they will have to make a greater tax effort and take stronger action to mobilize personal savings to generate substantial financing resources that can be supplemented by net capital inflows.

The Need for a Greater Tax Effort by Developing Countries. A fiscal policy designed to bring in more tax revenue is one of the major means of improving prospects for generating more resources for much-needed economic and social infrastructure and enabling developing countries to achieve a greater degree of financial self-reliance through their own efforts. Taxation is one of the three methods available to a country for mobilizing domestic savings, the others being financial intermediation and inflation. The experience of Latin American countries has shown that inflation is a dangerous option, and where inflation is out of control, there is a need for determined action to tighten fiscal discipline and curb monetary expansion.

As can be seen from Table 6, there is plenty of room in developing countries for increasing the ratio of aggregate tax revenue to gross domestic product. That ratio is commonly referred to as the "tax burden." However, the term "tax effort" seems more appropriate, since the payment of taxes should be viewed not as a burden imposed on the taxpayer but as the means by which he or she participates in a cooperative effort by contributing his or her share of the financial resources needed for the smooth functioning of the society in which he or she lives. In many developing countries, the tax effort represents less than 20 percent of GDP and in some of them less than 10 percent, that is, less than one-quarter of the tax effort of many industrialized countries. Of course, in countries where most taxpayers have low incomes, any increase in taxation that reduces their already low purchasing power may result in increased hardship, and it would therefore be both unfair and unrealistic to compare the tax-revenue performance of developing countries indiscriminately with that of industrialized countries. What is striking—indeed, disturbing—is that the tax efforts of many developing countries are not commensurate with their levels of development and per capita incomes. Some developing countries make a greater tax effort than others with a comparable or even higher level of development and/or with a similar or even higher per capita income.

As can be seen from Tables 7 and 8, the share of personal income tax in the national tax effort of many developing countries is extremely small, whether those countries are compared with industrialized countries or other developing countries. In many Third World nations, the bulk of tax revenue is derived from indirect taxes, the burden of which weighs heavily on the poor, who spend most of their income. This confirms the continuing relevance of the aphorism of the French jurist Gaston Jèze, *La classe au pouvoir échappe à l'impôt* ("The ruling class escapes taxation"). Within the framework of a greater national tax effort aimed at increasing their financial self-reliance, developing countries should place particular emphasis on augmenting the share of personal income tax in the total effort. In so doing, however, it is essential to steer a middle course between a tax system that discourages saving by siphoning off too large a proportion of an individual's income and a tax system depending almost entirely on indirect taxes that imposes a disproportionately large tax burden on the poor, leaving virtually untaxed the incomes of the rich, who often deprive their countries of the benefit of their savings by placing the latter abroad. Governments may therefore wish to endeavour to strike a reasonable balance by setting taxation at levels high enough to produce sufficient revenue for essential infrastructure projects but not so high as to discourage business and personal savings.

The question then arises, how high is "high enough" and at the same

Table 6
The World Tax League

Rank	Country	Tax Effort (Tax Revenue as Percentage of GDP)	Rank	Country	Tax Effort (Tax Revenue as Percentage of GDP)
1	Sweden	50.3	52	Seychelles	19.2
2	Norway	47.8	53	Fiji	18.8
3	Belgium	46.6	54	Indonesia	18.7
4	Netherlands	45.5	55	Yemen Arab Rep.	18.6
5	Denmark	44.0	56	Jordan	17.6
6	France	43.7	57	Costa Rica	17.5
7	Israel	41.1	58	Cyprus	17.2
8	Austria	41.0	59	Rep. of Korea	17.1
9	Ireland	40.5	60	Tanzania	17.0
10	United Kingdom	40.0	61	Peru	16.9
11	Italy	38.3	62	Singapore	16.7
12	Luxembourg	37.7	63	Mauritania	16.6
13	Fed. Rep. of Germany	37.3	64	Zaire	16.5
14	Finland	36.8	65	Bahamas	16.4
15	Canada	34.9	66	Papau New Guinea	16.2
16	New Zealand	34.0	67	Madagascar	16.0
17	Greece	31.7	68	Benin	16.0
18	Australia	31.6	69	Malawi	15.9
19	Portugal	31.1	70	Cameroon	15.6
20	Switzerland	30.9	71	Sierra Leone	15.2
21	United States	30.5	72	Gambia	15.0
22	Trinidad and Tobago	30.5	73	Nicaragua	14.7
23	Guyana	28.8	74	Pakistan	14.5
24	Swaziland	28.5	75	India	14.0
25	Egypt	27.9	76	Mexico	13.9
26	Japan	27.2	77	Oman	13.7
27	Congo	26.9	78	Honduras	13.5
28	Togo	26.7	79	Thailand	13.4
29	Tunisia	25.9	80	Upper Volta	13.3
30	Chile	25.6	81	Colombia	13.2
31	Surinam	24.9	82	Ghana	13.1
32	Spain	23.8	83	Sudan	13.1
33	Brazil	23.2	84	El Salvador	12.7
34	Jamaica	23.1	85	Mali	12.5
35	Liberia	22.6	86	Philippines	12.3
36	Zambia	22.3	87	Ethiopia	12.2
37	Sri Lanka	22.2	88	Niger	12.1
38	Malaysia	21.5	89	Ecuador	11.8
39	Mauritius	21.4	90	Dominican Rep.	11.6
40	Botswana	21.4	91	Burundi	11.3
41	Argentina	21.3	92	Syrian Arab Rep.	11.3
42	Morocco	21.2	93	Rwanda	11.1
43	Panama	20.9	94	Paraguay	11.1
44	Kenya	20.9	95	Burma	9.9
45	Gabon	20.7	96	Guatemala	9.4
46	Nigeria	20.6	97	Chad	9.3
47	Senegal	20.1	98	Haiti	9.3
48	Lesotho	20.1	99	Bolivia	8.6
49	Venezuela	20.0	100	Bangladesh	7.5
50	Grenada	19.7	101	Nepal	6.4
51	Turkey	19.3			

Source: Calculated on the basis of statistics from the Organisation for Economic Co-operation and Development and the International Monetary Fund. The figures for industrialized countries relate to 1982; those for developing countries are average figures for 1974-1976, 1975-1977, 1976-1978, 1977-1979, 1978-1980, 1979-1981.

Table 7
Industrialized Countries: Share of Personal Income Tax in the National Tax Effort
(Taxes on Personal Income as Percentage of Total Taxation)

	1965	1981
Australia	34.1	45.6
Austria	20.2	23.7
Belgium	20.5	34.8
Canada	23.0	33.8
Denmark	41.4	52.5
Federal Republic of Germany	25.9	29.0
Finland	35.8	45.8
France	10.6	13.3
Ireland	16.7	31.4
Italy	10.9	26.4
Japan	22.0	24.7
Luxembourg	24.8	27.8
Netherlands	27.6	24.7
New Zealand	39.4	61.4
Norway	39.7	26.3
Spain	14.3	20.2
Sweden	48.8	39.9
Switzerland	31.2	35.7
United Kingdom	29.8	29.3
United States	30.5	37.6

Source: Organisation for Economic Co-operation and Development, Revenue Statistics of OECD Member Countries, 1965-1982, p. 72.

time "not too high"? This question cannot be answered by providing one figure that is valid for all countries. However, some guidance can be obtained from an article written by Colin Clark that appeared in the December 1945 issue of the *Economic Journal* of London. In that article, Clark propounded the idea that for economic, political and psychological reasons, the level of taxation should not exceed 25 percent of net national income at factor costs. He contended that a higher level of taxation would increase costs by discouraging initiative and productive effort, prompt both businesses and individuals to engage in carelessly planned spending provided that the expenditure was tax deductible, and weaken the capacity of politicians to resist pressures. This idea was controversial when first published, at a time when the political and intellectual climate was strongly influenced by Keynesian economics. However, it has gathered a substantial measure of support since then, due to increasingly high levels of taxation in industrialized countries, which have at times been twice as high as the 25 percent limit mentioned by Clark.

The Need for a Greater Effort by Developing Countries to Mobilize Domestic Personal Savings. The Chief Economist of the Asian Development Bank, speaking at a press conference at the Bank's headquarters on 21 November 1984, observed:

Many Asian developing countries need to raise their level of investment if they are to achieve growth rates which are sufficiently high to create any significant improvement in the economic welfare of their populations. They face the problem of raising national saving to finance this level of investment. Other Asian developing countries which already have a high level of investment also must raise the national saving rate for they will not be able to depend on inflows of foreign savings to the same degree as they have in the past.[31]

A similar note had been struck earlier by the magazine *Afrique: Expansion*, which in the article "Indebtedness: The Fall-out from Rescheduling," published in the June-July 1984 issue, had observed:

As everybody knows, the world economy has now been locked into a vicious circle for more than ten years: industrial recession leads to a financial crisis which causes a decrease in trade that in turn aggravates the industrial recession. Africa was drawn into this vicious circle with a certain time-lag, but it is nevertheless completely entrapped by it today. . . . Does this mean that Africa has no alternative but to await the catastrophe that is always possible but never certain? The founders of *Afrique: Expansion* were willing to bet that there are sufficient human and natural resources in Africa to permit self-centered development. Africa can protect itself from the vicious circle of world recession by developing its food crops and industrializing to meet its own needs. And this development will necessitate the mobilization of African savings, which will make it possible to limit external indebtedness. The establishment of national agricultural banks . . . is already a step in this direction. There are grounds for optimism in the fact that various initiatives are being taken along these lines: for example, the United Nations is organizing from 10 to 15 December 1984 in Yaoundé a symposium on the mobilization of savings in developing countries.[32]

The Yaoundé Symposium, like earlier symposia in the same series and other gatherings on the subject of the mobilization of personal savings organized by the United Nations, concluded that a low level of income does not preclude the accumulation of personal savings. The first of these gatherings, the United Nations interregional seminar held in Stockholm in 1971, rejected the notion that because people are poor they are incapable

Table 8
Developing Countries: Share of Personal Income Tax in the National Tax Effort
(Taxes on Personal Income as Percentage of Total Taxation Averaged about 1979)

Turkey	46.8	Greece	11.0
Fiji	41.2	Congo	11.00
Papau New Guinea	28.3	Chad	10.6
Mauritania	25.5	Malaysia	10.4
Barbados	24.1	Burkina Faso	10.4
Jamaica	19.9	Bolivia	10.3
Seychelles	19.8	Chile	10.0
Zaire	19.7	Lesotho	9.9
Zambia	19.5	Ghana	9.8
Liberia	18.9	Ethiopia	9.4
Mexico	18.3	El Salvador	9.0
Costa Rica	15.4	Tunisia	9.0
Grenada	15.1	India	8.8
Malawi	14.7	Morocco	8.4
Cyprus	14.5	Thailand	8.3
Trinidad and Tobago	14.3	Madagascar	8.2
Guyana	14.2	Surinam	8.0
Philippines	14.2	Siera Leone	7.9
Rep. of Korea	13.9	Mali	7.9
Bangladesh	13.5	Dominican Rep.	7.8
Honduras	13.4	Rwanda	7.4
Mauritius	12.7	Burundi	7.3
Cameroon	12.1	Nepal	6.6

Table 8—*continued*

Swaziland	11.3	Nigeria	0.1
Parkistan	6.5	Argentina	0.1
Colombia	11.2		
Niger	6.1		
Togo	6.1		
Egypt	5.8		
Senegal	5.8		
The Gambia	5.6		
Yemen Arab Rep.	5.1		
Haiti	4.1		
Jordan	3.9		
Benin	3.9		
Venezuela	3.7		
Guatemala	3.5		
Sri Lanka	3.3		
Sudan	3.3		
Gabon	2.9		
Tanzania	2.8		
Peru	2.5		
Indonesia	2.3		
Uruguay	1.5		
Brazil	0.8		
Paraguay	0.2		

Source: International Monetary Fund, Government Finance Statistics Yearbook, vol. 6 (1982); World Bank, Atlas (1981).

of saving or are unwilling to save. The seminar noted that even in very poor countries, an increase in personal income was not used simply for consumption.

Of course, the ability to save depends on *disposable income*, that is, after-tax income, and on consumption requirements, which vary according to the number of dependents per income earner. However, there is convincing evidence that when people know that they themselves will have to provide for "rainy days," they often find a way to put aside precautionary savings, whatever their income level, although they will tend to save more as their income rises. Almost three decades ago Sir Arthur Lewis, firmly convinced that charity has never enabled a country to develop, appealed to the pride of his fellow West Indians by observing:

This opinion that the West Indies can raise all the capital it needs from its own resources is bound to shock many people, because West Indians like to feel that ours is poor community. But the fact of the matter is that at least half of the people in the world are poorer than we are. . . . It is not necessary for us to send our statesmen around the world begging for help. If help is given to us let us accept it, but let us not sit down and say nothing can be done until the rest of the world out of its goodness of heart is willing to grant us charity.[33]

Sir Arthur's remarks are, of course, applicable to a very large number of developing countries. Many of them state or imply in their development plans that they will rely less and less on external finance, but in fact such finance has accounted for a growing share of their gross capital formation. Others have virtually made external assistance the lynch-pin of their development strategy and their development plans have basically been no more than blueprints for foreign aid.

In many developing countries, the mobilization of personal savings is still greatly handicapped by a policy of artificially low interest rates (often negative real rates), inadequate financial intermediation, the absence of financial instruments targeted at households having no previous experience with financial institutions and the inefficient allocation of savings among alternative investment opportunities. On the whole, financial repression has led households that are anxious to preserve the purchasing power of their capital to hold their savings as real assets such as jewelry or gold and stocks of merchandise, rather than in the form of bank deposits and other income-yielding financial assets. It has led more sophisticated savers to devise ways to expatriate their capital and thus succeed in profiting from the rates of remuneration offered in the United States market and elsewhere. It has also led other savers to engage directly in moneylending, the riskiness of which is rendered acceptable only by the exorbitant loan rates in the curb market. In fact, as a result of financial repression, most savers in developing countries still constitute a group whose interests are sacrificed, not always on the altar of the general good.

If personal savings mobilization campaigns are to succeed to any significant degree, the institutional framework for the mobilization of savings will have to be strengthened in the following main ways:

—By encouraging existing savings-mobilization institutions to reach out to urban workers and dwellers in rural areas.

—By promoting the establishment of specialized grass-roots institutions such as savings banks, credit unions, cooperatives and rural banks.

—By creating a political and business climate that increases confidence in domestic financial institutions.

—By introducing new financial instruments targeted at potential new savers, who are often wary of entrusting their economies to institutions they do not completely understand.

—By improving the allocative efficiency of the financial intermediaries, which should enjoy more freedom in adjusting their investment patterns and lending rates so as to be able to offer higher rates of interest on savings.

—By resolving the interest rate dilemma so as to offer savers returns that compare favorably with other domestic yields and also with interest rates available elsewhere in order to encourage the diversion of savings from the curb market to the institutional financial sector and to discourage the overt or clandestine flight of capital to the United States and other world financial centers. (There are other reasons that prompt people to send their savings abroad, such as fear of political instability and fear of depreciation of the national currency.) Foreign interest rates could be ignored by the authorities when setting domestic interest rates by administrative decision only if it were possible to prevent domestic capital from leaving the country or to disregard indefinitely the continuing erosion of the exchange rate of the national currency.

Self-reliance and North-South Relations. Greater self-help efforts on the part of the developing countries would do much to enhance their image in the industrialized countries and strengthen their hand in international relations. In the absence of such efforts, the demands of the developing countries, no matter how justified, will continue to go unheeded. Unless the developing world is endowed with a remarkable capacity for self-deception, it must realize that only optimum mobilization and rational use of its material and human resources can prepare the way for a productive dialogue with the countries of the North, whose financial ability and political will to provide significant assistance or make significant trade concessions have dwindled appreciably. There is every indication that unless the South demonstrates a determination to undertake the necessary economic and social reforms, the North is prepared to continue living with the problems of hunger, illiteracy and disease in the South, stepping up aid only for humanitarian purposes in emergency situations.

After all, when the rich and powerful in so many countries of the South display shocking indifference to the tragic plight of their compatriots, what moral right do politicians from the South have to appeal to the compassion of taxpayers in the North? Similarly, when the rich and the powerful in the South, disregarding the lessons of history, refuse to see that it is in their enlightened self-interest to devote more of their countries' resources to bettering the lot of their own peoples, do politicians from the South really believe that they can convince political leaders of the North that it is in the enlightened self-interest of industrialized countries to allocate more of their resources to foreign aid and to agree that the South should receive a greater share of the gains from international investment and trade? In short, why should the developing countries expect the industrialized countries to act in accordance with the principle of interdependence among nations when they themselves often fail to abide by the principle of the interdependence of social groups within a single nation?

How can the developing countries expect their call in international forums for a new international economic order to be heeded when at home many of them are doing all they can to maintain the status quo? The willingness of some developing countries' governments to promote development that would benefit all social strata is suspect when they continue to waste human resources by violating human rights and, in particular, politically persecuting national technicians and other skilled personnel who refuse to condone corruption or who hold views different from those of the people in power.

The lack of popular support for some regimes in developing countries—of which political leaders in industrialized countries are well aware and which is widely publicized by the media in those countries—has undoubtedly weakened the bargaining power of the developing world in North-South negotiations. It is, after all, a basic principle of diplomacy that governments enjoying the full backing of their peoples are taken more seriously in international negotiations, for meaningful dialogue can take place only between truly equal political partners. More specifically, doubts about the degree to which the governments of a number of developing countries truly represent their peoples have certainly contributed to the increasing tendency to question the value of the results of the voting in international organizations ruled by the principle of one state-one vote. Those doubts also may have contributed to—or provided a pretext for—the decline in international cooperation in the areas of trade and finance that has occurred since the 1970s, indicating an apparent breakdown of the consensus on cooperation for development that prevailed throughout the 1950s and the 1960s.

The decline in international economic cooperation is reflected in the difficulties of developing countries in gaining wider access to the markets of the industrialized countries. Although the industrialized countries have not resorted to generalized overt protectionism, a more covert type of protectionism, involving ad hoc trade restrictions, has been expanding. These restrictions have included quotas, "voluntary" export restraints, and increasing bilateralism and countertrade. Industrialized countries have also been protecting their ailing industries by subsidies and their agriculture by farm support programs. Almost one-third of developing countries' agricultural exports to industrialized countries and almost one-fifth of their exports of manufactured goods to those countries encounter quota restraints or other nontariff barriers. There is a growing conviction in some circles that a trading system that is managed to some extent may be a better national policy tool than an open trading system that threatens a country's import-competing industries and export industries, although this conviction is in obvious contradiction with the Western countries' oft-proclaimed adherence to free market principles. In the United States, where those principles have by and large prevailed since the Second World War, increasing political pressure is being exerted on the Reagan administration to move to a more aggressive trade policy in order to reduce the country's trade deficit and stem the loss of jobs and markets to foreign competitors. It was in that context that in June 1985 five Cabinet officers including the Secretary of the Treasury and the Secretary of State sent every member of Congress a letter warning of the potentially harmful impact of a textile quota bill cosponsored by a majority in both the House and the Senate that would cut back textile imports by 36 percent. The letter pointed out that if enacted the bill would cost consumers $2 billion a year, violate international obligations, drastically cut imports from developing countries such as Brazil and Indonesia and lead to retaliation. Other studies have revealed, for example, that United States protection of the steel industry, in terms of the higher prices passed on to buyers, cost an amount approximately four times as large as the cost of compensation per job saved. The studies also showed that the ratio was even higher in the case of certain consumer goods. Nevertheless, there is broad support in the United States Congress for protectionist bills that would reduce imports of shoes from Brazil, the Republic of Korea and Taiwan, of cement from Mexico and of petrochemicals from Saudi Arabia. There is also support for bills that would impose a tariff surcharge of 15 to 20 percent on all United States imports and for bills that would limit imports of some products from industrialized countries, such as lumber from Canada, wine from France and Italy and telephones from Japan.

It may be recalled that under the rules of the General Agreement on Tariffs and Trade (GATT), about two-thirds of all imports from developing countries are admitted duty-free to the United States and the countries of the European Economic Community. Another one-fifth are eligible for preferential treatment under the Generalized System of Preferences (GSP). The ten most advanced developing countries account for the largest share of GSP exports. However, certain categories of products from some of the more advanced developing countries have been excluded from the GSP schemes of the United States and the European Economic Community. A number of imports from developing countries, including certain agricultural, leather and mineral products and footwear, which are judged to be fully competitive with similar products made in industrialized countries, bear duty at normal, not preferential rates.

All GSP schemes have been renewed beyond their initial ten-year period. Thus, on 28 June 1984 the Canadian Parliament enacted legislation extending Canada's scheme for another ten years. On 30 October 1984 the President of the United States signed into law the Trade and Tariff Act of 1984, authorizing the extension of the United States GSP scheme—which was to expire on 3 January 1985—for eight and one-half years. The extended United States scheme will thus cover a shorter period than the other time-bound schemes, which have been extended for ten years. However, the Trade and Tariff Act of 1984 made a number of changes in the scheme. One change denies GSP eligibility to any country that fails to take steps to afford its workers internationally recognized workers' rights, unless the President of the United States determines that such action would be contrary to national economic interest. As defined in the act, these rights include the right of association, the right to organize and bargain collectively, the right not to be subjected to any form of forced or compulsory labor, a minimum wage for the employment of children, and acceptable conditions of work with respect to minimum wages, hours of work, and occupational safety and health. Another change concerns the addition to the list of items excluded by statute from eligibility of footwear, handbags, luggage, flat goods, work gloves and leather wearing apparel; this exclusion is identical to that in the Caribbean Basin Economic Recovery Act.[34] A third change is aimed at terminating benefits under the scheme after a two-year phase-out period in the case of any beneficiary whose per capita GNP exceeds $8,500 (indexed to one-half the growth in nominal United States GNP since 1984). The act also provides that a beneficiary country will lose eligibility for preferential treatment for a particular product if its shipments of that product in the preceding calendar year exceed 50 percent of the value of total United States imports of the product or a specified amount, which grows in proportion to the previous year's growth of the GNP. The act empowers the President of the United States to negotiate concessions from developing countries in exchange for continued favored access for their exports to the United States market. However, a request for such concessions would clearly run counter to the GSP's basic principle of nonreciprocity.

The decline in international economic cooperation is also reflected in the fact that there are only a handful of commodity agreements, that is, multilateral agreements covering the production and international marketing of primary commodities that are produced mainly by developing countries. Similarly, the Common Fund for Commodities, negotiated within the framework of the United Nations Conference on Trade and Development, has yet to become operational and seems unlikely to do so in the foreseeable future. In effect, the Fund cannot begin functioning until its constituent agreement (adopted in 1980) has been ratified by 90 countries, and as of mid-1985 only eighty-three countries had done so. Moreover, the ninety ratifying countries must collectively account for two-thirds of the capital subscription, a condition that cannot be met unless either the United States or the Soviet Union is one of the ratifying countries, which gives them the power to decide the fate of the Fund. By mid-1985, the countries that had ratified the constituent agreement of the Fund accounted for 50 percent of the $470 million capital for the Fund's First Account, whose proceeds will be used to finance existing commodity agreements that provide for international buffer stocks. As to the Fund's Second Account, whose proceeds will be used for financial support for activities undertaken by international commodity bodies in such areas as research and development, productivity improvement and marketing, some $266 million had been pledged but could not be utilized because the Common Fund had not become operational.

The consequences of the lack of continued progress in North-South cooperation for development could be partially offset by greater progress in South-South cooperation. Regrettably, disputes and armed conflicts between neighboring developing countries, which would normally be expected to be allies in the developing world's war against underdevelopment, reduce the effectiveness of regional economic cooperation bodies and jeopardize the prospects for increased interregional economic cooperation in the South, in other words for greater collective self-reliance among developing countries. They lead to a waste of resources that could be used to alleviate hunger, disease and illiteracy and a further weakening of the South's moral, political and economic position in its dealings with the North.

To sum up, the position of the South would be greatly strengthened if the developing countries were to mobilize more domestic financial resources by increasing their tax efforts; by adopting economic and fiscal measures that would encourage people to hold their savings in the form of domestic financial assets rather than domestic real assets and creating an ethical and patriotic climate that would strengthen the confidence of their peoples in the future of their own countries and thus prompt them to invest their savings in the building of that future rather than to send them abroad; and by achieving greater collective self-reliance through increased regional and interregional economic cooperation among themselves, a process that would be greatly facilitated by the peaceful settlement of the disputes currently pitting neighboring developing countries against each other.

If the developing countries were thus to strengthen their collective position, it would considerably undermine the justification or pretext for resistance in the North to increased cooperation for development with the South, and it would help to dissipate the doubts about the developing countries' determination and ability to earn their way back to solvency and creditworthiness and to achieve and sustain economic growth through their own efforts. By putting the concept of interdependence into practice among the various social groups in each country and among themselves, the developing countries would bring moral pressure to bear on the industrialized countries to acknowledge that interdependence is not a hollow political concept invented by the Group of 77 in the United Nations as a device for extracting never-ending flows of financial aid and trade concessions from the North, but a practical reality that transcends narrow national interest and can benefit the North as well as the South.

Greater individual and collective self-reliance on the part of developing countries would mean not only stricter moral standards for officials but also greater realism, discipline and organization in the use of financial resources. This would constitute the best guarantee that any assistance the industrialized countries may provide will not disappear into a bottomless pit but will be used for constructive purposes, and that the developing countries are not relying solely or essentially on such assistance but regard it simply as a temporary supplement to their self-help efforts.

NOTES

1. The international bond markets are the foreign bond markets, in which bonds are usually issued and placed in a country other than that of the borrower and denominated in the currency of the country in which they are issued, and the Eurobond markets, in which bonds are issued simultaneously in more than one market by international syndicates of underwriters-selling groups and are denominated in a third country's currencies. The largest foreign bond market is that of the United States, where no authorization is required for the issue of securities. Other foreign bond markets tend to be subject to regulation, and some of them have at various times been closed to foreign borrowing to enable the government of the country concerned to meet its borrowing needs or to keep interest rates low, protect the balance-of-payments position or achieve other domestic policy goals. By the mid-1970s the Eurobond market was twice as large as the United States foreign bond market and almost as large as all of the foreign bond markets combined.

2. The Voluntary Foreign Credit Restraint Program administered by the Federal Reserve Board and the Foreign Direct Investment Program administered by the Department of Commerce were terminated; the effective rate of the Interest Equalization Tax was reduced to zero, and the legislation imposing the tax expired in June 1974.

3. Gaston Jèze, "*Les défaillances d'etats*," Recueil des cours de l'Académie de droit international de la Haye, 1935–III, Paris: Sirey, 1936, pp. 381, 386.

4. W. Arthur Lewis, *The Theory of Economic Growth*, London: George Allen & Unwin, 1955, p. 254.

5. Private firms as a whole account for more than 20 percent of Latin America's foreign borrowing.

6. Luis Burstin "Myths on Latin Upheavals," *The New York Times*, 9 February 1984, A31.

7. Bank for International Settlements, *Fifty-Fourth Annual Report*, pp. 111, 171.

8. Alexander L. Taylor III, "Where Did the Money Go?" *Time*, 2 July 1984, p. 40.

9. Eduardo Wiesner, "Domestic and External Causes of the Latin American Debt Crisis," *Financial and Development*, March 1985, 26.

10. Jeremy Bentham, *In Defence of Usury*, London, 1787.

11. The Federal Reserve System exerts jurisdiction over state chartered banks that are members of the Federal Reserve System, bank holding companies, and Edge Act Corporations engaged in banking. The Comptroller of the Currency has jurisdiction over banks with national charters, and the Federal Deposit Insurance Corporation has jurisdiction over state chartered banks that are not members of the Federal Reserve System.

12. Harold Lever, "The Road to Solvency," *The Wall Street Journal*, 7 June 1984.

13. The Monroe Doctrine derived from the message addressed to Congress on 2 December 1823 by James Monroe, who stated therein "The American continents by the free and independent condition which they have assumed and maintain, are henceforth not to be considered as subject for future colonization by any European power. . . . We could not view any interposition for the purpose of oppressing [the American republics or] controlling in any other manner their destiny by any European power in any other light than as the manifestation of an unfriendly disposition toward the United States."

In the corollary, first enumerated in May 1904 and repeated in a 6 December 1904 message, Theodore Roosevelt declared, "In the Western Hemisphere, the adherence of the United States to the Monroe Doctrine may force the United States, however reluctantly in flagrant cases of such wrongdoing or impotence, to the exercise of an international policy power."

14. Lewis, *The Theory of Economic Growth*, p. 155.

15. Walter Bagehot, *Lombard Street: A Description of the Money Market*, London, 1873.

16. Federation of Latin American Bankers Associations, "Declaration of the Commercial Banks of Latin America on the External Indebtedness of the Continent," *World of Banking*, January-February 1984, 12–13.

17. A loan is generally considered to become a nonaccural loan when the borrower falls behind on payments of principal or interest. Before June 1984 a number of United States banks classified loans as nonaccrual only when principal or interest payments were more than ninety days overdue on the day when they filed their income statements. They could thus record uncollected interest as income even for loans that were obviously not being serviced in accordance with the loan contracts. In June 1984 the Board of Governors of the Federal Reserve System and the Comptroller of the Currency sent the banks a joint statement explaining their policy

regarding the nonaccrual status of loans. According to that policy, loans are to be classified as nonaccrual on the day that principal or interest payments become ninety days overdue. When a loan is placed on nonaccrual status, any interest accrued but not actually collected must be deducted from income, and any additional interest is added to income only when interest payments are actually received. A loan retains its nonaccrual status until all principal and interest payments are up to date.

18. "Leaving the Debt Game While You're Ahead," *The Times* (London), 8 May 1984.

19. Commonwealth Secretariat, *The Debt Crisis and the World Economy*, London, July 1984, pp. 7, 13.

20. Harold Lever, "The Road to Solvency," *The Wall Street Journal*, 7 June 1984.

21. Henry Kissinger "Can There Be Life After Debt," *The Sunday Times*, 24 June 1984, 60.

22. "Strengthening U.S. Competitiveness," *World Financial Markets*, Morgan Guaranty Trust Company of New York, September 1984, 12.

23. United Nations, *World Economic Survey, 1968—Part One (E/4687/Rev.1; ST/ECA/118)*, New York, 1968, p. 63.

24. United Nations, *Foreign Investment in Developing Countries (E/4446)*, New York, 1968, p. 39.

25. Conference on International Economic Co-operation, Report of the Commission of Financial Affairs, 14 May 1977, p. 14.

26. Editorial, "The Shadow Over Latin America," *Financial Times*, 30 October 1984.

27. I.M.D. Little, "Thinkers and Doers," *Finance and Development*, March 1985, 48.

28. James Scheuer, "Playing Charades at Cancun," *The New York Times*, 28 October 1981.

29. Robert W. Kasten, Jr., "Our Alleged U.N. Friends," *The New York Times*, 17 June 1985.

30. Ibid.

31. Asian Development Bank, *Quarterly Review*, January 1985, 8.

32. "Indebtedness: The Fall-Out from Rescheduling," *Afrique: Expansion*, June-July 1984. The Yaoundé Symposium, of which I was the chairman, was the third in a series. The first International Symposium on the Mobilization of Personal Savings in Developing Countries was held in Kingston, Jamaica, in February 1980 and the second in Kuala Lumpur, Malaysia, in March 1982. All three symposia, as well as the earlier gatherings, were organized by the United Nations in cooperation with the International Savings Banks Institute and the Swedish Savings Banks Association. For the Yaoundé Symposium the original coorganizers were joined by three French entities, namely, the Caisse des Dépôts et Consignations, the Centre National des Caisses d'Epargne et de Prévoyance, and the Centre d'Etudes et de Recherche sur l'Epargne, les Patrimoines et les Inegalités.

33. Study Conference of Economic Development in Underdeveloped Countries, 5–15 August 1957, University of the West Indies, Jamaica.

34. The Caribbean Basin Economic Recovery Act, which came into effect on 1 January 1984 for twelve years, is aimed at expanding the productive capacity of

developing countries in Central America, northern South America and the Caribbean. It gives their products greater preferential access to the United States market and provides tax incentives for United States firms investing in those countries. The act allows exports from the Caribbean Basin (except textiles and clothing) to enter the United States duty free. Sugar exports are duty free only up to a certain limit, in order to protect the United States domestic sugar price support program.

4   Administered Interest Rates versus Market Interest Rates

The interest rate dilemma facing the developing world has arisen because on the one hand, developing countries have in most cases been setting their interest rates by administrative decision at levels too low to stimulate domestic personal savings in financial forms, while on the other hand, there is a danger that if interest rates were completely freed from government intervention, they might be driven so high by market forces that they would constrain economic activity.

To understand the options available to governments in their efforts to resolve the interest rate dilemma, it is necessary to review the process of interest rate determination and to analyze the arguments adduced in favor of administered interest rates and market interest rates.

THE PROCESS OF INTEREST RATE DETERMINATION

Interest rates may be considered to be determined by three main systems: the *administered interest rate system*, under which all interest rates are determined solely by administrative decisions; the *modified administered interest rate system*, under which most interest rates or major interest rates are determined by administrative decisions and/or interbank agreements but are modified as often as necessary in the light of market considerations and frequently in the light of the movement of world interest rates; and the *market interest rate system*, under which most interest rates or major interest rates are determined by the interplay of market forces, although the determination process may be influenced to a greater or lesser degree by central bank action. The extent to which market considerations influence administrative decisions concerning interest rates, or conversely the extent to which central bank action influences the determination of interest rates by market forces, indicates differing approaches to the control of the money supply.

The Administered Interest Rate System

Under the administered interest rate system, the interest rates on deposits and/or loans are set by the administration in the form of either absolute values or ceilings, often in a way that makes those rates extremely rigid, even in the face of wide fluctuations in the rate of inflation.

When ceilings are imposed only on the rates payable by banks to depositors, the rates on loans should in principle be determined by competition among financial institutions, although they will fluctuate in line with the rates payable on deposits. The more intense the competition, the smaller the differential between the interest rates charged on loans and the interest rates paid on savings will be, due account being taken of the need for profitability. When the lending institutions agree among themselves to charge the same rates of interest on loans, or when they are so few that a *de facto* quasi-monopoly situation exists, the differential between the average rate they pay to savers and the average rate they charge to borrowers is the widest possible.

Conversely, when ceilings are imposed on interest rates payable on loans, this inevitably entails restriction of the interest rates paid on deposits. A financial institution's ability to grant loans at least cost depends on its ability to mobilize savings at least cost. Therefore leading financial institutions are forced to set the rates of interest they pay on deposits at levels low enough to allow a margin between savers' and borrowers' rates that, after expenses and taxation, is sufficient to maintain adequate reserves. The fiercer the competition among financial institutions in the collection of savings, the smaller that margin will be. When the financial institutions agree that they will pay the same rate on deposits or when the financial institutions are few, the interest rate on deposits is the lowest possible.

The rates or ceilings may be set in legislation enacted by Parliament, in executive power decrees or in regulations issued by the monetary authorities—usually the central banks—in exercise of their statutory powers. Ceilings on lending rates are often set within the framework of usury laws. An administered interest rate system may even be extended to include bank charges and commissions, which are fixed in either relative or absolute terms. Administered interest rates are usually fixed at levels lower than those that would equilibrate the underlying supply of, and demand for, funds. Such levels often make the interest rates negative in real terms, that is, after correction for actual or expected price increases. However, administered interest rates are not necessarily always negative; they may be positive, particularly when they are set with a view to attracting more savings deposits.

Interest rates are automatically set by an administered system in countries with centrally planned economies. There, because of the heavy dependence on administrative control, interest rates, like all other prices, play only a limited role in economic decisions and performance. This is consistent with the Marxist premise that capital is not an independent factor of production but "past labor" and that it should not be allocated by the "invisible hand" of the financial market but should be under the control of the workers. Since there is no financial market, resources are allocated mainly through the state budget in accordance with the provisions of the plan; if unforeseen circumstances necessitate short-term adjustments, they, too, are made through the budget. Because the budget plays such an important allocative role, it is usually larger in relation to aggregate economic activity than in countries where the economy is not centrally planned.

In centrally planned economies, households possess more financial autonomy than enterprises, and consequently demand management has been aimed largely at preventing or counteracting inflationary trends in the household sector by controlling the amount of currency in circulation. The tools used for this purpose include the encouragement of saving by households, regulation of wage payments, limitation of budgetary payments entailing cash flows to households and control over the availability of consumer goods through the state distribution apparatus. Some centrally planned economies have introduced a degree of decentralized decision making and greater financial autonomy to improve performance. These countries increasingly recognize the need to allow interest rates to play a greater role in resource allocation, provided that this does not prove detrimental to other priority objectives, such as equity among groups or among regions. There is even increasing recognition that interest rates can be used as a tool to achieve better use of resources.

Interest rates are also set by an administered system in countries where government policy is socialist oriented. There too, because decision making concerning investments is centralized, interest rates play a limited role in the mobilization and allocation of resources and most equity investment is provided by the government directly through the budgetary process. As in all countries with an administered system, interest rate levels are not commensurate with the opportunity cost of capital in the economy, and rates on both savings deposits and loans do not correspond to the maturities and risks involved.

Interest rates are likewise determined by an administered system in market-oriented developing countries where government participation in business reflects the belief that it is the normal function of the public sector to carry out a wide range of activities to which the private sector is not attracted, to increase its involvement in the development of natural resources, to operate key industries and even to undertake other directly productive activities with a view to promoting economic growth or bringing about needed structural changes. These countries have often sought to foster the growth of the private sector by directly or indirectly providing credit facilities. They are generally characterized by an institutional financial sector that is very narrow compared with the noninstitutional financial sector and by the lack of corporate and government bonds or other interest-bearing assets that would give savers alternatives to bank deposits.

Owing to the lack of nonbank savings instruments, the interest on which would vary in response to the interplay of market forces, monetary savings tend to accumulate in the banks, which use them to finance commercial transactions and the construction and purchase of housing. Sometimes the banks find so few sound domestic investment opportunities that they have to let their funds lie idle or send them abroad. Since the banks are virtually the only source of financing apart from self-financing and family financing, the aggregate volume of credits channeled into the economy tends to fluctuate at an equal pace with the volume of funds on deposit with the banks.

The lack of a market for corporate bonds is partly a result of the relatively large size of the public sector and of a policy of channeling investment in public enterprises through the government budget, a policy that has greatly reduced the need for public enterprises to float bond issues. It is also partly the result of a reluctance to open closely held family businesses (especially in Latin America and Southeast Asia) to the public even by issuing bonds, let alone selling shares. Even in Asian countries with a relatively well-developed institutional financial sector, heavy dependence on provident funds as major mechanisms for mobilizing personal savings has impeded the development of a bond and share market in harmony with the level of financial development in those countries.

The lack of government bonds is a corollary of the practice of financing budget deficits by borrowing from the central bank, from the banking system (usually in the form of purchases of Treasury bills) or from foreign sources. The lack of both public corporate bonds and government bonds results to a certain extent from the fact that governments and public enterprises sometimes do not enjoy the degree of public confidence they need to be able to sell bonds on an open market. Another contributing factor in some countries is a policy inherited from continental Europe, where traditionally—in contrast to the practice in the United Kingdom and the countries that follow its tradition—the banks tend to play a much greater role in long-term financing than the financial market.

Market-oriented developing countries applying the administered interest rate system take a non-market approach to savings and credit policy. They do not resort to pricing tools such as variable deposit rates and frequent adjustments in the cost of credit. Rather, they have recourse to quantitative tools—such as overall credit ceilings for stabilization and balance-of-payments purposes and rediscounting ceilings for trade financing and other sector financing needs—with a view to influencing the allocation of financial resources in line with their development objectives. Typically, these countries are developing countries that have continued to apply a system originally introduced during the colonial era as an extension of the administered rate system applied in the metropolitan countries or that have adopted an interest rate system patterned mainly after the systems that formerly existed in the Federal Republic of Germany, France, the United Kingdom and the United States. However, the latter systems have evolved towards the modified administered rate system or the market rate system.

An administered interest rate system still exists in a number of industrialized countries. These countries generally have one or more of the following characteristics:

—Public sector investment is sizable, and public authorities tend to intervene in the allocation of financial resources to sectors and economic agents, frequently doing so under pressure from groups seeking advantages such as reduced borrowing costs.

—Public authorities are in a dominant position vis à vis the market and have many ways of ensuring that their borrowing needs are satisfied before those of all other borrowers.

—The deficiencies of the market as a financing mechanism stem from government intervention, and the public sector interferes significantly with private sector investment.

—Fiscal policy is used to regulate the supply of and demand for investment capital.

The Modified Administered Interest Rate System

Under the modified administered interest rate system, all interest rates or many interest rates are determined by administrative decisions but are adjusted in the light of market conditions and, where appropriate, the movement of world interest rates. A modified administered interest rate system may likewise be said to exist where all or most interest rates are agreed on or recommended within the framework of formal interest rate cartels or more informal interbank agreements. These cartels or agreements receive the tacit approval of the authorities, which find the rates set in this manner politically acceptable.

The interest rates determined by the modified administered interest rate system are usually set at levels that are very closely related to what the government regards as the prevailing requirements of the economy, to the constraints of the government's social priorities, or to what the government perceives as politically palatable limits. To avoid being obliged, by the pressure of market forces, to adjust interest rates upward to levels they consider incompatible with their economic and social goals, governments may subsidize interest rates on savings instruments through means such as tax exemption, premiums, and lottery prizes, which help to keep interest rates on loans below market levels. The adoption of a modified administered interest rate system usually reflects the authorities' belief that institutional, financial or other conditions necessary for applying a market rate system are lacking and that the market is incapable of generating what the government views as optimal interest rate levels. In other words, a modified administered interest rate system is generally seen as a second-best substitute for a market rate system rather than as an alternative.

The modified interest rate system operates in various ways. In some cases, rates are set in terms of absolute values or ceilings by administrative means, as in the administered interest rate system, but undergo frequent changes in line with a discretionary policy aimed at keeping them as close as possible to positive real rates or to the levels that would result from competition on an open market. In other cases, the rates are for the most part freed from regulation, but the monetary authorities prescribe ceilings for particular interest rates, especially loans to specific social groups or priority sectors, and/or issue guidelines on the basis of which interest rates are set by formal or informal interbank agreements.

Whereas the administered interest rate system is applied by many developing countries and a small number of industrialized countries with market economies, the modified administered interest rate system is applied by most industrialized countries with market economies and a few developing countries.

The Modified Interest Rate System in Industrialized Countries. The industrialized countries applying the modified administered interest rate system are generally those where government participation in business and government assistance to private enterprise are viewed as the most effective means of combating unemployment and providing services essential to the satisfaction of basic community needs. Consequently, as in most of the countries applying an administered interest rate system, there is a relatively large degree of state involvement in the economy, irrespective of the country's socioeconomic structure and political bent.

The countries applying a modified administered interest rate system tend to make wide use of direct government investment, production subsidies, tax incentives, government regulations, tariff protection and artifical pricing by public utilities. The public sector, which includes a significant portion of the industrial sector, has been entrusted with the tasks of promoting the continued growth of domestic industries, preventing strategic industries from being controlled by foreign interests, providing risk capital for innovative ventures and developing new industries in fields such as data processing, electronics, nuclear energy and space activities. The public sector has also been increasingly required to bail out ailing industries.

The industrialized countries with a modified administered interest rate system consider it their duty to control the use of the resources of both the money market and the capital market and to exert their influence to reduce the cost of borrowing, particularly long-term borrowing. To that end, they have sought to dominate the institutional financial sector, notably through their borrowing policy, their management of the public debt and their monetary and fiscal policies. They also intervene more directly in the market process to modify the conditions of competition between institutions and between instruments. They do so in various ways, in particular by regulating the rate of interest paid to lenders or depositors, by fixing the rates charged or paid by the public sector (for example, on loans from nationalized banks or on deposits with public sector savings banks) and by exempting from taxation the income derived from particular types of institutions (for example, savings banks as opposed to commercial banks).

Belgium provides a typical example of a modified administered interest rate. In that country, most of the rates payable by the main financial intermediaries (the commercial banks, the private savings banks and the semipublic credit institutions) are fixed after consultation and joint discussion within the framework of the Comité de concertation pour l'harmonisation des taux d'intérêt créditeurs, which operates under the supervision of the National Bank. According to the procedures of the Committee, each of the three above-mentioned groups of institutions has the right to take the lead for a given category of rates, as follows: the commercial banks: demand deposits, time deposits and deposits subject to withdrawal notice; the private savings banks and the Caisse Générale d'Epargne et de Retraite: savings deposits; and the semi-public credit institutions: bonds and short-term securities. The initiative for modification is taken by the "pilot group," and as a rule the others follow suit. However, for reasons of monetary policy, the National Bank has the right to impose a ceiling on the proposed rates.

The interest rates payable on sight deposits in Belgium are not influenced by money market trends or by changes in the discount rate of the National Bank. The interest rates payable on other bank deposits are set in the light of market conditions and the balance-of-payments position and have tended to fluctuate in line with the movement of the National Bank's discount rate for accepted bills domiciled at a bank. The rates on large deposits are more closely related than the posted rates to interbank market rates for corresponding maturities and are set by the banks individually. The interest rates payable on regular savings accounts are very stable; they are adjusted only when the differential between them and the rates on time deposits is deemed too large.

The interest payable on the bonds and short-term securities issued by the semipublic credit institutions are coordinated by the Council of Public Credit Institutions (Conseil des Institutions Publiques de Crédit). These rates are set in the light of market conditions, especially conditions in the market for new government securities. The interest rates payable on bonds and short-term certificates issued by the private banks and savings banks are usually aligned with those of securities issued by the semipublic credit institutions. The interest rates payable on bonds issued by industrial or commercial firms are, generally, somewhat higher than those payable on bonds issued by the financial institutions.

The interest rates payable on public debt bonds are fixed by the Ministry of Finance in the light of the conditions prevailing in the Belgian capital market and after consulting with representatives of the main banks. The market for medium- and long-term securities issued by the Government and the other public institutions is regulated (by appropriate buying and selling) by the Fonds des Rentes. Its action tends to smooth out fluctuations rather than influence the general trend. The interest rates payable on certificates issued by the Fonds des Rentes are set by tender, in the light of market condition and the policy of the Fonds, which is determined by the Committee of the Fonds des Rentes, consisting of representatives of the Ministry of Finance and the National Bank.

The interest rates on Treasury certificates with maturities of one month, two months and three months are set by the National Bank, which is responsible for issuing them. The National Bank sells the certificates to the institutions authorized to participate in the market whenever it believes this is justified by market conditions. The interest rates payable on Treasury certificates with maturities of six months, nine months and twelve months, which are issued by tender, are influenced not only by market trends but also by the policy adopted by the monetary authorities, which decide when the certificates are to be issued. The public is not allowed to buy Treasury certificates, which can be purchased only by authorized institutional investors.

The rates charged on bank loans are set by the banks, with noncompulsory reference to guidelines issued weekly by the Bankers' Association. These rates are based on a mix of administered and interbank interest rates. In the case of medium- and long-term loans, interest rates are usually aligned with the rates applied by the National Industrial Credit Corporation (Société Nationale de Crédit à l'Industrie). However, the banks do not apply the same rates across the board to all borrowers. The interest rates applied by the public credit institutions are set by those institutions themselves.

The Modified Administered Interest Rate System in Developing Countries. The developing countries that apply a modified administered rate system rely on the interplay of market forces in connection with the determination of prices in general to a greater degree than do the developing countries that apply the administered interest rate system. Although a sizable number of their institutions and enterprises may be owned or controlled by the government, these countries tend to foster private enterprise through fiscal and financial incentives, and by far the largest share of the gross domestic product is produced by the private sector. Similarly, although government decisions may strongly influence the level and composition of fixed capital formation and the aggregate demand for capital, these countries tend to have only limited recourse to price fixing and price controls. Many of the countries in this category, like many of the countries applying the administered interest rate system, often use certain credit tools to set limits indirectly on interest rates on loans in general or loans to specific categories of borrowers. The tools most frequently used are subsidized loan rates for priority sectors, preferential rediscount rates and credit floors and ceilings.

The Market Interest Rate System

According to standard economic theory, it is the function of the market to ensure that the equilibrium between the supply of, and the demand for, funds is maintained. In the absence of government intervention, the mechanism by which that equilibrium is achieved consists of fluctuations in interest rates induced by the free play of market forces. If the demand for funds outpaces the supply, interest rates will rise; if it falls short of the supply, the reverse will be true.

In practice, however, what is generally referred to as a market interest-rate system is far from being a system in which interest rates are determined by the unrestrained "invisible hand" of the market. Indeed, the "invisible hand" may be considerably restrained by the "visible hand" of the monetary authorities, wielding monetary tools. The free working of the market mechanism may be subject to the constraints of circumstances that cause the authorities to intervene indirectly to ensure that special economic and social priorities are met.

Because of the electorate's concern about unemployment and high interest rates on mortgage loans and other loans for purposes favored by the public, very few elected governments are genuinely enthusiastic about the virtues of the free market so far as the determination of interest rates is concerned. Only in recent years have certain countries taken steps to free interest rates to find their own levels through the relatively untrammeled working of the market mechanism. Even among those countries, generally, interest may still not be paid on demand deposits, although the interest rates payable on less liquid savings instruments have rapidly become increasingly flexible and responsive to market conditions. The countries applying what might be defined as a market rate system are few; of those few, two are particularly relevant to the issues dealt with in this book, namely: the United Kingdom, because it is a major financial center and in particular operates a vast offshore banking system; and the United States, because it, too, is a major financial center and because of the impact of United States interest rates on international interest rates.

The Market Interest Rate System in the United Kingdom. In September 1971 the United Kingdom took the important step of relaxing the controls on bank interest rates and at the same time abolished lending ceilings, which had until then been a major instrument of monetary control. Prior to September 1971 the Bank of England had influenced the conduct of all holders of assets through its control of the *Bank rate*: normally, the minimum rate at which the Bank of England was prepared to lend at last resort to a discount house having access to the Bank's Discount Office, either by rediscounting bills of approved quality or by lending against the collateral of such bills or of short-dated government securities. The Bank rate, which derived its importance from its impact on interest rates (which were either linked to it or fluctuated more or less in line with it), was announced by the Court of Directors of the Bank, usually on Thursday mornings; the Governor of the Bank did not ask the Court to approve a change in the rate until he had made sure that the Chancellor of the Exchequer would agree to the change. The Bank also influenced the conduct of holders of assets through the operations it undertook in the gilt-edged market as manager of the National Debt (selling gilt-edged securities from its Issue Department, which in effect underwrites government stock issues, and buying gilt-edged securities into the Issue Department).

A number of direct controls were applied to the London clearing banks, the Scottish banks, the Northern Ireland banks, other United Kingdom joint stock banks, and other deposit-taking institutions such as the trustee savings banks and building societies and also to nondeposit banks and other financial institutions. Such controls had impeded competition to such an extent that the Bank of England produced the Discussion Paper "Competition and Credit Controls," which recommended a revised system of credit control that was subsequently introduced in September 1971. The revised system of credit control involved the elimination of controls over interest rates and of lending ceilings.

Prior to September 1971 the London clearing banks (so called because they are members of the London Bankers' Clearing House), which handle nearly all domestic banking business of England and Wales, and which together with the Scottish banks and the Northern Ireland banks constitute the main domestic deposit banks, had adhered to a concerted policy on the terms of deposits in "deposit accounts" (the latter usually being called "time deposits" outside the United Kingdom).[1] The interest rate payable on deposit accounts and the period of notice for withdrawal had been fixed by agreement among the London clearing banks. The interest rate on deposit accounts had been set by reference to the Bank rate, and for a long time had generally been 2 percent lower than that rate. The interest rates chargeable on advances had been set according to a formula agreed with customers, usually a stated margin above the Bank rate, subject to a minimum. Most customers generally paid 1.0 percent above the Bank rate, subject to a minimum of 5.0 percent; exceptionally creditworthy private borrowers were charged only 0.5 percent above the Bank rate, and the nationalized industries, whose overdrafts were guaranteed by the government, were charged the Bank rate or 4 percent, whichever was the greater.

The Scottish banks, which handle the domestic banking business of Scotland, had operated as a cartel, fixing by agreement among themselves the rates of interest payable on savings deposits and deposit receipts, which were not necessarily linked to the Bank rate. They also fixed by agreement the rates chargeable on advances: the "cash account rate" for secured advances and the "unsecured overdraft rate," the latter being 0.5 percent above the former. The Scottish banks had also fixed among themselves at flat rates the commission charges on the working of current accounts, which were published; in England, on the other hand, such commission rates were neither agreed on by the banks nor published. The rates paid on deposits and charged on advances by the Scottish banks were less favorable than those offered by the English banks. The Scottish deposit receipt rate, which before the Second World War had usually been 2 percent below the Bank rate, was subsequently 2.5 percent below that rate, that is, 0.5 percent below the corresponding English rate. The rate on secured advances rose from 1.0 percent above the Bank rate before the war to 1.5 percent above that rate after the war.

Before September 1971 the Northern Ireland banks, like the Scottish banks, had decided among themselves what rates they would pay on deposits; those rates, too, varied in accordance with the Bank rate but more flexibly than in England.

Within the framework of the recommendations contained in the Discussion Paper "Competition and Credit Control," the London clearing banks, the Scottish banks, the Northern Ireland banks and other deposit-taking institutions decided to stop paying a common rate for small deposits. The London clearing banks abandoned their interest cartel in 1971; since then, each of those banks has had a single base rate, which may sometimes differ from those of the other banks. However, the large clearing banks tend to apply the same base rate, and if one decides to change its rate, the others almost automatically follow suit. The rates of interest charged by the London clearing banks on much of their lending are fixed at margins over their own base rate. A change in their own base rate generally entails a significant change in the level of short-term market rates; this explains why the base rate is widely interpreted as an indicator of the broad level of interest rates. A similar situation prevails in the case of the Scottish banks and the Northern Ireland banks. In fact, although the deposit banks no longer operate within the framework of interest rate cartels in which rates are formally agreed upon, their rates nevertheless tend to be more or less coordinated in practice, since their response to the pressure of market forces is sedate, and they refrain from engaging in frantic competition.

One year after the introduction of the revised system of credit control, market interest rates were being subjected to upward pressure as a result of the government's expansionary economic policies and its unwillingness to agree to an increase in the Bank rate. Consequently, the Bank rate was abolished in October 1972 and replaced by the *Minimum Lending Rate* (MLR), which was generally market determined, being calculated on the basis of a formula that fixed it at 0.5 percent above the average discount rate for Treasury bills at the most recent tender, rounded to the nearest 0.25 percent above. This move was prompted by the Bank of England's belief that the Bank rate had acquired excessive political and psychological significance and that its replacement by the MLR would remove routine monetary control operations from the political sphere. In May 1978 the automatic linkage of the MLR to the Treasury bill rate was eliminated, and there was a virtual return to the traditional Bank rate in the form of an explicitly administered MLR. Subsequently, the MLR rate itself was superseded, and by 1983 the Bank of England's operational aim was being established mainly in terms of an "unpublished band for very short-term interest rates."

In 1974 there was another major development in the banking system, involving the trustee savings banks, which originated in the many community savings schemes established in Britain during the nineteenth century in the aftermath of the Industrial Revolution. In 1974 the savings banks system underwent a radical reorganization, as a result of which the local savings banks were replaced by sixteen regional trustee savings banks and the Trustee Savings Bank Central Board, which coordinates matters of mutual importance. Each of the regional trustee savings banks is an autonomous unit, the policies of which are decided by its own Board of Trustees. Each bank operates two departments: the ordinary department and the special investment department. The *ordinary department*, intended principally for short-term savings, collects deposits at an interest rate set by the government and transfers them immediately to the National Debt Office for investment in government securities. This limitation is attributable to financial prudence in a country where there is no deposit insurance and trustee savings banks and building societies are debarred from buying company shares. The management expenses of the ordinary departments are defrayed by the Treasury at a rate arrived at by negotiation between the Treasury and the banks.

The *special investment department*, intended principally for long-term savings, collects deposits from savers who already possess a certain minimum balance in their accounts with the ordinary departments. The special investment departments are empowered to invest in a broader range of securities, including not only United Kingdom securities but those issued by local authorities and the governments of Commonwealth countries. The interest rates payable by the special investment departments are fixed by the banks themselves on the basis of the profitability of their transactions and the period of notice required for withdrawal of the deposit.

A further development in the banking system, involving the building societies, occurred in October 1983. The societies are "mutual" rather than "commercial" and mobilize funds by accepting deposits and issuing shares. In the building society movement the word *share* has a meaning different from that it conveys in the case of a joint stock company. In the case of a building society a *share* is virtually a deposit; it is not marketable but can be withdrawn on terms that do not differ greatly from those relating to deposits in a deposit account. The interest rate yielded by building society shares has been slightly higher than that yielded by deposit accounts with the societies.

Until October 1983 all building societies except the smallest followed the recommendations of the Building Societies' Association concerning interest rates; the interest rates tended to vary in accordance with the fluctuations in the rates paid on other investments (especially local authority securities and national savings securities) and in the Bank rate. The decision of the Abbey National building society to withdraw from the Building Societies' Association agreement in September 1983 rendered that agreement largely ineffective, and it was feared that the major building societies might engage in cut-throat competition for deposits, thus pushing up interest rates and hence mortgage rates. The Abbey National, however, was said to consider that the agreement had "outlived its usefulness" and to be interested in "healthy competition." The six large building societies had in fact been losing their share of the market to the medium and smaller building societies, which had been free to offer higher rates to investors.

The Building Societies' Association's response to Abbey National's decision was a review of the cartel to examine the system of recommended rates. Apparently as a result of that review, the Building Societies' Association announced on 21 October 1983 that its members would no longer stick to the recommended rates of interest payable on deposits and chargeable on mortgages, nor would they give one another twenty-eight days' notice of any planned changes. That announcement formally terminated an agreement that had been in existence for almost forty years. The building societies are now freer to change their rates and to compete with one another and with other financial institutions (while respecting the approved prudential "margin"), but they have nevertheless agreed to inform one another of any changes in their key rates for savers and borrowers, and the Association will still "advise" on rate levels in the hope of avoiding uncontrolled competition. This advice will probably be a moderating influence on the building societies' interest rates, if one takes into account the precedent set by the London clearing banks, which are still applying more or less identical rates even though they formally abandoned their interest rate cartel in 1971.

When the building societies' formal interest-rate cartel broke up, interest rates payable on mortgage loans were lower than the rates on long-term lending in the capital market. Some financial circles in London therefore thought that the termination of the building societies' cartel might prove beneficial to the economy as a whole, since the relatively low rates charged on mortgages had resulted in an excessive volume of resources being channeled into the housing sector, thus depriving the British manufacturing industry of funds greatly needed for modernization and expansion.

The year 1983 also saw major improvements in the operations of the National Savings Bank. Originally the Post Office Savings Bank, the National Savings Bank was separated from the Post Office in 1969, when the Post Office stopped being a government department and became a public corporation or nationalized industry. However, the National Savings Bank, which collects savings that help to finance government borrowing, continues to operate mainly through post offices, paying the Post Office Corporation an annual fee for its services under an agency agreement. It does not lend money or allow overdrafts and does not operate a personal checkbook system. Like the trustee savings banks, the National Savings Bank has two types of account, the ordinary account and the investment account. The rate of interest paid on deposits in ordinary accounts remained the same, 2.5 percent, from the establishment of the Post Office Savings Bank in 1861 until 1971. Withdrawals from ordinary accounts are allowed up to a specified amount of cash on demand at any post office. The investment account is aimed at attracting larger deposits from customers who can afford to give one month's notice of withdrawal. There is a limit on the amount that an individual can deposit therein; the limit was raised from £50,000 to £200,000 in 1981. In March 1983 ordinary accounts and investment accounts with the National Savings Bank represented just over 15 percent of the total stock of personal savings in the United Kingdom.

Since 1980 a number of steps have been taken to make the ordinary account attractive to a wider range of savers. The most important step was taken in January 1983, when a package of improved interest rates and withdrawal facilities was introduced. The 1982 Finance Act, which allowed the National Savings Bank to offer more than one rate of interest, had paved the way for such a package. The package included a two-tier interest system that pays 6 percent on ordinary accounts kept above £500 and 3 percent on lower balances. Because the interest is tax exempt, the effective return is in fact higher.

The Market Interest Rate System in the United States. Despite the widely proclaimed faith of the United States in self-correcting market forces, interest rates on deposits and loans have not only been regulated in the

United States but for the most part remained regulated for almost half a century following the Great Depression.

Strict anti-usury laws, placing ceilings on interest rates chargeable on mortgages and other loans, had long been imposed by many states, often since the time when they were still British colonies; in those states, the laws, which were patterned on England's maximum interest rate statutes, had continued to be enforced even after all statutory controls on interest rates had been removed in England and most European countries at the end of the nineteenth century. Nevertheless, the rationale for the full-fledged administered interest rate system that existed in the United States from the 1930s to the end of the 1970s was provided by the record number of banks (about 9,100) that failed or suspended activities from 1930 to 1933. This led Congress to adopt the Banking Act of 1933, commonly known as the Glass-Steagall Act. Section 19 of the Federal Reserve Act, as amended by the Glass-Steagall Act, provided that "no member bank shall, directly or indirectly, by any device whatsoever, pay any interest on any deposit which is payable on demand."

The practice of paying interest on deposits withdrawable on demand had been introduced early in the nineteenth century, when New York banks began paying interest on bankers' balances kept by country bankers and bankers in other cities for check clearing, investment and reserve purposes. The prohibition of interest on demand deposits lent credence to the wide-spread belief that paying such interest had had a destabilizing effect by prompting banks to pay interest to attract additional funds that they could invest in ventures that were riskier but yielded a higher return. With regard to that belief, the American Bankers' Association observed in its 1941 Reply to a questionnaire of the U.S. Senate Committee on Banking and Currency:

The justification for . . . [deposit interest] control is to be found in its history rather than in any defined tenet of economics or of the theory of money. Regulation Q came into effect after the banking crisis of 1933, and the primary reason for it was the recognition of the fact that excessive competition for deposits had developed among banks during the two decades prior to the banking crisis. In order to bid high for deposits, banks had in many cases invested in high yield bonds of low quality and had over-invested, impairing their liquidity. The control of interest was introduced as a means of discouraging unsound practices which the banking crisis had made so evident. Whether this sort of control will prove out under future conditions remains to be seen. In particular it will be interesting to study the long-term effect on savings habits.

A 1974 study published by the Federal Reserve Bank of New York and the New York State Banking Department noted that "there is little evidence that bank failures were associated with rate competition during the 1920s, the 1930s and even in more recent years." The report commented:

Although deposit interest ceilings have helped protect system safety and limit the diversion of funds from mortgages, they have also worked to the disadvantage of small savers who, because of inadequate expertise and information and/or the costs of making other investments, receive less interest for their deposits than they would in a free savings market . . . the prohibition of interest on demand deposits has resulted in the statutory grant of a source of interest-free funds to commercial banks only. Although checking account service charges do not cover the total cost of administering funds, the interest-free advantage enjoyed by commercial banks appears equal to between 40 to 50 basic points. Moreover, the combination of deposit interest ceilings and no demand deposit interest seems to favor large bank customers over smaller customers—for it is the large customer who can demand "free" services on return for his free demand deposit. The small customer, on the other hand, has no such power and also little mobility out of the institutional savings market and into the open market.[2]

The Glass-Steagall Act also provided that in the case of national banks the usury limit would be either 7 percent (the state limit) or one percentage point above the Federal Reserve's discount rate, whichever was the higher. The act also empowered the Board of Governors of the Federal Reserve System to regulate the maximum interest rates payable on deposits with member banks. Section 19 of the Federal Reserve Act, as amended by the Glass-Steagall Act, provided: "The Federal Reserve Board shall from time to time limit by regulation the rate of interest which may be paid by member banks on time deposits, and may prescribe different rates for such payment on time and savings deposits having different maturities or subject to different conditions by reason of different locations." In 1935 that regulatory power was extended to cover all commercial banks whose savings and time deposits were insured by the Federal Deposit Insurance Corporation (FDIC). The FDIC was established in 1933 to protect depositors against losses such as those incurred during the Great Depression, when banks went bankrupt and were unable to refund their depositors. Membership in the FDIC was to be compulsory for all Federal Reserve member banks but optional for nonmember banks and mutual savings banks. The FDIC was empowered to regulate maximum interest rates for those of its members that were not members of the Federal Reserve System. A similar power was vested in the responsible authorities in the various states for the other commercial banks.

In 1966 Congress adopted the Interest Rate Adjustment Act, bringing under regulation the interest rates payable on deposits with mutual savings banks, savings and loan associations and credit unions, known collectively as thrift institutions.[3] The act empowered the FDIC to set maximum interest rates on deposits with member mutual savings banks and granted a similar power to the Federal Home Loan Bank (which acts as a central bank for mutual savings and loan associations and a few mutual savings banks), in the case of deposits with savings and loan associations. From 1966 until the early 1980s, under Regulation Q, ceilings were imposed on interest rates on savings and time deposits with commercial banks and thrift institutions. The rate ceilings on deposits with the thrift institutions were slightly higher, the differential being designed to help them compensate for the greater competitiveness of the commercial banks. These ceilings were granted in view of the significant role played by the thrift institutions in efforts to attain the goal of "a decent home and suitable living environment for every American family."

The regulation of interest rates by limiting interbank competition was to have repercussions throughout the banking system. This situation was compounded by the repercussions resulting from the July 1963 imposition of the *interest equalization tax* (IET), an excise tax on purchases by United States residents of foreign fixed-interest securities, designed to equalize the return yielded by such securities with that from comparable domestic securities and whose rate varied according to the maturities of the securities purchased. Also compounding matters was the introduction in February 1965 of the voluntary Foreign Credit Restraint Program (under which United States banks and nonbank financial institutions were urged to limit their future foreign lending). The tax and the credit restrictions provided a major impetus for the Eurocurrency market, which the commercial banks began to use in 1969, when the Federal Reserve Board authorized them to establish shell branches overseas, thus enabling them to compete in that market.[4]

The strain on the banking system created by federal interest rate regulations intensified in the late 1960s, as mounting inflationary pressures placed depository institutions in an increasingly disadvantageous competitive position *vis à vis* nondepository institutions. The nondepository institutions such as money market mutual funds were not covered by the interest-rate regulations and could therefore offer market-related returns that tended to fluctuate in tandem with the inflation rate, thus enabling the institutions to entice substantial funds away from commercial banks and thrift institutions.[5] Similarly, foreign banks, which were likewise not bound by the federal interest rate regulations, benefited greatly by expanding their share of the market. Furthermore, the institutions that are members of the Federal Reserve System began to find that the opportunity cost of keeping noninterest-bearing reserves in order to satisfy the Federal Reserve's cash reserve requirements was an increasingly heavy burden. This caused a number of them to leave the System.

In a constantly intensifying effort to circumvent the interest rate regulations, the financial institutions began to use new methods of compounding interest that increased the effective return on savings deposits. They also introduced noninterest inducements to attract funds, including the offer of merchandise and even cash to savers for opening new accounts or depositing additional funds in existing ones.

As the need for a more flexible approach to setting interest rates became increasingly apparent, the Federal Reserve took further steps. The interest rate ceilings on various types of deposits were raised. The maximum rates on time deposits in denominations of $100,000 or more maturing in ninety days or more were suspended in May 1973 (the maximum rate for such deposits with maturities of thirty to eighty-nine days had been suspended in June 1970). Between 1 July 1973 and 31 October 1973, certificates maturing in four years or more with minimum denominations of $1,000 had no ceiling; however, the amount of such certificates that an institution could issue was limited to 5.0 percent of its total time and savings deposits. Sales in excess of that amount as well as certificates of less than $1,000, were limited to the 6.5 percent ceiling on time deposits maturing in two and a half years or more. As of 1 November 1973, ceilings were, however, reimposed on certificates maturing in four years or more.

The Federal Reserve also began allowing depository institutions to introduce new types of instruments that would enable them to pay interest at rates higher than those allowed under the existing regulations. One such instrument was the *repurchase agreement*, under which an institution sold government securities to an investor and committed itself to repurchase them at a set time and price. The fact that repurchase agreements were subject neither to interest-rate ceilings nor to cash reserve requirements made it possible for the issuing institutions to pay competitive rates of return on them. Another instrument was the *negotiable order of withdrawal (NOW) account*, which federally insured commercial banks, savings and loan associations, cooperative banks and mutual savings banks in Massachussets and New Hampshire were allowed to introduce on an experimental basis on 1 January 1974. The NOW accounts enabled the institutions concerned to pay some interest on checking accounts and thus to become more competitive with money market mutual funds. Their ability to compete was also enhanced when they were authorized to carry out automatic or telephone transfers to checking accounts and to install automatic teller machines at which direct deposits and withdrawals could be made. Authorization to introduce NOW accounts was extended to depository institutions throughout New England on 27 February 1976 and to depository institutions in New York and New Jersey on 10 November 1978 and 28 December 1979, respectively. Effective 31 December 1980, the Consumer Checking Account Equity Act of 1980 (Title III of the Depository Institutions Deregulation and Monetary Control Act of 1980) authorized depository institutions nationwide to offer NOW accounts where the "entire beneficial interest is held by one or more individuals or by an organization which is operated primarily for religious, philanthropic, charitable, educational or other similar purposes and which is not operated for profit."

A major step toward deregulation of interest rates was taken on 1 June 1978, when commercial banks, mutual savings banks and savings and loan associations were authorized to offer a new type of savings instrument with a maturity of twenty-six weeks. That six-month instrument, known as the *money market certificate*, was to be issued in a minimum denomination of $10,000 with a rate ceiling tied to the average auction rate on newly issued six-month Treasury bills. The rate ceilings were to fluctuate in line with the Treasury bills rate from week to week for newly bought certificates, but once bought, the certificates were to continue yielding until maturity the interest rates in force at the time of purchase. As in the case of most other types of savings and time accounts, there was an interest rate differential on the money market certificates. The commercial banks were limited to a rate equal to that of the Treasury bills, and the thrift institutions were allowed to offer a rate 0.25 percent higher. In March 1979 that differential was eliminated whenever the rate paid on Treasury bills was 9.0 percent or more. Furthermore, the thrift institutions were prohibited from compounding the interest on money market certificates. The main aim of these two moves was to provide cost relief to the thrift institutions, although simultaneously it adversely affected their competitiveness with the commercial banks and other institutions seeking funds in the open market.

The introduction of the money market certificates was not only an important step toward interest rate deregulation but a catalyst for growing pressure in favor of eliminating deposit rate ceilings altogether. The next steps were a series of measures that became effective on 1 July 1979 and included the introduction of a new market-linked four-year certificate of deposit with a ceiling rate 1.0 percent below the yield on four-year Treasury bills in the case of thrift institutions and 1.25 percent in the case of commercial banks.

The federal regulatory agencies had a specific reason for authorizing the introduction of the six-month money market certificate when interest rates on market instruments were rising and inflows of deposits to thrift institutions were declining. They wanted to avoid a replay of the scenario that had developed in earlier periods of high market interest rates (1969–1970 and 1973–1974), when fixed ceilings on deposit rates had prompted savers to withdraw their funds from depository institutions and invest them directly in market instruments. That process of disintermediation had resulted in a dearth of funds for housing loans, which in turn had led to a marked reduction in housing starts. The effectiveness of the money market certificates as a remedy for disintermediation had not been conclusively demonstrated when Congress adopted the Depository Institutions Deregulation and Monetary Control Act of 1980. Described as perhaps "the most important piece of banking legislation since the 1930s," the act was intended "to enhance the efficiency of financial markets, promote competitive balance among depository institutions and facilitate the implementation of monetary policy."

Title III of the act authorized depository institutions nationwide to offer interest-bearing checking (NOW) accounts. Title II of the act transferred the authority to establish maximum rates of interest payable on deposits to the Depository Institutions Deregulation Committee. That authority had previously been vested in the Board of Governors of the Federal Reserve System, the Board of Governors of the Federal Deposit Insurance Corporation, and the Federal Home Loan Bank Board. Perhaps the most important feature of the act, however, was the scheduled phase-out of interest rate ceilings on all time deposits of less than $100,000 (as noted above, ceilings on time deposits of $100,000 or more were eliminated in 1973). The schedule was the following:

Effective 1 August 1983, no ceiling was to be imposed on interest rates payable by commercial banks, mutual savings banks and savings and loan associations on deposits with maturities of four years or more.

From 1 August 1981 to 31 July 1982, commercial banks were to be allowed to pay interest on nonnegotiable time deposits with original maturities of two and a half years to less than four years at a rate not to exceed the higher of one-quarter of 1 percent below the average two- and a half-year yield for United States Treasury securities, as determined and announced by the Department of the Treasury before the date of deposit, or 9.25 percent (such announcements are made by the Department of the Treasury every two weeks). The average two- and a half-year yield was to be rounded by the Department of the Treasury to the nearest five basic points. The rate payable on any such deposit was not to exceed the ceiling rate in effect on the date of deposit. The mutual savings banks and savings and loan associations were still allowed a slight competitive edge in that they could pay on similar deposits a rate not to exceed the higher of the average two- and a half-year yield for Treasury securities, as determined and announced by the Department of the Treasury immediately before the date of deposit, or 9.25 percent.

Effective 1 August 1982, no ceiling was to be imposed on interest rates payable by commercial banks, mutual savings banks and savings and loan associations on deposits with maturities of three years or more. Also effective 1 August 1982, commercial banks were to be allowed to pay on deposits with maturities of two years to less than three years the average yield for two-year Treasury securities less one-fourth of a percentage point; mutual savings banks and savings and loan associations would pay on similar deposits the average yield for two-year Treasury securities.

Effective 1 August 1983, no ceiling was to be imposed on interest rates payable by commercial banks, mutual savings banks and savings and loan associations on deposits with maturities of two years or more. Also effective 1 August 1983, commercial banks, mutual savings banks and savings and loan associations were to be allowed to pay on deposits with maturities of one year to less than two years the average yield for fifty-two-week Treasury securities ("Bill rate").

Effective 1 August 1984, no ceiling was to be imposed on interest rates payable by commercial banks, mutual savings banks and savings and loan associations on deposits with maturities of one year or more. Also effective 1 August 1984, commercial banks, mutual savings banks and savings and loan associations were to be allowed to pay on deposits with maturities of less than one year the average yield for thirteen-week Treasury securities ("Bill rate").

Effective 1 August 1985, no ceiling was to be imposed on interest rates payable on deposits, irrespective of maturity.

The Depository Institutions Deregulation and Monetary Control Act of 1980 also preempts state usury laws with regard to interest rate ceilings applicable to federally related residential mortgage loans, although it empowers individual states to reenact such laws. This provision was designed to alleviate the cost pressures on financial institutions, which, although in a position to attract funds by paying market interest rates, were in many cases prohibited by usury laws from charging more than certain levels of interest on loans. The purpose of the preemption is to ensure that the availability of residential mortgage loans is not impeded in states having restrictive interest limitations. The preemption applies to loans, mortgages, credit sales and advances secured by first liens on residential real property, stock in residential cooperative housing corporations or residential manufactured homes.

Under the regulations, the provisions of the constitution or law of any state expressly limiting the rate or amount of interest, discount points, finance charges, or other charges that may be charged, taken, received or reserved are not to apply to any federally-related loan made after 31 March 1980 and secured by a first lien on: residential real property; stock in a residential cooperative housing corporation when the loan is used to finance the acquisition of such stock; or a residential manufactured home, provided that the loan so secured satisfies the requirements of the consumer protection rules for federally related loans, mortgages, credit sales and advances secured by first liens on residential mobile homes.

In 1982 Congress enacted the Garn–St. Germain Depository Institutions Act, which:

—Extended NOW accounts eligibility to funds deposited by governmental units (the Board of Governors of the Federal Reserve System amended Regulation Q accordingly[6]).

—Authorized all depository institutions to offer a new type of account, the money market deposit account (MMDA), to help them compete in both liquidity and rates of return with the money-market funds (MMDAs must have a $2,500 minimum balance determined over a period of up to one month and are not subject to reserve requirements and interest rate ceilings; holders of MMDAs can make unlimited withdrawals in person but can make only six automatic or telephone transfers a month).

—Authorized federally chartered savings institutions to choose either the savings bank or the savings and loan designation and to function either as mutual organizations or stock organizations (as a result, there has been a major restructuring of the United States savings industry, and all distinctions between savings banks and savings and loan associations have virtually disappeared; moreover, on 1 November 1983, the National Association of Mutual Savings Banks and the National Savings and Loan League were merged to form the National Council of Savings Institutions, a new central body for savings institutions).

—Broadened the investment authority of federally chartered savings institutions in the areas of commercial lending and leasing, consumer lending, and nonresidential mortgage loans and authorized savings institutions to offer demand deposit accounts to business loan customers.

On 5 January 1983 another new type of deposit account was introduced, namely, the Super-NOW account, which in addition to the features available in the MMDA offers unlimited checking.

The maximum interest rates currently payable on time and savings deposits are shown in Table 9.

THE ARGUMENTS IN FAVOR OF ADMINISTERED INTEREST RATES

The policy of keeping interest rates artificially low is popular with large segments of the public that benefit from such loans, for example farmers, small entrepreneurs and builders and owners of mortgage-financed homes, and therefore with politicians, who consider concessionally priced loans a convenient means of obtaining political support. The policy has been prompted partly by the tendency of governments to view interest rates primarily as a cost to the borrower and only secondarily as payment to the saver for his saving efforts and partly by their fear of an adverse political reaction on the part of borrowers and would-be borrowers. The following main arguments support a policy of administered interest rates that keep interest rates at artificially low levels:

—Personal savings are not markedly sensitive to changes in interest rates.

—Low interest rates reduce the cost of business borrowing and thereby promote investment and the creation of jobs and aggregate demand.

—Low interest rates reduce the cost of government borrowing, thus making it possible to spend more on the construction of public works and other forms of public consumption and hence to create more jobs.

Table 9
Maximum Interest Rates Payable on Time and Savings Deposits at Federally Insured Institutions (Percent per Annum)

Type of Deposit	Commercial Banks (In Effect 30 April 1984)		Savings and Loan Associations and Mutual Savings Banks (Thrift Institutions)[a] (In Effect 30 April 1984)	
	Percent	Effective Date	Percent	Effective Date
Savings accounts	5.50	1/1/84	5.50	7/1/79
Negotiable-order-of-withdrawal accounts	5.25	12/31/80	5.25	12/31/80
Negotiable-order-of-withdrawal accounts of $2,500 or more[b]	--	1/5/83	--[c]	1/5/83
Money-market deposit accounts[b]	--[c]	12/4/82		12/4/82
Time accounts by maturity				
7-31 days of less than $2,500[d]	5.50	1/1/84	5.50	9/1/82
7-31 days of $2,500 or more[b]	--	1/5/83	--	1/5/83
More than 31 days	--	10/1/83	--	10/1/83

Source: Federal Reserve Bulletin, May 1984

a. Effective 1 October 1983, restrictions on the maximum rates of interest payable by commercial banks and thrift institutions on various categories of deposits were removed.

b. Effective 1 December 1983, IRA/Keogh (HRIO) plan accounts were no longer subject to minimum deposit requirements.

c. Effective 14 December 1982, depository institutions were authorized to offer a new account with a required initial balance of $2,500 and an average maintenance balance of $2,500 not subject to interest-rate restrictions. No minimum maturity period is required for this account, but depository institutions must reserve the right to require seven days notice before withdrawals. When the average balance is less than $2,500, the account is subject to the maximum ceiling rate of interest for NOW accounts; compliance with the average balance requirements may be determined over a period of one month. Depository institutions may not guarantee a rate of interest for the account for a period longer than one month or condition the payment of a rate on a requirement that the funds remain on deposit for longer than one month.

d. Deposits of less than $2,500 issued to governmental units continue to be subject to an interest rate ceiling of 8 percent.

—The imposition of low interest rate ceilings by the monetary authorities prevents banks from engaging in collusive interest rate fixing or from becoming involved in cut-throat interest rate competition that may lead to bank failures and endanger the stability of the entire financial system.

The Interest Inelasticity of Personal Savings

The classical economists had theorized that saving is functionally linked to interest rates and that when those rates increase, savings increase and vice versa. They had also theorized that depressions would trigger an automatic self-correction mechanism, because they would cause interest rates to decline to a level where it would be profitable to make new long-term investments in plant, equipment and infrastructure. The Swedish economist Gustav Cassel, in his work, *The Nature and Necessity of Interest* (1903), had called into question the relationship between savings and interest rates postulated by the classical economists, arguing that when interest rates rise, it is no longer necessary to save as much as before if one is satisfied with a specific income, leading to the conclusion that an increase in interest rates may discourage saving, at least in certain cases.

Keynes pointed out that the rate of interest "cannot be a return to saving or waiting as such," for "if a man hoards his savings in cash, he earns no interest though he saves just as much as before." He linked the concept of interest with that of liquidity preference and observed:

The mere definition of the rate of interest tells us in so many words that the rate of interest is the reward for parting with liquidity for a specified period. For the rate of interest is, in itself, nothing more than the inverse proportion between a sum of money and what can be obtained for parting with control over the money in exchange for a debt for a stated period of time. . . . The rate of interest is not the "price" which brings into equilibrium the demand for resources to invest with the readiness to abstain from present consumption. It is the "price" which equilibrates the desire to hold wealth in the form of cash with the available quantity of cash:—which implies that if the rate of interest were lower, i.e. if the reward for parting with cash were diminished, the aggregate amount of cash which the public would wish to hold would exceed the available supply, and that if the rate of interest were raised, there would be a surplus of cash which no one would be willing to hold. If this explanation is correct, the quantity of money is the other fact, which in conjunction with liquidity-preference, determines the actual rate of interest in given circumstances.[7]

Keynes argued that the savings rate was essentially determined by the level of income. Most members of the classical school, he wrote, "would, presumably, not wish to deny that the level of income also has an important influence on the amount saved." He added that he, for his part "would not deny that the rate of interest may perhaps have an influence (though perhaps not of the kind which they suppose) on the amount saved out of a given income."[8]

Following Keynes, a number of prominent economists have maintained that, in the short term, savings are interest inelastic, and that even in the long term, it is very uncertain whether higher interest rates will induce households to save less or more. Some economists, notably Paul Samuelson, have argued that some people save less, rather than more, at higher interest rates, thereby implying that some people save with a view to reaching a certain level of income, and that higher interest rates make it possible for them to reach their desired level by saving less. This is known as the "target" or income effect. The fact that in the United States the higher interest rates prevailing in recent years, even when combined with the tax relief savings incentives embodied in the 1981 Economic Recovery Act, have failed to generate a higher savings rate, has raised the question whether higher returns simply prompt some people to save more and others to save less, thereby having a nil effect on saving.

Evidence apparently supporting the theory that personal savings are interest inelastic has emerged from the findings of a number of reports, surveys and studies. In the United Kingdom, the report of the Committee on the Working of the Monetary System (August 1959) stated that the Committee had "encountered extreme difficulty in testing the possibility that personal savings (which diminish the pressure of total demand) are directly affected by changes in interest rates," and that it had "noticed that witnesses concerned with the National Savings Movement stressed the power of relative interest rates on the distribution of savings between various channels but, when it came to encouraging the habit of saving, they emphasized anything but the rate of interest." The Committee acknowledged "that the evidence on the whole of this problem of the connection between interest rates and saving is unsatisfactory and Treasury witnesses showed themselves keenly aware of this."

Surveys of the motivations of savers and opinions about savings conducted in industrialized countries suggest that interest rates have only a minor impact on aggregate household savings. They indicate that households accord much greater weight to factors such as liquidity and safety of principal than to interest rates when it comes to deciding whether and in what form to save. A 1968 OECD study reported that from a sample survey concerning the form of investment best known in France, savings bank deposits, it appeared that only 27 percent of holders of savings-deposit books and 11 percent of persons without a deposit book knew the exact rate of interest paid by the savings banks; 43 percent of holders gave a wrong answer, and 30 percent admitted they did not know. However, 26 percent of the households interviewed (and 40 percent of persons in executive grades and liberal professions) considered the rate of interest on their savings deposits to be too low. The OECD study also reported that a survey made in 1957 by the Institut Dourdin covering a national population sample yielded similar information: 87 percent of heads of households did not know the characteristics of the Pinay 3.5 percent 1952 loan (indexed on gold) and the Ramadier 5.0 percent 1956 loan (indexed on the average price of securities): among holders of securities, that percentage fell to 55.0 percent.[9] A review of studies and evidence published in 1974 also reached the overall conclusion that savings are interest inelastic.[10]

The findings concerning the interest inelasticity of savings are not necessarily valid for all social groups in all countries and in all circumstances and are contradicted by the findings of other studies. Nevertheless, they have been seized upon by those who favor artificially low interest rates as a means to provide empirical justification for an interest rate policy that has greater political appeal and is not likely to be contested by savers, who have not sought to organize themselves into political pressure groups to lobby for higher interest rates. Perhaps savers tend to be secretive about their holdings and in some cases have ambivalent attitudes toward interest rates, since they are also borrowers.

Artificially Low Interest Rates as a Means of Reducing the Cost of Business Borrowing

In order to expand their installations and avoid being outpaced by the technical advances of their competitors, both domestic and foreign, enterprises usually need more funds than they can obtain from their own reserves, and they must therefore resort to borrowing. Similarly, skilled artisans and other potential small entrepreneurs wishing to start or expand a small-scale business and unable to obtain sufficient equity finance from their own resources or from friends and relatives must likewise resort to borrowing. A number of governments have sought to facilitate such borrowing through a policy of low administered interest rates, which are often negative in real terms; they have viewed this course as one of the main components of an economic strategy aimed at stimulating business innovation and competition, reducing job loss and expanding job creation. On the other hand, enterprises have sometimes been able to obtain credit at artificially low interest rates as a result of a policy of administered interest rates adopted by governments for the primary purpose of reducing the cost of their own borrowing.

In some instances, governments have adopted a policy of promoting the granting of credit at artificially low interest rates in order to foster certain economically or socially desirable activities or to benefit marginal economic or social groups. Thus a number of countries grant agricultural loans at preferential interest rates, either through the application of an administered rate policy to the agricultural sector alone or, when such a policy is applied across the board, through an agricultural credit subsidy system that makes it possible to grant agricultural loans at rates even lower than the general artificially low administered interest rate. Other countries provide special preferential rates for marginal groups. They may do so indirectly, for example, by refinancing loans granted to special groups by government-owned institutions, thus enabling the latter to lend at artificially low interest rates.

Artificially Low Interest Rates as a Means of Reducing the Cost of Government Borrowing

Governments have a tendency to spend more than they can collect in the form of taxes and must therefore use various methods to make ends meet. One common method is to finance budget deficits by the inflationary expedient of printing more money. Another method, likewise linked to inflation but more subtle and which might be termed a tax-cum-inflation method, is not to adjust tax brackets, which enables the government to take advantage of the phenomenon known as "bracket creep." The government then collects taxes at higher rates even though the taxpayers' income, which has increased in nominal terms, may have remained static in real terms or even declined. A third method that is widely used is borrowing on the domestic market and/or foreign markets. Government borrowing has become a gigantic operation involving annually thousands of millions of dollars in the richest countries and millions of dollars even in the poorest ones. David Hume, the eighteenth-century economist and philosopher, expressed concern about excessive borrowing: "It is very tempting to a minister to employ such an expedient as enables him to make a great figure during his administration without overburthening the people with taxes, or exciting any immediate clamours against himself. The practice therefore of contracting debt will almost infallibly be abused in every government."[11]

Given the magnitude of the loans involved, even small fluctuations in interest rates may mean substantial savings or additional servicing costs. Consequently, it is to the advantage of governments to keep interest rates artificially low in their own countries. It is also to their advantage if interest rates are kept artificially low in other countries, either because they may float loans there or because high interest rates in other countries may act as a magnet drawing capital out of their own countries or out of third-party countries, thus pushing up interest rates on the international capital markets.

Artificially Low Interest Rates as a Means of Preventing Collusive Fixing of Interest Rates

When the institutional savings and loan sector consists of a very limited number of financial institutions, for the most part foreign-owned, it is very likely that they will take advantage of their monopolistic situation and manipulate interest rates. Their objective is to set the rates on savings at the lowest possible level and the rates on loans at the highest possible level, while reducing the volume of transactions and services to a suboptimal level.

It is argued that a rational interest rate policy should take into account not only the return on investment but also the cost to the community of the capital used to finance such investment. A policy of administered interest rates is therefore said to be necessary to counteract possible adverse effects of the domination of the institutional sector by a limited number of financial institutions, on the remuneration of savings and the cost of borrowing.

Governments can also influence interest rates indirectly by nationalization or state ownership of a number of financial institutions that can wield sufficient power to prevent any attempt at collusive fixing of interest rates. In effect, the government-owned or government-controlled institutions are often provided with public funds and can thus lend at low subsidized rates in conformity with the government's priorities. Through those institutions, governments have sought to exert a moderating effect on the interest rates charged on loans by privately owned institutions.

Artificially Low Interest Rates as a Means of Protecting the Banking System against Financial Instability

A major argument for imposing ceilings on interest rates payable on deposits with the banking system is that it limits competition, in particular by preventing sudden shifts of funds prompted by interest rate differentials among various types of financial assets. It is claimed that interest rate ceilings are necessary to prevent institutions that are managed in an unsound manner from enticing customers away from prudently managed institutions by offering returns that cannot be provided without incurring excessive risks. In the United States, the main argument put forward in favor of interest rate ceilings on bank deposits, at the time when interest rate regulation was introduced in the 1933 Banking Act, was that they would prevent cut-throat competition among financial institutions. Such competition raised the cost of funds for the banks themselves and for borrowers and was believed to be one of the main causes of the widespread bank failures that had occurred in the late 1920s and early 1930s.

It is contended that in periods of rising interest rates, certain categories of institutions (for example, savings banks) lending funds for specific social or economic purposes such as the buying or building of houses start to suffer substantial capital losses if they offer competitive rates on deposits, because their assets are to a large extent tied up in loans granted at the lower interest rates prevailing before interest rate levels rose; on the other hand, if they do not offer competitive rates on deposits, they may not only fail to attract funds, but they may lose depositors, since the depositors will have a strong tendency to shift funds out of those institutions into others offering higher interest rates.

THE ARGUMENTS IN FAVOR OF MARKET INTEREST RATES

The following arguments can be adduced in favor of market interest rates: the increasing responsiveness of savers to changes in interest rates; the incompatibility of artificially low interest rates with a sound approach to financial management; and the aggravation of existing imbalances in income distribution.

The Increasing Responsiveness of Savers to Significant Changes in Interest Rates

A Roman emperor once observed, "one may expect agreement between clocks sooner than between philosophers," and Margaret Thatcher seems to take an equally pessimistic view of economists, for she once complained that "economists never agree." Nowhere has this tendency of economists to disagree been more evident than with regard to the question of the interest elasticity or inelasticity of personal savings. Keynesian economists have insisted that interest rates are not a determinant of the level of personal savings, which in their view depends primarily on income levels. However, more recent studies and empirical evidence, while not downgrading the importance of income level as a determinant of savings, indicate that interest rates play a much greater role in the mobilization of savings than is acknowledged in Keynesian economics in that an increase in the real after-tax return on savings would increase the rate of saving. One widely mentioned study carried out in the United States estimates that each percentage point increase in real interest rates pulls in between 0.3 and 0.4 percent more savings, thus revealing a relationship between the rate of saving and the rate of return that is surprisingly strong, given the negligible role hitherto attributed to the rate of return.[12]

An eminent French economist reached a conclusion that coincides with the findings of the United States study: he expressed strong disagreement with those economists who contend that savings are interest inelastic and that any increase in the rate of return on certain instruments will lead only to a shift of funds from one instrument to another and not to an increase in the overall volume of household savings. He argued on the basis of his own observations that if a savings instrument were made available that provided lenders with a suitable guarantee against a loss of purchasing power, while yielding an assured and predictable, albeit modest, rate of interest, there would be a marked increase in the rate of household savings in France. He observed that, with rare exceptions, there are currently only two reasons why people in France decide not to consume the whole of their income: first, to accumulate funds to buy a home, and second, to set money aside as a reserve for future unforeseen contingencies. He noted that apart from these two cases, people usually spend their disposable income on travel and durable consumer goods, because they fear, not without reason, that its purchasing power will be eroded by inflation.[13]

Similar findings concerning the interest elasticity of personal savings have emerged from studies of consumption and savings in rural households in Japan, which show "without exception" that such households "have had high average as well as marginal propensities to save, and that incentives played an important role in stimulating these savings."[14]

A number of studies have shown a significant degree of interest elasticity in developing countries and have provided theoretical support for the standard policy advice given by World Bank, IMF and United Nations experts and other foreign experts. The most notable of these studies are *Money and Capital in Economic Development*, by R. I. McKinnon, and *Financial Deepening in Economic Development*, by E. S. Shaw, both published in 1973. These studies recommend that real interest rates be raised to improve financial intermediation and increase investment by increasing the personal savings rate. In fact, the available evidence, based largely on the experience of Asian and Latin American countries, indicates that the personal savings rate will probably increase when interest rates rise, particularly when real interest rates become positive after being maintained at substantially negative levels by administrative controls. The experience of the Republic of Korea and Indonesia is of particular significance in this connection.

On 30 September 1965, the Monetary Board of the Republic of Korea announced that the basic lending rate of commercial banks would be increased from 16.0 percent to 26.0 percent a year and that the banks would pay interest at the rate of 2.5 percent a month (30.0 percent simple annual interest or 34.5 percent compounded annual interest) on 18-month time deposits. The differential between the interest rate on 18-month time deposits and bank loan rates was to be financed partly by subsidies from the central bank, partly by loan charges other than interest and partly by the banks of which the government is a partial owner. In October 1968 the interest differential between loans and long-term deposits was eliminated and an identical rate of 25.2 percent was applied for both types of transaction. In June 1969 the interest rate on loans was reduced to 24.0 percent and the rate on long-term deposits to 22.8 percent. According to the government of the Republic of Korea, the process of interest rate reform initiated in September 1965

was intended to boost the level of private saving in order to increase investment and control inflation, and would result in lower rather than higher interest costs to businesses because the greater supply of loans at bank interest rates would reduce their need to borrow in the private or curb market, where rates to established businesses were from 3.5 percent to 5.0 percent per month.[15]

Following the initiation of the interest rate reform, average annual real interest rates on long-term deposits rose sharply from negative levels in 1963 and 1964 (-13.2 percent and -17.0, respectively) to positive levels in 1965 (+11.0 percent), in 1966 (+17.1 percent) and in 1967 (+19.2 percent). It was reported that "the September 1965 interest rate changes caused an outcry in Korean business circles and predictions that contrary to the government's statement, the substantially higher level of commercial bank interest rates would lead to bankruptcy, reduced growth, inflation and other dire results." According to the same source, however, "none of these dire predictions came true," and "the faith of government policy-makers that higher interest rates would add to the availability of bank credit and to domestic savings seems to have been fully justified."[16] In effect, private savings rose from 3.9 percent of GNP in 1964 to 12.1 percent of GNP in 1969. Total time and savings deposits in all banks increased from 39 billion Won in 1964 to 566 billion Won in 1968, thus making it possible for commercial bank credit to increase 60 percent a year without any growth of the money supply. Deposits in agricultural cooperatives increased at about the same rate as total time and savings deposits in all banks.

An official of the Board of Governors of the Federal Reserve System of the United States, writing in his personal capacity, has drawn the following four conclusions regarding the interest rate reform in the Republic of Korea:

First, the relatively high and positive deposit rates have been a major factor contributing to the sharp increase in the volume of time and savings deposits. Second, the interest rate reform has contributed substantially to a significant increase in the national savings rate. Third, the rapid growth in time and savings deposits made it possible for the banking system to finance from non-inflationary sources a substantial increase in economic activity and real GNP. Fourth, Korea's "high" interest rates policy did not prove detrimental to investment spending, since investment expenditures—both absolutely and as a proportion of GNP—increased during 1966-69.[17]

According to another expert, the interest rate reform had a particularly noteworthy impact in the case of households with small farms, whose average propensity to save increased substantially from 1965 to 1974. Although "part of this increase was undoubtedly due to expanded incomes and to farm policies which increased the returns to on-farm investment . . . part was due to the more attractive incentives provided by financial markets."[18]

The success of the Republic of Korea's experiment with a policy of positive interest rates is believed to have played a significant part in the Indonesian government's decision to introduce a similar policy in October 1968. During the preceding fourteen months, time deposits with the state banks having a maturity of three months or more had yielded interest at the rate of 2.0 percent a month. As of 1 October 1968, that rate was doubled to 4.0 percent a month, and the state banks began paying interest at the rate of 5.0 and 6.0 percent a month on six-month deposits and twelve-month deposits, respectively. A number of other measures were introduced at the same time: the central bank undertook to guarantee payment of savings deposits; the interest on all savings deposits became tax exempt; the government let it be known that depositors would not be asked any questions about the source of the funds deposited; and the central bank undertook to subsidize part of the interest paid on six-month and twelve-month deposits. From a level of about 500.0 million rupiahs at the end of September 1968, the outstanding volume of time deposits with the state banks climbed to 6.8 billion rupiahs at the end of January 1969 and to 21.6 billion rupiahs in April 1969. As the rate of inflation decreased during 1969, the authorities concluded that the time deposit rate offered by the state banks could safely be lowered. The central bank therefore reduced the maximum rate on twelve-month time deposits from 6.0 percent to 5.0 percent a month on 17 March 1969, to 4.0 percent a month on 1 May 1969, to 3.0 percent a month on 10 July 1969, to 2.5 percent a month on 15 September 1969 and to 2.0 percent a month on 1 January 1970.

More recently, in June 1983, Indonesia introduced a number of liberalizing reforms to mobilize additional domestic personal savings. Those reforms included: the removal of ceilings on interest rates that the five state-owned commercial banks could offer on rupiah time deposits; tax exemption for interest earned on time deposits denominated in foreign currencies (similar to an existing corresponding rule concerning rupiah deposits); and the removal of all quantitative ceilings on bank loans.

The impact was immediate and tremendous, for time deposits with state-owned banks (which entirely dominate commercial banking in Indonesia) showed considerable increases: twelve-month deposits shot up from 41.2 billion rupiahs at the end of May 1983 to 111.9 billion at the end of June 1983 and 837.9 billion at the end of December 1983; six-month deposits climbed from 26.9 billion at the end of May 1983 to 119.3 billion at the end of June 1983 and 298.6 billion at the end of December 1983; three-month and less-than-three-month deposits soared from 8.1 billion at the end of May 1983 to 129.6 billion at the end of June 1983 and 449.1 billion at the end of December 1983; and total deposits (including twenty-four-month, eighteen-month, twelve-month, nine-month, six-month and three-month and less-than-three-month deposits) jumped from 911.8 billion at the end of May 1983 to 1,124.0 billion at the end of June 1983 and 2,125.8 billion at the end of December 1983.

According to an article published in the *Financial Times* on 16 September 1983, the Indonesian reforms "are believed to have attracted back a substantial part of the capital which fled Indonesia earlier this year." As the *Financial Times* observed, however:

> the money has been attracted back not only by the high interest rates on rupiah deposits but also by the tax exemption on foreign deposits. Thus, dollars have been returning from nearby financial centres like Singapore and have swollen both rupiah time deposits and the local dollar market, although rates on the latter are less than the Singapore inter-bank offered rates.[19]

In an address on 3 April 1984 to the Fourteenth World Congress of Savings Banks, held in Singapore, the president of the Asian Development Bank indicated that the bank had "made a study of financial development in a number of high and low saving Asian developing countries to identify problems which require consideration by these countries." He stressed that "the findings are noteworthy" and that "one is that higher real returns on savings, such as commercial bank savings deposits, and improved accessibility of financial institutions, are important determinants of savings behaviour." Another finding is that "greater financial intermediation has a strong effect on savings, investment and the rate of economic growth."

On the basis of both past and recent surveys and studies of the savings behavior of households, certain conclusions concerning the interest rate elasticity of personal savings can be drawn that might narrow the area of disagreement among economists:

—Those who save small amounts tend to be indifferent to modest changes in interest rates but are influenced by substantial changes in interest rates;
—Those who are saving for a specific purpose, for example, those who have joined a saving-for-housing scheme, tend to be indifferent to changes in interest rates, whatever their amplitude, because in this case the main incentive to save is the promise of a loan, often on preferential terms;
—Those who save substantial sums are definitely influenced by changes in interest rates;
—Those who are well informed about financial matters tend to be influenced by changes in interest rates.

The Incompatibility of Artificially Low Interest Rates with a Sound Approach to Financial Matters

A policy of keeping interest rates at artificially low levels would seem to be inconsistent with a sound approach to financial management. Any economic activity worth undertaking should be profitable enough to cover the full cost of the financing involved and hence should not need to be subsidized by the saver (by means of low administered rates on savings) or the taxpayer (by means of government subsidization of interest rates). If an economic venture is not basically profitable, its subsidization at the expense of the saver and/or the taxpayer merely serves to conceal this fact and leaves the basic problem of its economic efficiency unsolved and indeed unposed.

Low administered interest rates may, in the short term or even in the medium term, keep unprofitable ventures alive, thus preventing savings from flowing to potentially more efficient and more profitable ventures. However in the long term they cannot prevent those ventures from suffering the consequences of their own inefficiency in the form of default on the payment of loan interest and principal and even bankruptcy. It is for this reason that low administered interest rates have not proved to be an appropriate remedy for managerial imperfections that affect profitability.

The Distorting Effect of Artificially Low Interest Rates on Savings Allocation

Interest rates on financial savings that are not competitive with the yields of alternative domestic assets or with interest rates in the international financial markets discourage saving in the form of domestic financial assets. When such rates are not competitive, they prompt savers to buy gold, jewels, stocks of goods, art works, real estate and other physical assets or foreign financial assets or real estate situated abroad. The use of low administered interest rates to allocate savings to specific sectors or groups distorts that allocation and encourages enterprises to borrow for the sole purpose of protecting themselves against expected inflation. Such precautionary borrowing can channel savings toward projects of very limited profitability for the community as a whole, since the investment need not be particularly economically efficient to yield a return. Thus through such resource misallocation, inefficient activities can take up resources that could be employed for more worthwhile activities.

A policy of low administered interest rates may also promote the consitution of working capital and reserves far in excess of what is required for the continued successful operation of a venture. It may likewise, by unduly inflating the demand for capital, lead to a distribution of credit on the basis of strict security and financial profitability rather than on the basis of the economic and social requirements of the community.

Low interest rates tend to increase loan demand, thereby obliging lending institutions to ration their "bargain credit." That process lends itself to influence peddling and other forms of corruption. It also prompts the lending institutions to grant most of their loans to a relatively small number of borrowers who are important politically, have very high creditworthiness or are capable of satisfying exorbitant collateral requirements. This concentration of loans enables the financial institutions to reduce their lending costs to a minimum. The question of minimizing lending costs is particularly important in the context of high inflation or expectations of high inflation, since low interest rates that do not provide for a margin that will cover lending costs and may even be negative erode the loanable funds of the lending institutions and prevent them from engaging in an aggressive campaign to attract deposits. There is a great need for governments to pay more attention to the way in which public funds are allocated and to channel investment into schemes that will make the best possible use of available labor and financial resources. There is also a need to avoid prematurely initiating activities that cannot be efficiently operated and make unrealistic demands on a country's resources.

The Aggravation of Existing Imbalances in Income Distribution

A policy of low administered interest rates may induce investors to prefer capital-intensive projects to labor-intensive projects, thus increasing unemployment, aggravating underemployment and accentuating inequalities in income distribution. A policy of low administered interest rates aimed at orienting investment toward particular sectors or particular social or economic groups may lead, not to the expected goal of alleviating inequalities in income distribution, but to a greater concentration of income and wealth where the political system is such that only those in power and their friends are likely to benefit from any interest subsidization scheme. This kind of favoritism is morally reprehensible and has adverse material effects when the ventures thus subsidized are managed inefficiently. Such mismanagement often results in the maintenance of unprofitable activities at great cost to the community or in outright fraudulent bankruptcies that deprive the lending institution—often a government institution using taxpayers' money—of both the capital of the loan and the interest thereon. In the same perspective, it may be noted that high officials and other influential people in certain countries often deposit their funds abroad, either in foreign countries applying tight banking secrecy laws or in foreign countries where the rates on savings are very remunerative, and borrow from local financial institutions at low rates to build sumptuous villas for themselves or for rent at high rates to diplomats, foreign experts or foreign businessmen.

It is thus clear that a policy of administered interest rates, although prompted by good intentions, may become perverted and a source of influence peddling and corruption that aggravates existing economic and social injustice. This situation often increases apprehension about political instability that in turn provides a convenient pretext for further influence peddling and corruption, thus creating a vicious circle that inhibits any effort to tackle the basic problems facing the country concerned.

NOTES

1. The traditional role of the deposit banks has been to provide—usually in the form of bank advances—working capital or temporary finance for long-term capital projects pending the securing of funds from other sources. Since the 1960s, however, the deposit banks have been making available a growing volume of medium-term financing.

2. Leonard Lapidus, Suzanne Cutler, Patrick Page Kildoyle, and Arthur L. Castro, *Public Policy toward Mutual Savings Banks in New York State: Proposals for Change*, Federal Reserve Bank of New York and the New York State Banking Department, 1974, p. 110.

3. Mutual savings banks invest in mortgages and high-quality securities, savings and loan associations invest predominantly in mortgages, and credit unions use their funds primarily for personal loans to members.

4. The United States credit restrictions and the interest equalization tax were eliminated in 1974.

5. Money market mutual funds issue depositlike instruments called "shares" and invest only in short-term credit instruments; purchasers of their shares earn market-related returns and can write checks against their share accounts, which usually are required to have a minimum balance of $250.

6. Section 217.1 (e) (3) of Regulation Q now reads as follows:

(i) Deposits subject to negotiable orders of withdrawal may be maintained if such deposits consist of funds in which the entire beneficial interest is held by (A) one or more individuals, (B) a corporation, association, or other organization operated primarily for religious, philanthropic, charitable, educational, fraternal or other similar purposes and not operated for profit, or (C) the United States, any State of the United States, county, municipality, or political subdivision thereof, the District of Columbia, the Commonwealth of Puerto Rico, American Samoa, Guam, any territory or possession of the United States, or any political subdivision thereof.

(ii) Deposits in which any beneficial interest is held by a corporation, partnership, association or other organization that is operated for profit or is not operated primarily for religious, philanthropic, charitable, educational, fraternal or other similar purposes, or that is not a governmental unit described in subparagraph (i) (C) may not be classified as deposits subject to negotiable orders of withdrawal.

7 John Maynard Keynes, *The General Theory of Employment, Interest and Money*, New York, Harcourt, Brace and Company, 1936, pp. 167-168.

8. Ibid., p.178.

9. Organisation for Economic Cooperation and Development, *Capital Markets Study, II: Formation of Savings*, Paris, 1968, p. 125.

10. Paul David and John L. Scadding, "Private Savings: Ultra-rationality, Aggregation, and Denison's Law." *Journal of Political Economy*, 82 (March-April 1974), 225–249.

11. David Hume, Political Discourses (Edinburgh, 1752). Reprinted in E. Rotwein, *David Hume: Writings on Economics*, London: Nelson, 1955, p. 92.

12. Michael J. Boskin "Taxation, Saving, and the Rate of Interest," in *Research in Taxation*, published as supplement to *Journal of Political Economy* (Chicago), 86 (April 1978), Part 22, pp. S3-S27.

13. Jean-Marcel Jeanneney, "Indexer l'épargne à long terme," *Le Monde*, 29 March 1983.

14. Dale W. Adams, "Mobilizing Household Savings through Rural Financial Markets," *Development Digest*, April 1979, 12-23.

15. Gilbert T. Brown, "The Impact of Korea's 1965 Interest Rate Reform on Savings, Investment and Balance of Payments," in *CENTO Symposium on Central Banking, Monetary Policy, and Economic Development*, Ankara, Turkey, 1971, p. 190.

16. Ibid., p. 196.

17. Robert F. Emery, "Interest Rate Policy, Resource Allocation, and the Mobilization of Domestic Savings," in *CENTO Symposium on Central Banking, Monetary Policy, and Economic Development*, Ankara, Turkey, 1971, p. 187.

18. Adams, "Mobilizing Household Savings through Rural Financial Markets," 12-23.

19. Chris Sherwell, "Money Floods Back to Indonesia," *Financial Times*, 16 September 1983.

5   The Concept of a Just
              Interest Rate

From antiquity to the present, the question of interest has been approached essentially from two angles: discussion has focused on the ethical propriety of the basic principle of charging or taking interest or on the concept of interest as loan interest, that is, interest viewed as a cost to the borrower. Rarely has theorization on the question been concerned with interest on savings, that is, interest conceived as a reward to savers for sacrificing present consumption to future consumption. This bias was attenuated to some degree in classical economics but was subsequently accentuated in Keynesian economics.

Consciously or unconsciously, many today remain prisoners of the view derived from Keynesianism that interest on savings is "unearned income" and that since, for the benefit of the community as a whole, interest rates on loans should be kept at artificially low levels, the rate of interest paid to savers must also remain low. This mental conditioning makes it difficult to realize that interest is not only a cost to the borrower but the price paid to the saver for his savings, which in the case of the average saver are normally the product of self-denial. However, savers are becoming increasingly unwilling to accept an assessment of their self-denial that they consider unjust. This is vividly demonstrated by the number of savers in both industrialized and developing countries who have been transferring their savings to the United States — legally or illegally — to take advantage of the high interest rates available there. This trend has lent urgency to the generalized need for just interest rates.

The concept of a just interest rate is particularly important in view of the growing awareness that to promote an increase in domestic savings in developing countries to reduce their reliance on official development assistance and other forms of external financing, it is necessary to regard interest not only as a cost to the borrower but also as the price of a good, that is, of money obtained or accumulated as a result of labor, ingenuity and self-denial. In fact, saving and borrowing form a continuum: credit cannot come into existence unless savings have been accumulated and transferred from a saver to a borrower, directly or indirectly through an intermediary. Consequently, the question of interest rates must be considered from the standpoint of equity for savers as well as borrowers.

In so far as what may be considered a just interest rate for both savers and borrowers would be the rate arrived at through the unimpeded interplay of supply and demand, the concept of a just interest rate is implicit in the classical school's notion of interest rates. Irving Fisher may be considered to have touched upon the question of a just interest rate inasmuch as he was concerned with the distinction between the nominal and the real rate of interest and with the purchasing power of money. In his book *The Purchasing Power of Money*, first published in 1911, he raised the "question of justice between borrower and lender." In his view, "the ideal" was that "neither debtor nor creditor should be the worse off by being deceived through changes in the level of prices of goods bought and sold."[1]

However, the concept of a just interest rate per se has not been explicitly advocated in the economic literature, although the concept of a just price has existed since medieval times. The view of the scholastic school was that a just price is one arrived at through free bargaining conducted on the basis of a full knowledge of all relevant facts. The classical economists subsequently developed a similar concept, that of a market price determined under conditions of free competition and resulting from the equilibration of supply and demand. A related concept emerged in the 1970s in the United Nations within the context of the North-South dialogue, namely, that of prices deriving from "a just and equitable relationship between the prices of raw materials, primary commodities, manufactured and semi-manufactured goods exported by developing countries and the prices of raw materials, primary commodities, food, manufactured and semi-manufactured goods and capital equipment imported by them" and involving "a link between the prices of exports of developing countries and the prices of their imports from developed countries."[2]

In endeavouring to determine what may be regarded as a just interest rate, or more precisely a just interest rate structure—that is, an interest rate structure that comes as close as possible to the structure that would result from the interplay of supply and demand if the necessary conditions for such interplay existed—it is necessary to consider the question from the standpoint of the economic agents involved, namely, the saver, the financial intermediary and the borrower.

From the point of view of the saver, a just interest rate on domestic financial assets is a rate that keeps pace with inflation and compares favorably with the returns on alternative investments, due account being taken of the relative risks involved; depending on the saver's degree of financial sophistication, the alternative investments may be foreign as well as domestic.

From the standpoint of the financial intermediary, a just interest rate is a rate that will enable the institution to make what is considered an acceptable profit in the banking sector after paying interest to the savers who provide the loanable funds, defraying its own administrative costs and other overhead, and constituting reserves to offset the risk of delinquency on the part of its borrowers. However, the concept of a just interest rate may be modified in varying degrees by the fact that for many financial intermediaries the net difference between interest received and interest paid is not always the only source of earnings. The importance of sources of bank earnings other than loan interest is reflected in a 1980 report published under the authority of the Secretary-General of the Organisation for Economic Co-operation and Development (OECD). The report analyzed the profit and loss accounts of major categories of credit institutions operating in some eighteen OECD member countries and found that net income from other sources accounts for proportions of the gross earnings margin that vary between about 20 percent and 75 percent for commercial banks, between 2 percent and 30 percent for savings banks, and up to 60 percent for other credit institutions.[3] These findings relate to institutions in industrialized countries, but they have some relevance to comparable institutions in developing countries.

The concept of what constitutes a just interest rate from the standpoint of the borrower depends on whether the borrower is an individual, an enterprise or a government. In the case of borrowing by individuals for personal reasons, the interest rate the borrower considers just will depend not only on his capacity to repay (his general financial situation) but on the extent to which he needs the loan (whether for an emergency or for other reasons) and the benefit he derives from it (whether psychological, social or practical). Evidence has shown that consumer borrowing is more interest inelastic than is commonly recognized. People buying on credit often do not bother to ascertain the actual rate of interest they will be paying, and people seeking loans in an emergency are so anxious to obtain the needed funds that the interest rate is often of no concern to them at all.

In the case of borrowing by entrepreneurs, the concept of a just interest rate is more complex. Although there are no known econometric studies of the impact on investment of the high interest rates of recent years, some studies covering earlier years suggest that high interest rates may deter industrial investment. For example, the authors of a 1970 study on investment in United Kingdom manufacturing industry in the period 1956-1967 "found an interest elasticity of investment demand which lay well above unity, with an average lag of at least six or seven quarters."[4] The author of a study on inventory behavior in United Kingdom manufacturing in the period 1956-1967, also carried out in 1970, is reported to have "detected some interest-elasticity in inventory investment."[5]

Generally, although recent years have witnessed a significant reduction in the difference between the average return on investment and the cost of funds, the aggregate interest payments tend to represent a relatively small proportion of an enterprise's turnover, so interest rate levels may, after all, have relatively little influence on production costs. Furthermore, the interest paid is expressed as a percentage of the nominal amount of capital borrowed. In a period of inflation, the real value of the principal borrowed and of the interest paid is constantly being eroded, so interest payments come to be a gradually diminishing burden. It is faulty management technique to consider self-financing as being free of charge and a loan as being costly because it involves the payment of interest. It can be argued that if an entrepreneur considers that interest rates are so high that he cannot afford to borrow to invest, he would do better to give up his business and seek other ways of using his capital. On the other hand, recent experience in the United States has shown that market interest rates combined with lower inflation can make corporate executives better managers in that they are obliged to become more efficient: when an enterprise has to pay more realistic interest rates or market interest rates and cannot raise prices because of low inflation, it must increase its profits by raising its productivity or go out of business.

As a general rule, the decision of an enterprise to borrow to invest seems to be affected less by interest rate differentials than by one or more of the following considerations:

— The investment is needed to keep pace with the projected expansion of the market for the goods or services involved;

— The investment is considered essential for the survival of the business or required by the state of the market, which makes it necessary to modernize to keep up with the competition or to install new plant and equipment in response to changes in customers' technical specifications;

— The cost of the interest can be included in the price of the goods or services and passed on to the customer (especially in industries that enjoy monopoly privileges or where competition is not keen);

— The burden of interest payments is expected to be lightened considerably by inflation over the life of the loan. (This reasoning is based on the experience of the past twenty-five years, during which the real value of interest payments has indeed dwindled substantially as a result of inflation);

— The borrowing is necessary to reconstitute stocks, particularly in times of high consumer demand;

— The cost of the interest can be offset by using the firm's production capacity to the fullest extent possible, for example, by trying to work the plant around the clock without paying the workers time and a half or double time.

In the case of government borrowing (whether at the central or the local level), as in the case of borrowing by entrepreneurs, if a loan has been contracted for a sound purpose, that is, a purpose that is directly or in-directly productive, the interest payments should be more than offset by the benefits derived from the loan. Hence the question of a just interest rate for borrowing is closely linked to the sound use of the loan and the proper choice on a cost-benefit basis of the projects to be financed; it is also linked to the quality of investment spending, which may be adversely affected by dishonesty in public administration and unsound fiscal, financial and monetary policies. If loans are contracted for sound purposes, they should be expected to generate directly or indirectly enough returns for repayment, provided the economy is properly managed.

Clearly, it is not easy to determine what constitutes a just interest rate since savers, financial intermediaries and borrowers see the question from different vantage points. Nevertheless, some indication can be inferred from the views expressed in recent years by various officials, politicians and economists who, apparently reasoning independently, seem sponta-neously to have adopted lines of thinking that converge on a surprisingly narrow range of figures. The Minister of Finance of New Zealand, in an address delivered to the New Zealand Bankers Association on 27 July 1983, observed that "the rate of inflation has dived from about 16 percent to about 4 percent in twelve months" and went on to say: "It is my belief, and it is my intention, that the whole interest structure should follow the rate of inflation down, and that we cannot and must not be faced with a massive increase in real interest rates, that is to say, the amount by which interest rates exceed the rate of inflation." He then announced: "What I now propose to do is take off the market tomorrow the Government tap loan at 14 percent, and replace it by a loan at 8 per cent." The Minister of Finance thus implied that an acceptable rate of interest for loans was 8 percent minus the rate of inflation (4 percent), that is, a real rate of 4 percent. A more direct answer was provided by the Managing Director of the International Monetary Fund, who according to *The Times* of London of 8 December 1983 told a French foreign trade symposium on 7 December 1983 that "interest rates in the seven largest economies were more than 5 percent above inflation when the difference should be no more than 2 percent."[6]

These comments, which refer essentially to loan interest, could be in-terpreted as relating to interest rates that are appropriate or just for bor-rowers, who should be enabled to benefit from a decline in the inflation rate. However, this is only one aspect of the interest rate question: the other concerns savers, who are likewise affected by inflation but deserve protection against an increase in the inflation rate.

The question of the protection of savers, particularly small savers, against inflation, was raised as early as 1955 by Sir Arthur Lewis in his book *The Theory of Economic Growth,* in which he commented: "If the community is . . . using inflation for the purpose of capital formation, with the result

that the value of money is falling, there is something to be said for guaranteeing the real value of small savings; otherwise small savers are dis-
criminated against (since the value of other assets rises as prices rise), and
small savings are discouraged." He further commented that "partly because
the cost of collecting and using small savings tends to be high," there might
"well be a case for subsidizing the rate of interest offered on small savings."[7]

Almost twenty years later, in 1974, another proposal aimed at guaranteeing the real value of savings while striking an equitable balance between
the interests of savers and those of borrowers was made by Michel Rocard,
a leader of the Socialist Party of France, who subsequently became Minister
of Agriculture in the Mitterand Government. According to Rocard,

borrowers should repay the real value of what they have borrowed, in other words
all savings and the principal of all loans should be indexed, together with the interest
on both savings and loans, but interest rates should not exceed 5 percent. This
would encourage longer-term loans and financing charges would be reduced. However, such a policy would make it necessary to disregard many vested interests,
current strategies and even ingrained habits.[8]

The need to protect the assets of small savers was emphasized by Valéry
Giscard d'Estaing, then President of France, in a letter addressed to the
Prime Minister in 1978, in which he observed:

The inflationary situation of the world economy in recent years has a direct bearing
on saving. . . .

In these circumstances, I feel it would be useful to devise for small savers, whose
primary concern is to protect their assets, a simple and specialized savings instrument which would ensure the durable security of their assets in exchange for a
limited interest rate and effective stability of the deposits.

I am not suggesting comprehensive indexation of savings, which would be bound
to weaken the ability of our economy to overcome inflation.[9]

It is clear that what the President had in mind was a savings instrument
that would protect the economies of small savers against inflation while
yielding a "limited" but positive real rate of interest. The President of
France did not define what he regarded as a "limited" rate of interest, but
specific figures were mentioned in a proposal along the same lines made
in an article on the indexation of long-term savings. There the President
of the Observatoire français des conjonctures économiques suggested that
the index linking of loan principal would make it possible "to revert to
real interest rates known with certainty in advance, which would range
from 2 to 4 percent per annum, being immediately compatible with the
profitability of investments and at the same time remunerative enough to
attract savings."[10] Historical experience, too, indicates that in Western

countries a just interest rate for savers would be a real interest rate in the range of 2 to 5 percent.

In Belgium, during the seventy-five-year period between 1835 and 1910, the average annual yield on the "2.5 percent rent" long-term government securities never exceeded 5.05 percent, which it reached in 1850; the lowest average yield, recorded in 1895, was 2.57 percent.

In England the average annual yield of long-term government securities known as "3.0 percent consols" (consolidated annuities) ranged from 4.48 percent in 1815 to 2.44 percent in 1900. During the first half of the twentieth century, the average annual yield of the "2.5 percent consols" ranged from 2.54 percent in 1900 to 5.32 percent in 1920. On the whole, the average annual yield of consols was in the neighborhood of 2.75 percent for about a century. The idea that this constituted a just interest rate seems to have been accepted at that time. In his "Translator's Preface" to the English version of Böhm-Bawerk's *Kapital und Kapitalzins* (published in 1890), William Smart, lecturer on political economy in Queen Margaret College, Glasgow, observed:

There is . . . in every country, although varying from country to country, a certain annual return which can be obtained by capital with a minimum of risk, without personal exertion of the owner. Its level is usually determined by the market price of the national security. We count the 2 3/4 per cent interest of Consols an absolutely safe return, because the British Constitution is pledged for the annual payment of this amount of interest on its debt—on the capital borrowed by the nation from its members in past years. This we should probably consider the proper economic interest for capital invested in Great Britain. Any return above this level we should consider, either as due to the insecurity of the capital as invested (i.e. as a premium for insurance), or as that still vague quantity called "profit." Thus we should probably consider the 4 per cent of our railway stocks as consisting of, say 2 3/4 per cent for interest proper, and 1 1/4 per cent insurance or equalisation of dividend.[11]

Although the yield of consols remained close to 3 percent, a rate of 5 percent, which for generations was the maximum legal rate under the usury laws, continued to be the standard rate for bank loans throughout much of the country well into the twentieth century. As the Committee on the Working of the Monetary System (known as the Radcliffe Committee) observed in its August 1959 report presented to Parliament by the Chancellor of the Exchequer, the "hold on people's minds" of 5 percent as a rate charged by banks was so "strong" that "even the Stagnation Thesis of the 1930s could not entirely destroy" it.[12] After affirming that "it is not surprising that any general breakthrough of lending interest rates beyond that level causes people to decide that rates have become 'high' and that any pronounced fall of lending rates well below 5 per cent creates a general view that rates have become 'low,' " the Committee observed: "When interest rates change, the main effects that are brought about through a change of people's attitudes—the psychological effects, as they are often called—can be produced only by this kind of breakthrough."

In France, from the end of the Napoleonic Wars to the outbreak of the First World War, the annual average official discount rate (which is indicative of short-term interest rates) remained in general in the range of 3.0 percent to 4.0 percent, although it rose to 4.44 percent in 1855 and fell to 2.10 percent in 1895. The average annual yield of the "5 percent rent" long-term government securities ranged from 4.17 percent to 5.09 percent during the twenty-five-year period 1825-1850, whereas the average annual yield of the "3 percent rent" long-term government securities never exceeded 5.33 percent or fell below 2.96 percent during the period 1825-1920.

In Germany, from 1835 to 1890, the annual average official discount rate rose no higher than 4.94 percent, a level it reached in 1865, and never fell below 4.0 percent. In that country, as in France and elsewhere in Europe, the annual average official discount rate fell at the end of the nineteenth century, dipping to 3.14 percent in 1895. The average annual yield of the Prussian State 4.0 percent bonds remained close to 4.0 percent during the period 1825-1880; subsequently, the Deutsches Reich 4.0 percent bonds yielded an average annual return of close to 4.0 percent from 1880 to 1895.

In the Netherlands, the average annual official discount rate remained below 3.0 percent for most of the nineteenth century, reaching its highest level (4.25 percent) in 1870 and its lowest level (2.0 percent) in 1835.

The nominal rates of interest mentioned above were for the most part real or near-real yields, because during the whole or most of the nineteenth century and the early twentieth century, inflation was very low, and in some cases there were even relatively long periods of deflation.

In fact, from the sixteenth century until the early twentieth century, inflation in Europe as well as in the United States was, generally, neither widespread nor pervasive, although it became a problem at certain times as a result of special circumstances, particularly increases in the supply of gold and silver and large-scale wars. In the sixteenth century, for example, inflation became rampant in Europe as gold and silver from the New World flooded into Spain and from there percolated into other countries. Similar, though less dramatic, bouts of inflation occurred after gold was discovered in California, South Africa, Australia and elsewhere. Inflation likewise rose as a result of the instability caused by the French Revolution and the Napoleonic Wars.

More specifically, in England, the Silberling's index of commodity prices (base 1790 = 100) climbed constantly from 1792, reached a peak in 1801, decreased and then rebounded to reach its highest peak (198) in 1814. Even so, during the twenty-five years running from the French Revolution to the defeat of Napoleon at Waterloo, the average annual increase in the index was only 4.0 percent, which in the light of contemporary experience is a very modest rate of inflation. Moreover, starting in 1828, the index fell to a pre–French Revolution level. In France from 1700 to 1800, prices rose only at an average annual rate of 0.7 percent. Subsequently, the retail price index (base 1900 = 100) rose from 74 in 1810 to 85 in 1840-1849 and 99 in 1860-1869. Even that modest increase was offset by a long period of falling prices between 1860 and 1890. Inflation became a problem in the first half of the twentieth century: prices were multiplied by 4.07 between 1900 and 1920 (an aggregate increase of 307.0 percent) and by 14.5 between 1940 and 1950 (an aggregate increase of 1,350.0 percent), the latter being the period with the highest recorded inflation rate in France's history. Prices were multiplied by 1.48 between 1960 and 1970 (an aggregate increase of 48.0 percent) and by 2.5 between 1960 and 1970 (an aggregate increase of 150.0 percent).

Thus in the light of both the opinions of contemporary economists and politicians and historical experience, annual real interest rates in the range of 2 to 5 percent may be considered just for both savers and borrowers in industrialized countries. In the developing countries, however, the range should be broader, as part of a rational financial policy to encourage households to save the largest possible proportion of incremental income and to promote a shift in the composition of household savings away from real assets and toward financial assets. The interest rate structure might begin with annual real interest rates of, say, 2 to 4 percent for financial instruments with short maturities that are virtually as liquid as cash (current account deposits, money market accounts, savings accounts from which withdrawals can be made without notice or at very short notice and so on). Real interest rates would increase as maturity periods lengthened and the financial instruments become progressively less liquid, rising as high as 10 to 15 percent in the case of virtually risk-free government bonds with maturities of ten years or more or comparable risk-free instruments and as high as 15 to 20 percent for riskier financial instruments.

Substantial real interest rate differentials between short-term, medium-term and long-term financial instruments are necessary even in industrialized countries to encourage savers to forgo liquidity by tying up their funds in instruments with longer maturities. The interest rate differential incentive is even more necessary in developing countries, where there is in most cases no secondary market that would provide investors with liquidity by enabling them to trade their instruments. At the same time, it would be desirable for the authorities in developing countries to devise arrangements under which long-term financial instruments could be redeemed in certain circumstances, usually at a penalty rate. Such arrangements might encourage more savers to buy long-term instruments.

Annual real rates of interest rising as high as 10, 15 or even 20 percent would be realistic in the light of the conditions prevailing in most developing countries and would be sufficiently remunerative to encourage households to save and to hold their funds in the form of domestic financial assets rather than real assets or foreign assets. Such an interest rate structure would reflect the fact that savings are needed not only for short-term purposes (for example, to finance seed-time to harvest-time working capital for peasant farmers, loans to small merchants and consumption loans) but also, and perhaps more importantly, for long-term investments in agriculture and industry that generate incremental real income in the medium and longer term.

If a given interest rate is to be considered just or realistic by savers, it must compare favorably with returns from alternative domestic investments, particularly returns from investment in housing and returns from the curb market (due account being taken of the risks involved in curb market lending) and with interest rates in major financial centers.

In developing countries, as in developed countries, investment in housing constitutes by far the most important component of personal savings. Impressionistic evidence indicates that the share of residential buildings in total gross capital formation, although much lower than in most industrialized countries, is nevertheless highly significant. In the mid-1960's, it was estimated that in Mexico and other countries with a similar level of economic development, about one-tenth of gross capital formation consisted of residential buildings, that most residential buildings were purchased by households, and that mortgage debts accounted for a substantial although not predominant part of the purchase price.[13] Saving in the form of housing, while contributing to the attainment of an important social objective, siphons off resources that could be used for projects that might have greater priority in the context of development, particularly when housing is purchased primarily as a hedge against inflation or for speculative purposes. The following extract from a 1978 statement by the Governor of the Bank of Greece describing the housing situation in his own country is probably of relevance to the situation in many other countries:

Investment in housing is not conducive to the expansion of the economy's production potential. The rapid growth of housing investment in recent years has turned the construction sector into a serious source of inflation. Labour shortages in this sector lead to fast increases in money incomes, which then spread throughout the economy. The rise in the prices of urban real property stimulates speculative demand, creates excessive profits in the construction sector, and attracts savings which, if channelled into investment in manufacturing and agriculture, would help expand the country's production potential.[14]

The curb market functions outside the sphere of control of the monetary authorities and is characterized by the high interest rates charged by lenders who operate mainly with their own capital. Nominal interest rates of 10 to 15 percent a month are not uncommon in the curb market in countries with low or moderate rates of inflation. The rationale sometimes advanced for such usurious rates is that curb market lending involves exceptionally high risks, but the lack of adequate collateral that usually characterizes noninstitutional moneylending is offset to some extent by the fact that the moneylenders are well acquainted with local conditions and generally are in a good position to assess a borrower's creditworthiness.

As to interest rates in foreign countries, experience has shown that funds tend to flow from countries with low interest rates to countries with high interest rates and that the magnetic power of the high rates draws funds out of developing countries even when "strict" foreign exchange controls are supposedly in effect.

Annual real rates of interest of up to 20 percent, plus a margin for the cost of bank intermediation, would not be so high that they would deter potential seekers of personal loans or preclude a just return to those borrowing funds for direct investment in agriculture, industry, trade and housing for sale or rental. For those wanting loans for personal consumption or to finance small businesses (trade, handicrafts, and so on), annual real rates of interest ranging up to 20 percent or slightly more would compare favorably with the rates charged by moneylenders in the curb market. Annual real rates of interest ranging up to 20 percent or slightly more would also be a bargain for small farmers, who in developing countries often obtain "interest-free" loans from a middleman in exchange for a promise not only to reimburse him but also to sell him their next crop. The difference between the low price at which the middleman buys the crops and the price the farmer could have obtained had he been free to sell his crops to the highest bidder is often equivalent to an annual rate of interest much higher than 20 percent.

Entrepreneurs seeking loans for productive ventures do not necessarily need to be treated as privileged borrowers and granted loans at rates that depart too much from those in industrialized countries. Indeed, positive real interest rates or market or near-market rates may help innovative entrepreneurs improve their productivity by forcing them to adopt more advanced technologies. It has even been argued that the introduction of such technologies, combined with the fact that most ventures in developing countries have a relatively small capital base, often results in projects in developing countries yielding a higher investment return than projects in industrialized countries. The World Bank has estimated that in the 1970s the developing countries obtained annual rates of return on investment in the neighborhood of 20 percent. Although the rates of return fell below 20 percent in some of those countries in the late 1970s and early 1980s, the developing countries as a whole have a significant potential ability to achieve high rates of return. This potential can be realized provided that new technologies are employed and management is improved.

Annual real rates of interest rising as high as 10, 15 or even 20 percent would reflect the scarcity of savings and particularly savings channeled through bank and nonbank intermediaries as well as the risks of lending. They would also be more competitive with the yields obtainable from nonfinancial assets and investments in foreign countries. Such an interest rate structure would reduce the exceptionally high degree of financial dualism so evident in the wide interest rate differentials between the institutional and noninstitutional financial sectors. It would encourage the banks to become more involved in agricultural lending, through supervised production loans. In effect, a major argument advanced by banks in developing countries for not lending to small economic units, especially in rural areas, and for confining their lending to a limited number of relatively large economic units in urban areas is the high cost of obtaining the information needed to assess the creditworthiness of small borrowers and the high administrative costs involved in processing numerous small loans. More realistic interest rates on bank lending would make it easier for banks to absorb these costs and might encourage them to make banking facilities available in the countryside. At the same time, more realistic interest rates on deposits might attract to banks the funds of moneylenders, who might find those rates, combined with the security offered by the banks, preferable to the higher rates and higher risks of curb-market lending.

An idea that might be worth exploring is that of a kind of partnership between the banks and the moneylenders that would make it possible to provide more credit facilities for numerous small borrowers, especially in remote rural areas, where it might prove difficult to open bank branches. A bank would advance funds to a moneylender to supplement the latter's own capital, and the moneylender in turn, possibly under the supervision of the agricultural extension service or within the framework of the cooperative movement, would use his funds or at least the portion thereof provided by the bank to make loans available to farmers at rates lower than the normal curb rates but high enough to allow him to make a reasonable profit after paying interest to the bank. This partnership would in effect make bank funds available to rural borrowers at lower overhead for the banks, which would also benefit from the moneylender's knowledge concerning local conditions and the creditworthiness of many would-be borrowers, thus paving the way for the further expansion of bank intermediation in rural areas.

The experience of industrialized countries indicates that bank intermediation as measured by the ratio of bank offices or bank windows to population reinforces the impact of realistic interest rates on personal savings. Thus in Japan the noncorporate sector saves about 21 percent of its disposable income—the highest rate in the world. More than 60 percent of the sums thus saved are held in the form of financial assets, mostly bank deposits, which constitute about 80 percent of total financial savings. This high savings rate is partly due to the scope of the financial intermediation network: there is one bank office per ten thousand Japanese, about seven thousand offices of credit associations and credit cooperatives; almost seven thousand labor, agricultural and fishing cooperatives; and twenty-two thousand offices of the postal savings system. In Switzerland, where gross savings represent just under 30 percent of the gross national product, there is one bank window for about fourteen hundred inhabitants. Another country with a high saving rate is the Federal Republic of Germany, which has one bank window for about sixteen hundred inhabitants. These three countries all have higher savings rates than the United States, which has one bank window for about six thousand inhabitants.

The demand for increased financial intermediation in developing countries is likely to intensify as more and more primary and secondary entrepreneurs discover that their own accumulated savings are no longer sufficient to finance the desired degree of expansion of their undertakings and as unincorporated enterprises are increasingly transformed into incorporated enterprises. There is also likely to be a demand for increasing financial intermediary activity as more and more households seek to acquire more durable consumer goods or to purchase housing and hence to enter into commitments involving sums larger than their accumulated savings and exceeding the credit-supplying capability of the seller.

An appropriate expansion of the financial intermediation system, by increasing the options available to savers, may prompt households to invest their savings in financial assets rather than non-productive physical assets. Similarly, diversification of financial intermediaries may be expected to offer potential entrepreneurs a wider variety of credit facilities, so that they are more likely to find a type of loan adapted to the requirements of their ventures in terms of maturity, security and cost. However, as was noted at the United Nations International Symposium on the Mobilization of Personal Savings in Developing Countries, held in Jamaica in February 1980,

It would be unrealistic to expect that a simple increase in financial intermediation, in the sense of the creation of a greater "density" of financial institutions (creation of more institutions of the present kind), could alone provide a solution, for a number of reasons: First, the access to financial intermediaries is a matter of geography as well as of economics: the policy problem will clearly be quite different in a country with a scattered population and a high concentration of wealth, and in one with a more geographically even distribution of population and a less skewed pattern of income-distribution. Second, the multiplication of facilities (such as bank offices) is costly in real terms, and there is no reason to expect that of itself it will generate greater confidence in financial institutions. Thus, we can say only that increased density of financial institutions will for many less developed countries be one of the necessary conditions for economic development. But it may not evolve "naturally": and it may impose a short-run resource cost on the entire economy greater than the resources captured through new saving and mobilization of existing savings. It is possible that financial intermediation does not voluntarily expand in certain geographical areas of a country because the effective demand for its services

is insufficient to attract profit making financial institutions. Government intervention will be socially beneficial only if, once established, financial intermediaries can
stand on their own feet.

Even if appropriate policies are devised to deal with this problem, there remains
the question, almost ignored in the relevant literature, of whether the savings
"released" from private tangible assets will not simply remain dormant in govern-
ment-subsidized financial institutions. In sum, greater density of financial institutions will for many countries be a *sine qua non* of economic development: but it
is at best a partial answer to the problem.[15]

In developing countries, as in developed countries, the maintenance of
a just interest rate structure entails keeping interest rates at levels that are
positive in real terms. This can be done by setting interest rates on both
savings and loans at levels commensurate with the expected rate of inflation. It would require that an assumption be made concerning the probable
rate of inflation over the life of each savings instrument or type of loan.
That figure then would be added to current real rates of interest as determined by reference to the most recent twelve-month increase in the index
that reflects most accurately the overall trend in prices (the consumer price
index, the wholesale price index, the gross national product deflator or the
gross domestic product deflator). Since the rate of inflation over the duration of a savings instrument or a loan contract cannot be determined in
advance with any precision, the real rate of interest cannot be calculated
accurately until the end of the period covered by the saving instrument or
loan contract. As the rate of inflation is fundamentally erratic and unpre-
dictable, real rates of interest determined on the basis of *ex ante* calculations
can constitute no more than a makeshift solution in the case of medium-
term and long-term savings instruments and loan contracts.

The technique of trying to anticipate the expected rate of inflation during
the life of financial instruments and adding the result to current rates of
interest may disappoint either the saver or the borrower. Savers whose
assets are locked into long-term instruments will suffer if the rate of inflation
exceeds the rate of interest paid on their savings. The higher the expected
rate of inflation, the higher the rate of interest on such instruments will
have to be in order to be considered just by savers. The question of expectations concerning the future is naturally particularly important in a
market interest rate system, where long-term interest rates are greatly
affected by subjective assessments of possible future developments on the
part of savers and other economic agents.

In the context of rising inflation, expectations about inflation may be so
high that they render any real rates of interest based on current inflation
too low to attract savers. By and large, savers and lenders have learned
by experience that a certain degree of inflation is tolerated and even welcome: "better 5 percent inflation than 5 percent unemployment," as the
Chancellor of the Federal Republic of Germany said in 1972.

The notion of the effect of expected inflation on interest rates was expanded upon by Irving Fisher, who propounded the doctrine that a market interest rate consists of two components: a fairly steady real interest rate and a margin representing the expected rate of inflation. In his 1930 book *The Theory of Interest*, Fisher observed: "When prices are rising, the rate of interest tends to be high but not so high as it should be to compensate for the rise; and when prices are falling, the rate of interest tends to be low, but not so low as it should be to compensate for the fall."[16] This relationship between interest rates and inflation, which is known as the Fisher effect, suggests that when savers, particularly sophisticated savers, anticipate higher inflation rates, they expect the increase in those rates to entail a comparable increase in nominal interest rates. If that increase is not forthcoming, savers may direct their savings away from domestic financial assets to uses that are nonproductive from the standpoint of the national economy. On the other hand, the borrower will suffer if the rate of interest charged on his loan is greater than the rate of inflation. Uncertainty about the future course of inflation and the possibility that changes in government policies will bring inflation down may make interest rates calculated by reference to the expected rate of inflation appear too high to him.

The technique may be made more acceptable to both savers and borrowers by adjusting current interest rates whenever the actual rate of inflation is deemed to deviate too significantly from the projected rate. An even simpler solution to the problem of achieving a just interest-rate structure in which interest rates would remain positive in real terms might be through indexation, that is, periodically and automatically readjusting interest rates to reflect variations in a chosen base reference such as the price of gold or an appropriate index.

Implementing a strategy for mobilizing domestic financial resources that would place great emphasis on a shift in the composition of household savings toward financial as opposed to real assets requires that interest rates and other savings incentives (for example, premiums) be kept under active review so that such rates and incentives retain their real value. Flexible interest rates have been enjoying growing popularity not only among banks and other institutional investors but among individual savers and other private investors. In the United States, for example, these rates have been embodied in a number of formulas that include the following: the *variable rate mortgage loan*, under which the lender is allowed to change once a year the interest rate and the monthly payment on an outstanding loan in accordance with any change in the cost of funds (the maximum increase allowed on the interest is 2.5 percent during the duration of the loan); and the *renegotiable rate mortgage loan*, under which the interest rate and the monthly payments are changed every three, four or five years (the maximum increase allowed on the interest during the duration of the loan is 5 percent).

Flexible interest rates are considered responsible for the success of the floating rate notes issued in recent years on the Eurobond market. Despite the elimination in 1984 of the United States withholding tax on interest income payable to foreign investors holding United States domestic fixed-interest securities, the Eurobond market set a new record in that year.

If interest rates are to be reliable indicators of the relative scarcity of investible funds, they should as much as possible be freed and allowed to be determined by market forces. However, many, if not most, developing countries are not in a position to choose between freeing interest rates to find their own levels and discretionary management of interest rates. The size and structure of the financial market and other conditions in developing countries tend to impede effective market competition. Freeing interest rates from all controls would enable a few financial institutions to take advantage of their monopolistic position to create new distortions in the financial structure or exacerbate existing ones by widening disproportion-ately the spreads between deposit interest rates and lending interest rates and thus continue to keep interest rates on savings instruments abnormally low. Discretionary management of interest rate levels on the basis of the guidelines proposed earlier in this chapter may help to resolve the interest rate dilemma by making it possible to set interest rates at just levels, that is, levels approximating those that would exist in a financial environment resulting from undistorted market competition.

NOTES

1. Irving Fisher, *The Purchasing Power of Money*, New York: Augustus M. Kelley, Bookseller, 1963, p. 233.

2. United Nations, General Assembly, Resolution 3202 (S-VI), Section I, paragraph 1(d).

3. Organisation for Economic Co-operation and Development, *Costs and Margin in Banking: An International Survey, 1980*, Paris, 1980.

4. The first study was carried out by A.G. Himes and G. Catephores and the second study by P.K. Trivedi. Both studies are mentioned in A.D. Bain, *The Control of the Money Supply*, 3d edition, Harmondsworth, Middlesex, England: Penguin Books, 1982, p. 122.

5. Ibid.

6. "Faster World Growth and a Diminishing Debt Problem," *The Times* (London), 8 December 1983.

7. W. Arthur Lewis, *The Theory of Economic Growth*, London: George Allen & Unwin Ltd., 1955, p. 229.

8. Quoted in G. Charles, "Indexation de l'épargne: nouvelle offensive," reprinted in *Problèmes Economiques*, 4 December 1974, 23.

9. Quoted in G. Malignac, "La Réglementation des Indexations,", *Journal de la Societé de statistique de Paris*, 119:2 (1978), 149.

10. Jean-Marcel Jeanneney, "Indexer l'épargne à long terme," *Le Monde*, 29 March 1983.

11. William Smart, Translator's Preface, in *Capital and Interest*, by Eugen von Böhm-Bawerk, New York: Augustus M. Kelley Publishers, 1970, p. vii.

12. According to the committee, "the Stagnation Thesis is that in a rich country continuing to increase in wealth (through accumulating capital and technical improvements) opportunities for further and further profitable capital development will tend to decline while the disposition to save will be at least maintained, and that this combination of circumstances is likely to produce a chronic tendency to underemployment of the country's resources."

13. Raymond W. Goldsmith, *The Financial Development of Mexico*, Paris: Organisation for Economic Co-operation and Development, Development Centre Studies, p. 43.

14. Bank of Greece, Summary of the Statement of Governor Xenophon Zolotas at the Annual Shareholders' Meeting, 30 April 1979, Athens, 1979, p. 12.

15. United Nations International Symposium on the Mobilization of Personal Savings in Developing Countries, *The Mobilization of Savings in Developing Countries*, Working Paper No. 7, pp. 62, 63.

16. Fisher, *The Theory of Interest*, New York: The Macmillan Company, 1930, p. 43.

Selected Bibliography

DOCUMENTS

International

African Development Bank, *Annual Report.*
Asian Development Bank, *Annual Report.*
———, *Asian Development Review*, biannually.
Bank for International Settlements, *Annual Report; Quarterly Analysis of International Banking.*
Inter-American Development Bank, *Annual Report.*
———, *Economic and Social Progress in Latin America: External Sector*, annually.
International Bank for Reconstruction and Development, *Annual Report.*
———, *World Debt Tables.*
———, *World Development Report.*
International Monetary Fund, *Annual Report.*
———, *Exchange Rate Volatility and World Trade*, Occasional Paper No. 28 (1984).
———, *Government Finance Statistics.*
———, *IMF Survey*, biweekly.
———, *Interest Rate Policies in Developing Countries*, Occasional Paper No. 22 (1983).
———, *International Financial Statistics*, monthly.
———, *World Economic Outlook*, annually.
International Savings Banks Institute, *International Information*, monthly.
———, *Savings Banks International*, quarterly.
Organisation for Economic Co-operation and Development, *Costs and Margins in Banking: An International Survey*, Paris, 1980.
———, *External Debt of Developing Countries*, Paris, 1982.
———, *Financial Market Trends*, quarterly.
United Nations, *Foreign Investment in Developing Countries*, Sales No. E.68.II.D.2.
———, *Savings for Development: Report of the International Symposium on the Mobilization of Personal Savings in Developing Countries*, Sales No. F.81.II.A.6.
———, *Savings for Development: Report of the Second International Symposium*

on the Mobilization of Personal Savings in Developing Countries, Sales No. E.84.II.A.1.

———, *United Nations Model Double Taxation Convention Between Developed and Developing Countries*, Sales No. E.80.XVI.3.

National

France, La Documentation française, *Le développement et la protection de l'épargne*, Rapport au Ministre de l'économie et des finances et au Ministre délégué chargé du budget de la Commission présidée par David Dautresme.

———, *Problèmes Economiques*, weekly, Paris.

France, Institut national de la statistique et des études économiques, *Economie et statistique*, monthly.

France, Ministère de l'économie et des finances, *Statistiques et ètudes financières*, monthly, Paris.

United Kingdom, *Committee on the Working of the Monetary System, Report*, 1959.

———, Bank of England, *Quarterly Bulletin*.

United States, *Federal Reserve Bank of St. Louis Review*.

———, *Federal Reserve Bulletin*.

———, *Records of Policy Actions of the Federal Open Market Committee*.

———, Federal Reserve Bank of Kansas City, *Economic Review*, monthly.

United States, Federal Reserve Bank of New York, *Central Bank Views on Monetary Targeting*, Papers presented at a conference held at the Federal Reserve Bank of New York, May 1982.

NEWSPAPERS AND PERIODICALS

Afkar–Inquiry (London)
Afrique: Expansion (Paris)
Arabia–The Islamic World Review (London)
The Economist (London)
Financial Times (London)
O Globo (Rio de Janeiro)
Jeune Afrique (Paris)
Le Journal de Genève (Geneva)
The Middle East
Le Monde (Paris)
Le Moniteur des Travaux Publics et du Bâtiment (Paris)
La Nación (Buenos Aires)
The New York Times (New York)
La Prensa (Buenos Aires)
The Times (London)
El Universal (Caracas)
La Vie Française (Paris)
The Wall Street Journal (New York)
The Washington Post (Washington)

BOOKS AND ARTICLES

Aronson, Jonathan David, *Debt and the Less Developed Countries*, Boulder, CO: Westview Press, 1979.

Avramovic, Dragoslav, et al., *Economic Growth and External Debt*, Baltimore: International Bank for Reconstruction and Development, The Johns Hopkins Press, 1964.

Bailey, Norman A.; Luftt, R. Donald; and Robinson, Roger W., "Exchange Participation Notes: An Approach to the International Financial Crisis," in Thibaut De Saint-Phalle, ed., *The International Financial Crisis: An Opportunity for Constructive Action*, Washington, DC: Center for Strategic and International Studies, Georgetown University, 1983.

A. D. Bain, *The Control of the Money Supply*, 3d ed., Harmondsworth, Middlesex, England: Penguin Books, 1982.

Baird, Jane, "The Mexican Nightmare," *Institutional Investor*, November 1982, 81–87.

Belliveau, Nancy, "Heading Off Zaire's Default," *Institutional Investor*, March 1977, 23–30.

Benoît, J. Pierre V., *1804–1954: Cent cinquante ans de commerce exterieur d'Haiti*, Port-au-Prince, Haiti: Institut d'Haiti de statistique, 1954.

————, *Evolution budgétaire et développement économique d'Haiti*, Port-au-Prince, Haiti: Editions Henri Deschamps, 1954.

Böhm-Bawerk, Eugen von, *Capital and Interest*, New York: Augustus M. Kelley, Publishers, 1970.

Boskin, Michael, "Taxation, Saving, and the Rate of Interest," *Journal of Political Economy*, 86 (April 1978), Part 2, pp. S3–S27.

Buffie, E. F., "Financial Repression, the New Structuralists, and Stabilization Policy in Semi-industrialized Economies," *Journal of Development Economics*, 14: 3 (April 1984).

Burdeau, Georges, *Le libéralisme*, Paris: Editions du Seuil, 1979.

Chandavakar, Anand G., "Some Aspects of Interest Rate Policies in Less Developed Economies: The Experience of Selected Asian Countries," *Staff Papers*, 18:1, Washington, DC: International Monetary Fund, 1971.

Chappey, Joseph, *La crise du capital*, Paris: Librairie du Recueil Sirey, 1937.

Cline, William R., "Mexico's Crisis, The World's Peril," *Foreign Policy*, Winter 1982–1983, 107–117.

Datta, G., and Shome, P., "Social Security and Household Savings: Asian Experience," *The Developing Economies*, 19:2 (1981), 143–160.

Davis, Christopher, *Financing Third World Debt*, London: Royal Institute of International Affairs, 1979.

Deaver, J. V. "The Chilean Inflation and the Demand for Money," in D. M. Meiselman, ed. *Varieties of Monetary Experience*, Chicago: University of Chicago Press, 1970.

Delamaide, Darrell, *Debt Shock*, London: Weidenfeld and Nicolson, 1984.

Denison, E. F., "A Note on Private Saving," *Review of Economics and Statistics*, 40:3 (1958).

Fisher, Irving, *The Purchasing Power of Money*, New York: Augustus M. Kelley, Bookseller, 1963.

————, *The Theory of Interest*, New York: Macmillan Company, 1930.

Friedman, Milton, "The Quantity Theory of Money: A Restatement," in *Studies in the Quantity Theory of Money*, Chicago: Chicago University Press, 1956.

————, "The Role of Monetary Policy," *American Economic Review*, 58 (March 1968), 1–17.

Fry, M. J., "Money and Capital or Financial Deepening in Economic Development?" *Journal of Money, Credit, and Banking*, 10:4 (1978).

————, "Saving, Investment, Growth, and the Cost of Financial Repression," *World Development*, 8:4 (1980).

Galbis, Vicente, "Inflation and Interest Rate Policies in Latin America, 1967–76," *Staff Papers*, 26:2, Washington, DC: International Monetary Fund, 1979.

————, "Money Investment and Growth in Latin America, 1961–1973," *Economic Development and Cultural Change*, 27:3 (1979), 423–443.

Gide, Charles, and Rist, Charles, *Histoire des doctrines économiques*, Paris: Librairie du Recueil Sirey, 1947.

Giovannini, A., "The Interest Elasticity of Savings in Developing Countries: The Existing Evidence," *World Development*, 2:7 (1983), 601–607.

Gupta, K. L., "Personal Saving in Developing Nations: Further Evidence," *Economic Record*, 46:114 (1970), 243–249.

Heins, A. James, *Constitutional Restrictions against State Debt*, Madison: University of Wisconsin Press, 1963.

Hirsch, Richard G., *The Way of the Upright*, New York: Union of American Hebrew Congregations for the Commission on Social Action of Reform Judaism, 1973.

Johnson, G. G., "Aspects of the International Banking Safety Net," Washington, DC: International Monetary Fund, DM/82/85 (1982).

Kafka, A. "The Brazilian Stabilization Program 1964–66," *The Journal of Political Economy*, 75:4, August 1967, Supplement, 596–631.

Karsten, Ingo, "Islam and Financial Intermediation," *Staff Papers*, 29, Washington, DC: International Monetary Fund, March 1982.

Keynes, John Maynard, *The General Theory of Employment, Interest, and Money*, New York: Harcourt, Brace and Company, 1936.

Lewis, Arthur W., *The Theory of Economic Growth*, London: George Allen & Unwin, 1955.

McKinnon, R. I., *Money and Capital in Economic Development*, Washington, DC: The Brookings Institution, 1973.

Mikesell, R. F., and Zinser, J. E., "The Nature of the Savings Function in Developing Countries: A Survey of the Theoretical and Empirical Literature," *Journal of Economic Literature*, 11:1 (1973), 1–26.

Miracle, M. P.; Miracle, D. S.; and Cohen, L., "Informal Savings Mobilization in Africa," *Economic Development and Cultural Change*, 28:4 (1980), 701–724.

Mussa, M., "U.S. Macroeconomic Policy and Developing Country Borrowing," Paper presented at the Cato Institute Conference on World Debt and Monetary Order (Washington, D.C., January 20–21, 1984).

Nellor, D.C.L., "Tax Policy, Regulated Interest Rates, and Saving," Washington, DC: International Monetary Fund, DM/83/59 (1983).

Shaw, E. S., *Financial Deepening in Economic Development*, New York: Oxford University Press, 1973.

Siegel, J. J., "Notes on Optimal Taxation and the Optimal Rate of Inflation," *Journal of Monetary Economics*, 4:2 (1978).

Tanzi, Vito, "The Deficit Experience in Industrial Countries," Washington, DC: International Monetary Fund, DM/85/10 (1985).

———, "Quantitative Characteristics of the Tax Systems of Developing Countries," Washington, DC: International Monetary Fund, DM/83/79 (1983).

Wellons, P. A., "Borrowing by Developing Countries on the Euro-Currency Market," Paris: Development Centre of the Organisation for Economic Cooperation and Development, 1977.

Index

About the Author

J. PIERRE V. BENOIT, formerly an official in the Ministry of Finance and a bank manager in his native country, Haiti, is Chief of the Fiscal and Financial Branch of the United Nations Secretariat. In the course of his career, he has written numerous studies and reports dealing with fiscal and financial issues at both the international and national levels. He has also advised governments of developing countries and chaired many United Nations seminars, workshops and symposia concerned in particular with policies and techniques for mobilizing personal savings. He received the Gold Medal of the International Savings Banks Institute.